2/49

hb text ip 35⁰⁰

hb text ip 35⁰⁰

Myth,

Rhetoric,

and the

Voice of

Authority

Myth, Rhetoric, and the Voice of Authority

A Critique of

Frazer,

Eliot, Frye,

& Campbell

Marc Manganaro

YALE UNIVERSITY PRESS

NEW HAVEN & LONDON

Published with assistance from the Mary Cady Tew Memorial Fund.

Designed by Jill Breitbarth and set in Bembo type by Brevis Press, Bethany, Connecticut.
Printed in the United States of America by BookCrafters, Inc., Chelsea, Michigan.

Library of Congress Cataloging-in-Publication Data
Manganaro, Marc, 1955–
    Myth, rhetoric, and the voice of authority : a critique of Frazer, Eliot, Frye, and Campbell / Marc Manganaro.
      p. cm.
    Includes bibliographical references (p.   ) and index.
    ISBN 0-300-05194-8
    1. Literature and anthropology. 2. Mythology—Historiography.
    3. Narration (Rhetoric) 4. Myth in literature. 5. Frazer, James George, Sir, 1854–1941. 6. Eliot, T. S. (Thomas Stearns), 1888–1965. 7. Campbell, Joseph, 1904– . 8. Frye, Northrop.
    I. Title.
    PN51.M267 1992
    809'.915—dc20   91-34974
                                          CIP

10 9 8 7 6 5 4 3 2 1

For Lisa

A mighty maze! but not without a plan.

Alexander Pope
An Essay on Man

Contents

Acknowledgments

Anyone trying to write a book on the work of several authors with encyclopedic tendencies will end up owing much to many people. First I should thank William Harmon at the University of North Carolina, who one spring day in the early 1980s dumped a dozen weighty works of anthropology in my lap and told me to go off and read them and then come back again. And I also need to thank Joseph Flora (chair of the English department at Carolina then) as well as my partners in the travails of graduate study: Bill Gargan, Meg Harper, Rose Haskell, and others. Many people at the University of Hawaii, in one way or another, encouraged this project in its early stages: Tom Caramagno, Russell Durst, Craig Howes, Joseph Kau, Anne Simpson, Joe and Beth Tobin, and other members of the Department of English theory group (1986–89), and the late Jack Unterecker (who read an initial version of this project with great diligence and insight). I am also thankful to the University of Hawaii for providing me research and travel funds in order to work on this book, and to Rutgers University for providing me a leave to complete it. And I am grateful to friends and colleagues at Rutgers who have provided me with so much support: Rick Barr, Marjorie Howes, Marcia Ian, John McClure, Michael Moffatt, Bruce Robbins, Jo Tarvers, and especially Barry Qualls.

I could not have completed this work in the given time frame were it not for a Fellowship for University Teachers from the National Endowment for the Humanities. And I wish to thank those whose own work made a difference to the way this book is shaped, and whose commentary and encouragement is greatly appreciated: James Boon, Ross Chambers, James Clifford, Clifford Geertz, Richard Hardin, Jacob Korg, Michele Richman, George Stocking, Marilyn Strathern, Stephen Tyler, and John Vickery. And I need to acknowledge the influence that the work of Eric Gould has had on this project and thank him for his excellent suggestions on the book. Thanks to Robert Segal as well for his careful reading of the Frazer and Campbell chapters. And I am thankful to Susan Laity, manuscript editor at Yale University Press, for her careful and intelligent suggestions. But I especially am grateful to Ellen Graham, retired senior editor at Yale University Press, who from the beginning believed in this project and worked unflaggingly to help bring it off.

Thanks go to journals that first published material appearing in this volume. A portion of the Frazer chapter was published as " 'The Tangled Bank' Revisited: Anthropological Authority in Frazer's *The Golden Bough*" in *The Yale Journal of Criticism* (Fall 1989); and material from the Eliot chapter was published as " 'Beating a Drum in a Jungle': T. S. Eliot on the Artist as 'Primitive' " in *Modern Language Quarterly* (December 1986).

I wish to thank my families, in (the unlikeliest of geographical combinations) Beirut, Nebraska, and Wisconsin, for their love and support: especially my father- and mother-in-law, Elie and Phyllis Salem, my grandmother, Nettie Manganaro, and my parents, Ross and Alice Manganaro. This book was urged forward out of love for my three small children, Anthony, Thomas, and Rania, who at times also gave the process of completing it a certain edge. And to Lisa, for everything, as always.

Introduction:
Being There/Being Everywhere

This book concerns the rhetorical authority of the comparative method used by four successive modern authors: James Frazer, T. S. Eliot, Northrop Frye, and Joseph Campbell. Thirty years ago a study of four writers, with Frazer at their head, undoubtedly would have focused, in myth-critical fashion, on tracing the influence of the ritual *content* of anthropology, exemplified by *The Golden Bough,* upon the literary canon. Such a stress reflected, as John Vickery has observed, the "critical shift . . . from rhetoric to myth" that in the 1950s and 1960s engendered myth criticism and sounded the death knell for New Critical approaches to literature.[1] Myth-critical emphasis did not abandon the priority of literary *style,* however: from that perspective *The Golden Bough* was worthy of study because it influenced the literary giants. The ways it did so were then used, retroactively, to canonize Frazer's book as a literary masterpiece.

This study engages in a reversal of that flow. First, it does not assume an evolutionary framework in which prepubescent literariness in anthropology matures into a full grown body of literature. Literariness is not valorized as a terminus, just as anthropology is not conceived of as a means to a glorious aesthetic end. Second, this book reverses the movement from rhetoric to myth, insisting that the mythic or ritualistic is capable of discursive analysis because it is contained in text. For this reason the reader may be surprised to find little attention paid, for example, to the importance of vegetation ceremonies on Eliot and much paid to the rhetorical function of tropes, the chief of which, this study maintains, is the comparative method itself. When anthropological concepts, such as totemism and androgyny, are discussed, they are not treated simply as "influences," and are certainly not valorized as vessels of "mythic consciousness," but rather are conceived of as figures that say much about the ideological and semiotic assumptions that govern the text and engender its authority.

This book would not be possible without recent anthropological writing questioning the authority by which cultures are represented in social-scientific texts, primarily by pointing to the discursive nature of those texts.

1

Of course to a degree anthropology has always been perceived as a writerly activity, and cultural anthropology in particular has never really been regarded as an exact science. And yet this relative shift in perspective, from perceiving anthropology as a science in which cultural "facts" are gathered and attractively presented to assessing it as an eminently interpretive textual process, still marks a fundamental change, one that would not have been possible without challenges to the easy referentiality of language made within semiotics, phenomenology, structuralism, and deconstruction.[2]

The "results" of anthropology, recent anthropological theory holds, are something other than the unmediated transfer of cultural information from a native culture to a civilized public. As James Boon puts it, the fact that anthropology is manifested "*as writing* suggests the fundamental symbolic remove from whatever immediacy or presence anthropological discourse presumes to embody." And, according to James Clifford, that anthropologists have taken so long to discuss collectively "the constructed, artificial nature of cultural accounts" only underscores "the persistence of an ideology claiming transparency of representation and immediacy of experience."[3]

Recent cultural theory has emphasized that this insistence upon an unmediated presentation (versus mediated representation) has motivations and effects other than hermeneutic naïveté, nostalgia, or optimism (though such logocentric impulses do play a part). Central to this book is the notion, conceived by Friedrich Nietzsche and rearticulated by Jacques Derrida, that the "will to truth" is actually a "will to power" whose very authority is enabled by an essential "dissimulation": "truth" is, in an oft-quoted phrase of Nietzsche's, "a mobile army of metaphors, metonymies, anthropomorphisms" that exert power for the user precisely because of their capacity to disguise themselves as transparencies.[4]

More specifically, notions of power and otherness in contemporary critical and social theory, especially as articulated by theorists such as Michel Foucault, Edward Said, and Tzvetan Todorov, have been brought to bear upon anthropology's own relation to its "objects" of inquiry. Such studies suggest, among other things, that offering the *interpretation* of another culture as transparent presentation obscures the power that readers of culture hold in being able to construct their own version of these objects: those "other" peoples, tribes, "savages," what you will. That ability to fashion suggests as well the wider hold that the West as a whole has upon the "natives" of other cultures. Johannes Fabian has written specifically of such patterns of domination as they have worked in anthropology since its in-

ception, and George Marcus and Michael Fischer, among others, have written of the uses, both negative and positive, to which the anthropologists'
treatments of the cultural Other have been put.[5]

The assertion that anthropological texts are something other than se-
miotically transparent and ideologically neutral transmitters of cultural
"facts" has led anthropological theorists to speculate, then, on the animus
of the authority emerging from writing that purports to represent other
cultures. Clifford Geertz in *Works and Lives: The Anthropologist as Author*
holds that "the ability of anthropologists to get us to take what they say
seriously has less to do with either a factual look or an air of conceptual
elegance than it has with their capacity to convince us that what they say
is a result of their having penetrated (or, if you prefer, been penetrated by)
another form of life, of having, one way or another, truly 'been there.'"
James Clifford similarly focuses on the authority of the ethnographer
whose field experience supposedly shapes the text. Primarily through the
claim that "I was there" (in the field, face to face with the cultural subject),
the modern ethnographer exerts what Clifford terms *ethnographic authority*
in order to become the voice of culture, effectively consolidating the power
to represent cultures by displacing other sources.[6]

Geertz, Clifford, and other recent anthropological theorists center on
modern ethnography, with its emphasis upon participant observation, as a
site for analyzing the relation between cultural representation and the authority of those who represent. In the preface to *Works and Lives* Geertz
explains that "the term 'anthropology' is used here mainly as equivalent
to 'ethnography' or 'works based on ethnography.'" He is fully conscious,
he states, of his emphasis upon "sociocultural anthropology, and particularly to that part of it that is ethnographically oriented," and also notes his
omission of the other three branches of anthropology ("archaeology, comparative linguistics, physical anthropology") which are "not, or not necessarily, ethnographically based" (v). Similarly, although Clifford defines
ethnography rather broadly as writing about culture, or "writing culture"—"the making of ethnography is artisanal," he notes in his introduction to *Writing Culture,* "tied to the worldly work of writing" (6)—his
notion of ethnographic authority quite specifically denotes the rhetoric of
the twentieth-century cultural anthropologist come from the field, whose
textual parameters are significantly bound to the ritualized experience of
participant observation.

Now Geertz, Clifford, and others are not in error or in any way mis-
leading. But it needs to be asserted that ethnography as defined (socio-

cultural anthropological writing based primarily upon participant observation) represents a fairly narrow band of anthropological representation.
This is true of modern anthropology (with its fourfold division, institutionalized early in this century) but especially true of the history of anthropology, which in the broadest sense reaches back to antiquity. The
surfeit of attention paid to Bronislaw Malinowski in the increased interest
in anthropology's linked "poetics and politics" (the term is Clifford's) is
highly significant here, for Malinowski figures, whether triumphantly or
pejoratively, as the architect of modern ethnography as it has come to be
recognized. In this respect *Writing Culture* tends to reduce the history of
Anglo-American anthropology, providing brief discussions of modern anthropology before Malinowski and citing its oddly dissonant relation to
mature ethnography (though it is sometimes consonant: pre-Malinow-
skians also wrote, and some even ventured into the field!). Occasionally
Clifford even selects an "oddball" text from the pre-Malinowskian period
(Codrington's *The Melanesians,* Cushing's *Zuni*) that, in its less self-
fashioned discursivity, might serve as a cue toward reorienting the discipline and discourse.[7]

This book focuses specifically on the rhetorical authority of evolutionary
comparativism, the method that prevailed in anthropology before the
emergence of a functionalist ethnography. While the standard discursive
product of classic ethnography, the monograph, concentrates on the function of cultural items or features *within* a particular culture, the evolution-
ary-comparativist text by definition compares two or more (usually more)
cultures, or particular items from different cultures, based largely upon the
reconstruction of a hypothetical evolutionary sequence, ranging from the
least to the most "civilized." The monograph centers upon the controlling
persona of the ethnographer, gaining narrative authority from presence in
the field; the early comparativist texts comprised a more encyclopedic gathering of sources that found their synthesis in the mind of the armchair
gatherer: if the ethnographer gains authority from being "there," as Geertz
suggests, then the comparativist is empowered by being everywhere.

In a sense this book takes a step backward—to the rhetoric of comparative anthropology that reigned before the emergence of the Malinowskian
monograph, especially as centered in the work of James Frazer. And yet it
also takes a step forward, to the perpetuation of that comparativist rhetoric
during the reign of the monograph and beyond, as sited in the works of
T. S. Eliot, Northrop Frye, and Joseph Campbell. This cross-disciplinary
grouping of writers—whose texts fan out from anthropology to literature,
literary criticism, folklore, and myth—does not simply attest to the uni-

versality of comparativism as a rhetoric. Rather, the wide cross section of represented fields illustrates the manner in which this powerful mode of authority became largely obsolete in anthropology with the rise of the monograph and consequently became displaced to institutional spaces within the humanities, where, I maintain, it wielded an authority that had deeper and more dramatic implications than did the rhetoric of the monograph.

One can appreciate the limitations of evolutionary comparativism as perceived by the functional anthropologists. A figure such as Frazer was perceived as the "armchair" anthropologist par excellence, the scholar who plundered antique accounts as well as contemporary missionary and travelers' reports that made their way into his study in order to draw gross evolutionary comparisons between the present-day "savage" and our Western ancestors. For anthropologists after Malinowski, the barrier placed between the comparativist theorist and his "man on the spot" fieldworker generally posed an insurmountable obstacle to ethnographic accuracy, to capturing the native in the pure state.

As Clifford and George Stocking have shown, modern ethnography's response to armchair comparativism was to close the gap by creating the narrator-persona of the anthropologist fieldworker, who becomes the singular "voice" of culture by welding theorist and fieldworker. Drawing his terms from Mikhail Bakhtin, Clifford describes how modern ethnographic discourse becomes monologic, since its single narrative point of view inevitably subsumes all "other" voices—most notably, those of the native subjects. Clifford's description of the modern ethnographer's strategies emphasizes the Bakhtinian notion of the closing off of voices: "The tasks of textual transcription and translation along with the crucial dialogical role of interpreters and 'privileged informants' [are] relegated to a secondary, sometimes even despised, status."[8]

Critics such as Clifford, in attempting to shatter the illusion of post-Malinowskian ethnography as a transparent window to the anthropological subject, have clarified the empowering metaphysics of presence that has made orthodox the representational fieldwork account known as the monograph. According to Clifford, the modern ethnographer's insistence on disregarding previous written accounts bolsters his authority by demanding a logocentric transformation of native "experience" into First Text: "The fieldworker, typically, starts from scratch, from a research *experience,* rather than from reading or transcribing. The field is not conceived of as already filled with texts."[9]

The monographic denial of prior texts seems a deliberate reversal of what one could call the essential intertextuality of a book such as *The Golden Bough,* which is literally bursting with previous writings and points of view. Now this plurality of voice hardly means that a functionalist ethnographer completely silences all other voices while a pre-Malinowskian comparativist permits total freedom of voice and self-representation to "native" and source. But the ethnographically unfortunate gap between the armchair comparativist and his informants does create a rhetorical situation in which the author *depends* on other sources to an extent not usually found in a modern monograph. Indeed, for the comparativist such as Frazer texts are his only "field." The result is anything but what Clifford calls the "integrated portrait" that the modern ethnographer wrests from "the research situation's ambiguities and diversities of meaning" (PC 40). Rather, a text such as Frazer's *Golden Bough,* published in various versions from 1890 to 1922, necessarily opens itself to other "voices" in ways that suggest the polyphonic.

The manifest profusion of voice and source in the armchair theorist's text goes far in explaining the appeal of a Frazer over a Malinowski to a literary Modernist such as Eliot. The historical and multicultural range of *The Golden Bough* offered a much wider vista to readers than did Malinowski's account of the natives of a particular time and place. And yet this comparativist appeal goes deeper than mere receptivity to source and voice and has much darker implications. Indeed, a key contention of this book is that such openness is integrally tied to appropriative cultural representation, that a will to power operates not only within but because of the profusion of source and voice in these comparativist texts. The nature of that power owes much, in Nietzschean fashion, to the mystification of the metaphorical nature of the comparative method itself, to the capacity of these comparativist texts to disguise their "metaphors, metonymies, anthropomorphisms" as the voices and sources of truth.

The authority of this representation, in other words, gains power from the illusion of transparent openness to cultural subject and reader, and it is in this respect that Clifford's notion of "ethnographic authority" must be extended, even altered. Clifford's fairly firm polarization of *open* versus *closed* texts does not make sense of the Modernist comparativist text, which opens *so that* it closes, which proliferates voices in order to control them and protect the author. And it is not enough to say that if a text's ultimate end is to protect the author, then it is closed. Rather, it becomes necessary to pose openness itself not as a bedrock of anthropological virtue, but, in the Foucaultian manner, as a shifting, rhetorical ploy situated in a network of power relations.[10]

The aim here, then, is not to trumpet comparativism over ethnography, nor yet to castigate the comparative method, but rather to suggest the directions in which recent insights into what Clifford terms the "poetics and politics" of anthropology can be used in understanding the power of at least one strain of comparativism as a discursive force. In order to do that it seems necessary to premise with a simple observation: in the history of anthropology, and in fact of social science in general, the role of comparativism has been as fundamental as that played by ethnography.

The general principle of comparativism is of course fully operative within the other three branches of anthropology, and it extends well beyond anthropology. Alan Dundes in "The Anthropologist and the Comparative Method in Folklore" makes the point that most academic disciplines are "comparative in nature and scope" and that although "the comparative method in [cultural] anthropology was essentially abandoned by the majority of anthropologists by the middle of the century," many fields, such as folklore, still hold comparativism as a governing principle.[11] And within the field of anthropology, comparativism is certainly as venerable a method as ethnographic participant observation. Though Clifford's statement that "ethnography's tradition is that of Herodotus and of Montesquieu's Persian" (WC 2), is not incorrect—Herodotus *did* fieldwork—it underscores the tendency within even recent anthropological theory to accentuate experience in the field and to downplay comparativism as an originary discursive feature of anthropology. For Herodotus's *Histories* is an eminently comparativist text. Dundes cites Herodotus as a key case in point for his assertion that "anthropology in its beginnings was unmistakably comparative," pointing to his "keen interest in comparing Greek customs with those of neighboring peoples" ("Anthropologist and Comparative Method" 125).

Establishing the work of Herodotus as either comparativist or ethnographic is not the crucial issue here. Obviously anthropological texts can be both ethnographic, in the sense of being written out of experience "with" the people, in the field, *and* comparativist, setting whole cultures (or items from them) next to or against each other in order to support generalizations on cultural difference or similarity. The concepts as practiced are hardly mutually exclusive. Indeed, that ethnography and comparativism welded so often and so easily in the history of anthropology is itself quite telling: for it is only with the orthodoxy of the monograph in the twentieth century that comparativism was made virtually taboo in cultural anthropology. And, to be fair, that exclusion was in part a reaction against the armchair comparativists who, in general, never entered the field but used the observations of others instead. In any case, reading Herodotus as ethnography, as Clifford correctly does, nonetheless still carries the resonance of earlier attempts to place comparativism closer to the margin of anthropological consciousness.

A principal objection to comparativism within anthropology has always been that cultural comparison (especially though not exclusively as practiced by comparativists of the evolutionary persuasion) has tended to hunt for uniform laws about cultures, generalizations that discount the genuine differences existing between those cultures. In this respect Andre Köbben has noted that, for functional anthropologists in particular, the fieldwork experience has made them "unwilling to see the society, whose uniqueness they have established with such infinite care, treated as just one more specimen of a genus."[12] On the other hand, proponents of comparativism, even at the height of functionalism's reign in the 1940s and 1950s, have asserted that without the implementation of an eventual, overarching comparativism, the thousands of isolated case studies of discrete cultures will remain stranded in their particularity, unattached to any larger theory of cultural integrity or change.

James Boon, following the lead of Geertz, characterizes the comparativist urge to establish a cultural common denominator as the effort, crystallizing in the Enlightenment, toward "converting cultural diversity into uniformity." This tendency in anthropological comparativism, Boon warns, "among all other traditions," is "one that would most thwart our own [ethnographic] enterprise"; indeed, he asserts that "the comparison of cultures requires not that we reduce them to platitudinous similarity but that we situate them apart as equally significant, integrated systems of differences."[13] And yet, as Boon well realizes, the search for difference in the anthropological comparison of cultures often produces the oppositional Other, the convenient construction that embodies a society's hates and fears, locating foreignness in a figure or complex of figures attached to strangers. Said's *Orientalism* (1978) is of course a crucial text illustrating the Western tradition of the programmatic representation of Orient as Other, and Todorov's *Conquest of America: The Question of the Other* (1982) charts a similar construction of dark difference that moves from East to West.

But while Said stresses the oppositional and negative character of the relationship between anthropologist and Other, others emphasize how the anthropological enterprise enables us to explore difference in other cultures sincerely and through that experience find things of value that can be brought to bear upon our own culture. Clifford in this respect criticizes

Said for neglecting "a sympathetic, non-reductive Orientalist tradition" (PC 261) and thus attempts to combat the notion that encounters with the Oriental Other are intrinsically oppressive. And Marcus and Fischer's *Anthropology as Cultural Critique* focuses on the positive use of the Other in anthropology "as a form of cultural critique for ourselves" (1). In this respect the "difference" that marks another culture becomes in a sense eliminated by a bridge that anthropologists build between that culture and their own.

There are of course hazards affiliated with the promotion of cultural critique within the anthropological enterprise. Who, for example, determines the political correctness of a particular use of a culture? Certainly an anthropologist can read a tribal custom as a text open to various ideological applications, just as a cultural critic can read an anthropologist's rendition of tribal custom to support either liberal or conservative causes: see as an example how Emile Durkheim's theories of primitive collectivity are appropriated by both the Collège de Sociologie and T. S. Eliot in the service of leftist and rightist causes, respectively.

But it is not simply a matter of good and bad politics, for whichever way the appropriation turns, we need to deliberate over the fate of the integrity of the actual people being used to make the point. It may be true that in one important sense cultures are constructed in the act of depicting them, just as it is undeniably fallacious that in the representation of another culture "observers can fully escape culture and history to gain, Enlightenment-like, rarified objectivity" (Boon, *Other Tribes* 30). Nonetheless, people exist before the pen is put to paper, or, put another way, do not go away once represented by the anthropologist; and we cannot avoid responsibility for the effects of such figurings by simply stating, in generalized postmodernist fashion, that a cultural construction is not the same thing as the culture itself.[14] It is a critical underpinning of this book that the process of cultural interpretation is fraught not simply with inaccuracy (for that implies that pure presentation is somehow possible) but with the hazards of seriously misrepresenting others.

Herodotus's text follows the track of Greek trading routes, and in the tradition of Herodotus, anthropology has followed the lines of exploration and conquest and found there cultural contrast (real or imagined, transparently obvious or complexly constructed) that engendered the comparative moment. While anthropology, in Derridean terms, was born (and borne) out of difference perceived, those cultural contrasts would consequently be used for different purposes and be read as differences or similarities (or, as Boon terms them in the title of his recent book, affinities and extremes). In either case, that Other culture is appropriated as it was by Herodotus, according to Jacob Gruber—"in a comparative way[,] to provide the reflecting backdrop against which Western society could better view its own." A fundamental function of that backdrop has been as a base from which the Other culture, usually conceived in this case as "primitive," is equated to earlier stages of our own civilization.[15] The cultural Other is thus figured as a historical reconstruction of our past, a key to our much elegized heritage.

Historians of anthropology have indicated one genesis of comparative anthropology or "ethnology" to be reconstructionist texts that chronicle cultural contact with natives of the New World: a prominent example of such a text is Father Lafitau's *Moers des sauvages ameriquaines, comparées aux moers des premiers temps* (1724). The title indicates the search for origins at work. Lafitau himself states that "knowing the nature of the Indians" was not enough; he "sought in these practices and customs vestiges of the most remote antiquity."[16] But of course Lafitau was hardly the first to sketch a comparative history containing developmental or conjectural arguments about origins. In this regard, Boon makes a fundamental assertion concerning the beginnings of such speculation. Enlightenment efforts toward reducing cultural diversity to uniformity by "constructing an artificial platform" across cultures (as Lafitau and later developmentalists and evolutionists do) must be read against, and in conjunction with, the Medieval-Renaissance tendency to "reveal a scriptural similitude" beneath varying customs (*Other Tribes* 34). If we perform a comparative study of civilization's own comparativisms, we find we cannot say that the Enlightenment drive toward a scientistic set of standards of measurement is necessarily more objective than the search for a "lost unity."

Perhaps the critical point of Boon's analysis is that the eminently logocentric pre-Enlightenment efforts to recover prelapsarian speech, "to restore total intelligibility to the diversity of languages, alphabets, and customary usages documented in history and travel" (*Other Tribes* 30) are in comparative anthropology inextricably tied to abstract Enlightenment procedures of charting difference as uniformity. "Comparative anthropology is caught between eras—or epistemes—just as it is caught between cultures" (44), Boon notes, so that pulling away from Enlightenment practices makes us gravitate toward the logocentric search for unity. Indeed, the history of modern comparativism reads as a narrative of such oscillations, a chronicle of shiftings between progressive chartings and regressive longings for the lost chord.

Degeneration theories, in which humankind was seen to be in progressive decline from its origin, were often conservative, hearkening back to pre-Enlightenment tendencies. According to Frazer's biographer Robert Ackerman, the implicit claim often made in such theories is that "the best we can do now is to recover [the Golden Age] shards and be inspired by the gleams of divinity that continue to suffuse them." Such thinking served as a base in the search for the roots of the Indo-European language families, often thought to have initiated with Sir William Jones's statement, in 1786, on the comparative significance of the Sanskrit languages. Andrew Tuck holds that Jones's emphasis on comparison is the clue to his reputation as the founder of comparative philology. Jones's implication that Europe could, by these studies, learn things about itself proved "a far greater motivation . . . than learning about an utterly, culturally-unrelated civilization." Jones was followed by such seminal figures in comparative philology as Friedrich and August Wilhelm Schlegel, Franz Bopp, and Jacob Grimm, all of whom used the principle of bringing together cognate lexical items in order to reconstruct an ur-language. Significantly, comparative philology later became comparative linguistics, one of the four institutionalized branches of anthropology.[17]

An influence on comparative philology, and a fundamental predecessor of the comparative method in evolutionary anthropology, was the comparative anatomy and biology of the early part of the nineteenth century, especially as embodied in the work of Georges Cuvier and, later of course, Charles Darwin. Comparative anatomy enjoyed great status in the first half of the nineteenth century: Edwin Ackerknecht has referred to it as "the glamor science of the day."[18] Of course the increasingly evolutionary character of the field had a great impact upon the institutionalization of anthropology as a discipline. Physical anthropology, separating from cultural anthropology in the middle of the century, was really a direct descendant of comparative anatomy, and yet *both* physical and cultural anthropology became evolutionist mainly under the influence of comparative anatomy ("On the Comparative Method" 121).

Though the "harder" sciences of anatomy and biology were manifest influences upon cultural anthropology during the latter half of the century, cultural anthropology did not simply owe its existence to them. As Stocking has so persuasively argued, the evolutionary comparativists of Victorian anthropology were perhaps more closely aligned with the "pre-Darwinian developmental tradition" than to Darwinian theory per se. Edward Tylor himself denied the manifest influence of *The Origin of Species,* but of course Darwin readily accepted anthropologists' "contribution" to evolutionary theory. Still, the centrality of biological evolution as the precedent that established the legitimacy of sociocultural anthropology should not be minimized. Darwin's work clearly encouraged studying man in terms of evolutionary process; indeed, at the end of *The Origin of Species* Darwin calls for the application of the principles of his evolutionary theory to the study of humankind (see Ackerman, JGF 77). *Evolution* as a term did not gain currency through Darwin, however, but through a social scientist, Herbert Spencer, who applied a developmental schema to human social processes.[19]

Anthropology did not really gain academic acceptance until Tylor in the 1870s and 1880s convinced his peers that anthropology was a systematic science capable of implementing a rigorously consistent comparative method. For this reason, as much as any other, Tylor is considered the founder of modern anthropology. In a famous paper delivered to the Royal Anthropological Institute in 1889, Tylor argued that "the great need of anthropology is that its methods should be strengthened and systematized." Tylor advocated a "strict" use of the comparative method that would demonstrate that "the problems of anthropology are amenable to scientific treatment," as is the case in "mathematics, physics, chemistry, and biology."[20]

But, in a move that was repeated many times in the genealogy of comparativist rhetoric, Tylor's push for anthropology's status as science depended upon the transfer of evolutionary theory from the hard to the social sciences. He insists upon that connection as early as 1871, in his classic *Primitive Culture,* when he holds that mankind follows the same fundamental rules of growth and evolution as do other material substances and living beings: "The history of mankind is part and parcel of the history of nature . . . our thoughts, wills, and actions accord with laws as definite as those which govern the motion of the waves, the combination of acids and bases, and the growth of plants and animals."[21]

More generally, underlying all of Tylor's work is the reconstructionist motive of comparing past and present cultures in order to erect a model of evolutionary development. Behind that model lies the assumption that "the savage state in some measure represents an early condition of mankind, out of which the higher culture has gradually been developed or evolved, by processes still in regular operation as of old" (*Primitive Culture* I: 32). Of course Tylor's criteria for ascendancy from primitive to civilized are highly ethnocentric. In the opening of *Primitive Culture,* for example, he confidently asserts: "the educated world of Europe and America practically settles a standard by simply placing its own nations at one end of the social series and savage tribes at the other, arranging the rest of mankind between these limits according as they correspond more closely to savage or cultured life."[22]

Tylor more than any other anthropologist set out the methodological configurations of evolutionary comparative anthropology. Central to this emergent endeavor was the uniformitarian notion of unity of mind, the rather easy assumption that human cultures could be hierarchically arranged according to evolution because in fact they represent variations on the same theme. This assumption helped to shape the other characteristics of evolutionary comparativism as they were exhibited in the methods not only of Tylor and, later, Frazer, but also by other major figures such as John Lubbock, John McLennan, and Henry Maine. Stocking provides a succinct summary of the tenets of what he terms "classical evolutionism" in anthropology, which, along with the notion of unity of mind, include:

> that sociocultural phenomena, like the rest of the natural world, are governed by laws that science can discover; that these laws operate uniformly in the distant past as well as in the present; that the present grows out of the past by continuous processes without any sharp breaks; that this growth is naturally from simplicity to complexity; . . . that other sociocultural phenomena tend to develop in correlation with scientific progress; that in these terms human groups can be objectively ordered in a hierarchical fashion; that certain contemporary societies therefore approximate the various earlier stages of human development; that in the absence of adequate historical data these stages may be reconstructed by a comparison of contemporary groups; and that the result of this "comparative method" can be confirmed by "survivals" in more advanced societies of the forms characteristic of lower stages. (VA 170)

Once Tylor first articulated the prospect of a science of culture built upon evolutionary principles and operating through a comparative method, cautions about both the method and its assumptions were raised and continued to surface with increasing intensity, until the eventual supplanting of evolutionary comparativism with functionalist ethnography. Many of the objections were built on the premise that cultural evolutionary theory lacked the empirical bases of evolutionary theory in the physical sciences. Discredit was brought to cultural evolutionism because of what was perceived as badly displaced scientism. According to Ackerknecht, the fall from grace came to evolutionary comparativism because it was "far more vulnerable than biological evolutionism. . . . The archaeological foundations of cultural evolutionism were different from and weaker than the paleontological foundations of Darwinism. Cultural anthropology had no embryology to support its arguments" ("On the Comparative Method" 122).

The validity of the comparisons came under question early. Francis Galton in an important reply to Tylor's 1889 paper noted that the historical relation of items compared might invalidate or radically change the grounds of the comparison, for then the issue of cultural diffusion arises, which can and often does run at odds with the comparative project. Similarly, through the 1890s and early years of the twentieth century, Franz Boas battled what he considered indiscriminate comparativism in much evolutionary anthropology. In a notable paper presented in 1896, entitled "The Limitations of the Comparative Method in Anthropology," Boas, anticipating Malinowskian functionalism, asserts that "a detailed study of customs in their relation to the total culture of the tribe practicing them" would provide "much greater accuracy than the generalizations of the comparative method will permit."[23] Boas, calling for more careful *historical* analysis of the connections between varying tribes, rejects the "fundamental assumption" among evolutionary comparativists that "the occurrence of the same phenomenon is always due to the same causes, and that thus it is proved that the human mind obeys the same laws everywhere" (275). He concludes that comparisons of cultures should "be restricted to those phenomena which have been proved to be effects of the same causes" (275) and that distinctions be made between the effects of cultural diffusion and other modes of similarity. "In short," Boas claims, "before extended comparisons are made, the comparability of the material must be proved" (275).

Boas's criticism of the uses of evolutionary comparativism does not translate into a call for the end of comparison altogether, or, for that matter, for the death of evolutionism in all its forms: he is simply demanding a more limited and careful basis of comparison and a new emphasis in anthropology upon respecting the integrity of separate cultures. Ackerknecht points out that in the 1930s Boas sought "'a cultural morphology founded on comparative studies of similar forms in different parts of the world'"; only "the functionalist school of Malinowski broke completely with the comparative method" ("On the Comparative Method" 122). And Stocking similarly observes that while Boas "retained a sense of the diversity of the writers who were later classed as 'evolutionist,'" his disciples, chiefly Ruth Benedict and Margaret Mead, began their training during "the battle against evolutionism" and thus had no such tolerance for them (VA 291).

And yet Benedict and Mead cannot be classified as simply anticomparativist. Joseph Tobin makes the point that the two ethnographers, authors of *Patterns of Culture* and *Sex and Temperament in Three Primitive Societies,* respectively, "were themselves comparativists, but comparativists who focused on whole cultures rather than on cultural traits ("HRAF as Radical Text" 477). But they were resolutely opposed to the brand of evolutionary comparativism in which an isolated "trait" from one culture was placed against a similarly excised trait from a different culture. In a famous and quite useful analogy, Benedict likens such comparison to the surgical procedures of Doctor Frankenstein:

> Studies of culture like *The Golden Bough* and the usual comparative ethnological volumes are analytical discussions of traits and ignore all the aspects of cultural integration. Mating or death practices are illustrated by bits of behavior selected indiscriminately from the most different cultures, and the discussion builds up a kind of mechanical Frankenstein's monster with a right eye from Fiji, a left from Europe, one leg from Tierra del Fuego, and one from Tahiti, and all the fingers and toes from still different regions. Such a figure corresponds to no reality in the past or present.[24]

The criticisms of Galton, Boas, Benedict, and others point to the seemingly dramatic nature of the break with evolutionary anthropology, a rupture most palpably felt with the publication of Malinowski's *Argonauts* in 1922. And yet Stocking acknowledges that the break between the old comparativism and the new ethnography has often been dramatized and exaggerated, for, among other things, it ignores the earlier, persistent criticisms of the comparative method, and it also discounts the real continuity, versus the simple break, in fieldwork practices. In "The Ethnographer's Magic" Stocking attempts to historicize Malinowski by placing him "in the context of earlier British fieldwork" (71). Though a significant shift undoubtedly occurred between participant observation and armchair culling of sources, Stocking reminds us that the "evolutionary anthropologists were very seriously concerned with improving the quality and quantity of their empirical data" (71). Stocking points to the emergence of *Notes and Queries* in the 1870s, which over the subsequent decades provided guidelines for those in the field; he underscores the efforts of Tylor and Frazer to improve the quality of data; and he chronicles the fieldwork done by Boas, whom he calls the "first important agent in the field" (74).

That such continuities exist compels us to consider shifts outside of the domain of fieldwork or method proper, and brings us back to the conclusion with which this introduction began: anthropology is given shape in discourse, so it must be considered as such. What shifted in the transition

from evolutionary comparativism to functionalist ethnography was perhaps not so much the method itself as the discursive form that contained
that method. This is not an entirely original observation. Boon and Stocking are of course pointing in this direction, as is Robert Thornton when he
notes that what emerged from Malinowski was "a new discursive space for
ethnographic argument."[25] And Marilyn Strathern, commenting that "if
we look to practice, we could do worse than look to anthropological writing," similarly focuses on Frazer's readability, asserting that a significant
difference between Frazer and Malinowski lies in the contrasting relations
of writer to reading audience: Frazer establishes a cozy relationship with
his readers, while Malinowski consciously creates a more "modernist" distance ("Out of Context" 84, 105–07).[26]

These critics are correct in focusing on such discursive gaps, and this
book similarly keys on writerly difference by essentially contrasting comparativist and ethnographic authorities. And yet a discursive perspective
brings to light continuities as well. We cannot forget, after all, that Malinowski drew inspiration from Frazer's writerly ways. Writing from the
Trobriand islands while doing fieldwork for *Argonauts,* Malinowski reports
to Frazer (in a manner that suggests the deference of the fieldworker to his
armchair master) that through *The Golden Bough* "I have come to realize
the paramount importance of vividness and colour in descriptions of native
life" (quoted in Thornton, "'Imagine Yourself'" 8). Indeed, Thornton
holds that the "new discursive space" created by Malinowski was made
possible by Frazer, for Malinowski first found his trope of travel in *The
Golden Bough* (10).[27]

Malinowski, however, produced a different kind of text. Whether we
perceive it as realist ethnography or romantic quest narrative, or something
of both, we cannot forget Malinowski's own authorial aspirations: after all,
Malinowski proclaimed that W. H. R. Rivers is "the Rider Haggard of
Anthropology: I shall be the Conrad!"[28] But we also cannot ignore the
essential difference between the quality of Malinowski's and Frazer's aesthetics. One way of putting this contrast is to note that while Malinowski,
in the realist vein, attempts to mystify his authorial figurings in the guise
of a seeming transparency (I was there, and this is what I saw), Frazer's
blatant, florid show of figures conceals an aesthetic that is at bottom transparent and reductive. The full nature and extent of Frazerian transparency
will be defined and expanded below (indeed, it is a recurring concern of
this book), but for now it is patent that Frazer's grandiloquent, explicitly
writerly ways encouraged humanist, and more specifically, Modernist literary uses, in ways that Malinowski's text did not.

Frazer's literariness, however, does not translate simply into a series of "literary influences"; indeed, the reciprocal relation of Frazerian anthropology and "literature" underscores the appropriative nature of such borrowing. Frazer's literary borrowings, in other words, go both ways: literature and literary criticism use Frazer, but Frazer uses literature. In this respect the powers of Frazerian comparativism are inextricably tied to the allure of the literary, the anthropological and the aesthetic functioning symbiotically within a grand stratagem of control. For an anthropologist like Frazer, for example, the use of a "literary" style ultimately became a defense, when faced with attacks on theories and methodology, that his texts were artistic creations; for a literary Modernist like Eliot, borrowing social-scientific "facts" from anthropology heightened the institutional legitimacy of literature and literary criticism. Together these eminently effective strategies, welding "hard" cultural study with appropriately ambiguous figurality, promoted the power of writer over cultural "subject" (who doubled as both native and reader).

The comparativist text, as exemplified in the writings of Frazer, Eliot, Frye, and Campbell, encourages multiple weldings of seeming contraries (literature and anthropology), as the encyclopedic tendency to move outward is complemented by the urge toward fusion and thus becomes a way of extending one's grasp. Rationalist evolutionism combined with poetic fervor may seem contradictory but they do roll toward the same authorial end. A profusion of voices may stand out as diversity, but they ultimately move toward the system or idea that unites, destroying variation in the process. In this respect, Frazer and Eliot, and especially Frye and Campbell, are noted for far-ranging encyclopedic texts that, in uniformitarian fashion, persuade through their very scope that human nature and endeavor can be reduced to a few fundamental ideas.

1

James Frazer: Facts and Figures

The absence of speculation [in *The Golden Bough*] is a conscious and
deliberate scrupulousness, a positive point of view. And it is just
that: a point of view, a vision, put forward through a fine prose
style, that gives the work of Frazer a position above that of other
scholars of equal erudition and perhaps greater ingenuity, and
which gives him an inevitable and growing influence over the
contemporary mind . . . this will not fail to have a profound effect
upon the literature of the future.

—T. S. Eliot, 1924

The Golden Bough purports to be a work of anthropology, and yet it
has had more influence on literary criticism than in its own alleged
field, and it may yet prove to be really a work of literary criticism.

—Northrop Frye, 1957

Apparently primitive custom and belief caught Frazer's imagination
as no literature ever did, and we can see the range and complexity
of his poetic imagination . . . in his compilations on magic and
religion. Late in his life Frazer defined "the highest poetry" as
characterized by "that flight of imagination, that outburst of lyrical
rapture." For him, the highest poetry was the curious behavior
of man.

—Stanley Edgar Hyman, 1962

Quite explicitly [Frazer] thought of himself as making a contribution
to literature rather than to science, and it does not seem to have
occurred to him that in "improving" his sources he might also be
distorting them.

—Edmund Leach, 1966

THE FACTS

For well over half a century literary audiences have listened to modern artists and critics speak of Frazer's literariness and its salutary effects upon
Modern art and criticism; Eliot found Frazer's literary "vision" and style
an essential component of the emerging Modernist temperament, and by

the early sixties Frye and Hyman brought to a culmination the literary usefulness of Frazer's graceful text for myth and ritual studies. Typical of interdisciplinary relations, however, was the lag (or break) between social-scientific production and aesthetic appreciation and appropriation: Eliot's plaudits of Frazer in 1922 (in his Notes to *The Waste Land* as well as in the famous review of Joyce's *Ulysses*) coincided with the publication of Bronislaw Malinowski's *Argonauts of the Western Pacific,* a model for the emerging functionalist monograph that would have little use for Frazer's self-confessed brand of literary social science.

And yet Malinowski's work hardly constituted a radical break with a dominating Frazerian school. As we have seen, evolutionary comparativism had been roundly attacked by leading anthropologists since the turn of the century. Boas of course had steadily assaulted the comparative method that Frazer had inherited from Tylor and others, and Leach claims that by 1910 "Frazer had ceased to matter," as diffusionism and the French sociologists took center stage of anthropological attention. In any case, Leach's condemnation of Frazer in 1966 was anything but a novel statement in anthropological circles; in fact, the position required such a restatement only because a colleague, I. C. Jarvie, had attempted a positive reappraisal of the author of *The Golden Bough.*[1]

Indeed, the assumptions of Frazerian comparativism were scorned by many anthropologists well before the time that the literary critics were canonizing Frazer: the modern ethnographer was purportedly interested in the "true" voice of the native, not the convenient fictionalization. In the postmodern era, however, some polarities have curiously reversed. As Marilyn Strathern so well illustrates, the figurality that cursed Frazer in the eyes of modern anthropologists now holds itself teasingly in front of those who criticize anthropology as a window to the world, and indeed the bang and clatter of voices and the encyclopedic range of *The Golden Bough* do justify our looking there for more varied representations than meet the monograph-ic eye.[2]

Whether our predilection toward many-sided and multivoiced cultural representation makes us see in Frazer's fictions what we wish to see, clearly a good part of the power of Frazer's writing derives from its apparent profusion of voice and source. Conversely, in ethnography after Frazer, the controlling authors to a great degree translate the voices of the sources into their own words. And yet these voices, however much the ethnographic authoritarian tries to contain them, bleed out onto the margins of the page. The other voice always has its say if one listens. Clifford, alluding to Malinowski, states that "one may also read against the grain of the text's dominant voice, seeking out other half-hidden authorities" (PC 53). But in Frazer's case the background noise is deafening, because of the sheer multitude and variety of cultural accounts that he draws, in encyclopedic manner, from historians, mythographers, missionaries, fieldworkers, translators, and native informants, often quoting them at great length.

Frazer himself articulates those instances where polyvocality is most possible in *The Golden Bough* as moments of weakness. Whenever he gives in to the impulse to play tale-teller or ventriloquist, he then openly rationalizes and publicly defends his indulgence. For example, a fundamental organizational oddity in *The Golden Bough* is the imbalance between the great multitude of legends, stories, songs, and reports, and the theory on Arician priesthood that supposedly unites the whole work. It is incredible to see Frazer proclaiming, in the opening to the first two-volume edition (1890), that he is providing the literally thousands of cultural accounts spanning the globe and the centuries for the purpose of answering just two questions: "first, why had the priest [at Nemi] to slay his predecessor? And second, why, before he slew him, had he to pluck the Golden Bough?" Having stated his purpose, Frazer adds: "it remains to try whether the survey of a wider field may not yield us the clues we seek" (I: 6)—and he tries, in ever-expanding editions, over the next quarter-century.

This imbalance did not go unnoticed. In 1901 a reviewer of the second edition of *The Golden Bough* quipped that the Golden Bough itself (that originary mistletoe, that ur-branch of his ultimate fifteen-volume effort), was "too slender a twig to sustain the weight of learning hung upon it." And a generation ago myth critic Stanley Edgar Hyman, in *The Tangled Bank,* commented on how Frazer "tells myths, legends, folk tales, and similar stories on every occasion, whether or not they are relevant." Similarly, Ackerman consistently recounts Frazer's general "excessive use of examples that only tenuously exemplify" (JGF 25), and most recently Steven Connor has commented on how "the flood of examples" in *The Golden Bough* "threatens to swell beyond the control of the narrative."[3]

In one sense, Frazer simply could not maintain control over his line of argument, could not keep the myriad legends and fieldwork accounts tied to his thesis or in line with his method. This of course did not stop him from retelling those tales, but at least he felt some remorse over his compulsion. Ackerman well documents Frazer's apologies and justifications in the correspondence to his publisher of fifty years, George Macmillan, concerning what Ackerman refers to as the "pattern of uncontrollable swelling" that "became the rule in all his best-known works" (JFG 57). And Frazer's prefaces to the multiple editions of *The Golden Bough* illustrate the varied attempts to justify the ever-increasing multitude of accounts. In the preface to the first edition, for example, he comments that "a justification is perhaps needed of the length at which I have dwelt upon the popular festivals observed by European peasants," and, rather lamely, he provides one: "despite their fragmentary character" they are "the fullest and most trustworthy evidence we possess as to the primitive religion of the Aryans" (ix–x).

The digressiveness that more fastidious critics castigated and Frazer himself felt compelled to excuse nonetheless had a powerful rhetorical effect upon Frazer's readership, a magnetizing pull that Frazer clearly was not willing to sacrifice for the sake of efficiency and concision. As Frazer spins out myth after myth, the reader's attention gradually shifts from whatever generalization ostensibly brought forth the need for illustration and onto the various stories themselves. Their intrinsic interest justifies their presence. Ackerman holds that the "labyrinthine quality" of Frazer's text is due to Frazer's "unbridled willingness to digress": the resultant "profusion of data" creates a rhetorical context "in which virtually any topic, as in a dream, may turn into any other" (JGF 99). Indeed, Frazer's tellings can at times resemble a Lacanian fantasy: a mad jostling of signifiers, each linked by a thread to the one before and after, but often with no firm connection to the supposed purpose for the chain.

The first chapter of the first edition of *The Golden Bough*, published in 1890, exemplifies this process of digressive drift. In the first edition, Frazer used topic headers—phrases placed at the top of each page to identify subject matter. The use of such headers acknowledges that this is a text that requires firm tags identifying meaning or content, reader's aids for signification. With the heading of "Rain-Making," for example, the author is announcing to his readers that yes, despite the babble of strange stories stuffed with distracting exotica, ranging in origin from Roumania to China to Peru, this is what I am talking about, this is my point. The markers serve, in effect, as guides for the wide-eyed tourists liable to lose their way.

And yet once these markers of meaning are read in sequence, are linked one to the other in a slender chain, a wholly different rhetorical effect emerges. In a sequence that comprises seventeen pages of text (I: 12–29), "Rain-*Making*" becomes "*Making* Sunshine"; "Making *Sun*shine" becomes "Staying the *Sun*"; "Stay*ing* the Sun" becomes "*Making* Wind"; "Making *Wind*" becomes "Fighting the *Wind*." The italics, my own, indicate the middle terms, the linking signifiers in each relation, but the middle term links only that particular pairing of signifiers. The second of the pair and the term preceding the first of the pair usually have no or little bonding, and the relation between the first signifier in the sequence, "Rain-Making," and the last, "Fighting the Wind," resembles the dissonance or drift between the first and last messages in a children's game of telephone.

This slippage of signification, like the proverbial snowball down the hill, only increases the impetus toward digression; indeed, it creates a context in which yet another tale needs telling in the effort to come to that ever-elusive close. Early readers of *The Golden Bough* were aware of this rhetorical tendency; indeed, one of the earliest assessments of the book, published in the *Edinburgh Review* in 1890, comments: "Mr. Frazer delights to lead us on, like an Oriental story-teller, who ends each tale with an event or allusion that requires another one to explain it."[4]

With the multivolume third edition of *The Golden Bough* Frazer apparently felt an even greater need to provide markers for his readers, aids to signification, so he not only retained the topic headers but added marginal glosses. The glosses are attempts to underline the text's coherence, its logical progression, and in a sense they do contain the text, mark off its margins. But on the other hand, the glosses deceive, because the digressions in the voluminous volumes of the third edition increasingly spill over, overrun their borders, become in their insistence the object of attention.

An example of the increasing digression in the third edition can be found in the opening section of *Taboo and the Perils of the Soul,* the third of the edition's twelve volumes. There Frazer's chronicle of "Royal and Priestly Taboos" leads him to consider "Taboos observed by African kings"; which leads him to discuss the prohibition upon the king "to see the sea"; which leads to observations of how "Egyptian priests loathed the sea"; which leads to sources commenting on how the Indians of the Peruvian Andes, "sent by the Spaniards to work in the hot valleys of the coast," were horrified at the specter of the ocean opening before them; which leads to "the inland people of Lampong in Sumatra," who "are said to pay a kind of adoration to the sea, and to make it an offering of cakes and sweetmeats" (9–10). In richly descriptive swells, Frazer has surged his way from taboos on kings to sea-worship. And crammed at the bottom of the page, we find the sources for these (to Frazer) compelling narratives, including a Chief Native Commissioner for Mashonaland, the renowned van Gennep, a Father Porte from the *Missions Catholiques,* and Plutarch.

Frazer's discontinuousness, however, cannot be attributed simply to bad organization. On the one hand, he was caught up in the stories he read, consumed by the voices he had heard, and he marched out justification, excuse, and rationalization to legitimate his retelling, or more accurately, his rewriting. On the other hand, Frazer clearly realized the rhetorical effects of this, at the least, seeming inability: the steady sales of his books, for one thing, indicated that a reading public enjoyed participating in this discursive obsession of projecting multiple voices that might just lose track of the argument proper.

Deliberate or not, Frazer's digressiveness produced rhetorical effects that, importantly, promoted the authority and credibility of the author and defended his ideas against the opposition. That is why simply labeling Frazer's digressive drift obsessive or even deconstructive misses the important ways in which apparently compulsive and elusive tale-tellings act as formidable power mechanisms of authorial dominance. In this respect it is crucial to recognize that Frazer's digressiveness performs fundamentally defensive rhetorical functions. Quite simply, Frazer attempts to win over his audience, and in the process mute his opposition, through the sheer massiveness of his train of examples. Frazer's contemporaries were not wholly confused by this tactic. One of them, R. R. Marett, a critic of Frazer but a staunch supporter of his reputation, acutely noted that Frazer does not "shift his ground" when faced with opposing views but instead "is compelled by the sheer amount of his additional material to demonstrate the strength of his material, and to leave adverse, or at any rate qualifying, considerations more or less out of sight."[5]

The point is not just that Frazer's contemporaries recognized Frazer's tactic but that they, in large part, were nonetheless still swept away by it even as they recognized his argumentative shortcomings. Ackerman's recent assessment is that Frazer's books were remarkable successes, in terms of wide readership, *in spite of* their argumentative flaws: note his final assessment of *Folk-Lore in the Old Testament,* that "despite the fact that most of the work thus constitutes a gigantic piece of pseudo-argumentation, it was very popular" (JGF 275). But it is critical to see that Frazer's texts succeeded in this respect not despite but *because* of his rhetorical tactic, that the power of Frazer's comparative rhetoric was integrally tied to such apparently inane or compulsive rhetorical habits.

The power of Frazer's massive accumulations lies in his habit of adding stories, "facts," and theories while never, or rarely, discarding. This tendency runs throughout his career. In *Totemism and Exogamy,* published in 1910, Frazer resolves the problem of his own thrice-shifting views on the issue of totemism by publishing everything he has had to say on the issue to date, in spite of the fact that his earlier theories are in total contradiction to his current position. Hence the original volume, *Totemism* (1887), is reprinted alongside two essays (published 1899 and 1905) that are meant to refute it. Frazer's rationale, as stated in the preface, assumes that a resolution to contradiction can be achieved not through the deletion of the old but through the accretion of the new: "I felt that to reprint *Totemism* without noticing discoveries which had, in my opinion, revolutionised the whole aspect of the subject, would be unpardonable; hence my decision to add the essays in question as an appendix to the reprint."[6]

This rhetorical habit of accumulation, referred to by Ackerman as "Frazer's obsessive trait of discarding nothing and recycling everything" (JGF 220), goes far to explain the massiveness of Frazer's corpus, and ultimately must be read in the light of rhetorical effect.[7] To what degree and how often Frazer really did change his mind on anthropological issues is highly debatable, but what is inscribed in the text is the sum total of Frazer's collections and considerations. Relevant here is Robert Alun Jones's observation on the "palimpsest character" of the later editions of *The Golden Bough*, which enables us to "read" the third, multivolume edition as "a history of the development of Frazer's mind—a history filled with 'fossils'" of the varying "'stages' of his thought."[8] Frazer is the ultimate pack rat: fossil by fossil he builds a museum of relics that, so the rhetoric implies, contains all body parts and hence contains all possible explanations. If it holds multiple, contradictory theories, then very well; it is large, it contains contradictions.

The review of the first edition of *The Golden Bough* in the *Edinburgh Review* attacked Frazer for pushing his theories too hard, claiming that the author "spoils an interesting theory by straining it" and "presses his points too far; he makes too much play with fanciful resemblances" (559, 557). One important defense against such attacks, a stratagem that only increased in use over time, was to attach several possible, even contradictory theories to a single problem. If one theory does not convince, then no need to press too hard: there are several others to choose from. Vickery holds that "Frazer's habit of entertaining several alternative hypotheses" illustrates Frazer's "more cautious" temperament and "both contributed to and reflected the intellectual confusion and uncertainty of the age."[9] Clearly, there is more to these wafflings and logical inconsistencies than what Vickery sees as the harbinger of "modern skepticism or relativism" (24) or the "confusion" that Frazer attributes to his "savage." Indeed, Frazer's apparently obsessive layering of theory upon theory, like his piling of story upon story, builds a clumsy edifice that in its utterly massive inclusiveness powerfully resists attack.

In a fundamental sense, Frazer collected contradictions because, by containing them in bulk within his own comparativist discursive form, he
made them incapable of disarming him. The comparativist masterwork
through accretion grew larger than any mere idea. But the rhetoric reads
differently, of course, promoting a humility that disguises the authority at
work. Indeed, Frazer's many prefaces to the various editions and volumes
of *The Golden Bough* are filled with seemingly humble statements that
downplay his own abilities and inclination toward "authority" by making
the value of his work dependent upon the reliability and usefulness of anthropological "facts" gleaned from his sources: "My contribution to the
history of the human mind consists of little more than a rough and purely
provisional classification of facts gathered almost entirely from printed
sources" (*Balder* vi). In fact, Frazer's defense often takes the form of a grandiloquent gesture of humility, such as the following, taken from the Preface
to *Taboo and the Perils of the Soul*: "The facts which I have put together in
this volume . . . may perhaps serve as materials for a future science of
Comparative Ethics. They are rough stones which await the master-builder,
rude sketches which more cunning hands than mine may hereafter work
up into a finished picture" (viii).

Frazer's apparent humility rests upon an institutional assumption, evolutionary in nature, that anthropology is "still in the collecting stages"
and hence a master of the "science" of anthropology is not yet possible.
Since "it is essential that a period of collection should precede a period of
generalization," Frazer maintains, then "the prime want of the study is not
so much theories as facts."[10] Again, Frazer's seeming humility projects the
possibility of a future master, a great Theorist who can emerge only when
induction has clicked into the proper evolutionary stage: "The great think-
ers, the Newtons and Darwins of Anthropology, will come after us. It is
our business to prepare for them by collecting, sifting, and arranging the
records in order that when, in the fullness of time, the master-mind shall
arise and survey them, he may be able to detect at once that unity in multiplicity, that universal in the particulars, which has escaped us" (31).

John Vickery acutely sees in Frazer's call for the "master-builder" the
implication "that perhaps in some unforeseeable, miraculous fashion someone in the future will be able to master and utilize the quantities of data he
has amassed" (*Literary Impact* 24); but he does not discuss Frazer's minimizing of his own accomplishments as a stance that attempts to enshrine
while it humbles, plotting the anthropologist-author a place in history by
unassumingly constructing a history in which he himself would have value
(in which the "master" is, after all, a projection of himself).

The future master, then, must be seen as allegorical, as a figure who functions as authorial projection and masks, through humility, the will to dominance at work in the text. And Frazer's future master is integrally tied to another anthropological figure, what Clifford refers to as the "allegory of salvage," that "rhetorical construct" that perpetuates the value of anthropology by saying to its reader that "the other [the 'native'] is lost, in disintegrating time and space, but saved in the text" (wc 112). For in evolutionary anthropology, according to Frazer, "the prime want of the study is not so much theories but facts" not only because, inductively, one needs facts first in order to erect grand theories, but because the ultimate source for those facts, the "savages" themselves, are daily disappearing from our lives:

> Contact with civilization is rapidly effacing the old beliefs and customs of the savage, and is thereby obliterating records of priceless value for the history of our race. The most urgent need of anthropology at present is to procure accurate accounts of the existing customs and ideas of savages before they have disappeared. When these have been obtained . . . the philosophic historian will be able to formulate, with a fair degree of probability, those general laws which have shaped the intellectual, social, and moral evolution of mankind. (*Man, God, and Immortality* 31)

Frazer's allegory of salvage makes urgent the preservation of a record that is essential to the coming master, as it compels the anthropologist's audience to envision a future apocalypse in which "the savage . . . will then be as extinct as the dodo" (*Man, God, and Immortality* 20). Frazer's rhetoric of ethnological extinction replicates the assumptions of a determined evolutionism, as in this passage, where the colons pound out an inexorable progression: "The sands are fast running out: the hour will soon strike: the record will be closed: the book will be sealed" (20). But, crucially, Frazer's clarion call to beat the evolutionary clock functions not so that the savages can be preserved: they, sadly or not, are foredoomed, thanks in part to the fieldworkers whose contact with them makes Frazer's collection possible. Rather, Frazer seeks to justify the preservation of the ethnological "facts" and hence carve out an institutional significance and future fame for the collector. And in fact the rhetoric of projection in the above passages becomes an explicit entreaty (appropriately charged with harsh juridical metaphor) for the increased institutionalization of Frazer's brand of collecting:

And how shall we of this generation look when we stand at the bar of posterity arraigned on a charge of high treason to our race, we who neglected to study our perishing fellow-men, but who sent out costly expeditions to observe the stars and to explore the barren ice-bound regions of the poles, as if the polar ice would melt and the stars would cease to shine when we are gone? Let us awake from our slumber, let us light our lamps, let us gird up our loins. The Universities exist for the advancement of knowledge. It is their duty to add this new province to the ancient departments of learning which they cultivate so diligently. (20–21)

Frazer's plea for a university-sanctioned discipline rests ultimately upon the assertion that anthropology is a legitimate science. Indeed, Frazer was a central figure in what Ackerman calls the attempt "to raise [social sciences] to the standards already achieved in the natural sciences." The main thrust of that claim had to do with the application of Darwinian evolutionism to human cultures, a pioneering transfer involving of course not only Frazer but Tylor and the other evolutionary founders of anthropology. Still, referring to Frazer as a scientist strikes some as stretching the term, especially since the shift from Frazerian to Malinowskian anthropology is often characterized as the point at which the field got whipped into scientistic shape.[11]

Although, as Vickery perceptively notes, "the aligning of Frazer with science seems curious and unlikely" if we insist upon a narrow, more contemporary conception of science replete with "mathematical formulae, intricate experiments, and concepts that either flout or beggar common sense," what is important is that like Darwin and Freud "Frazer thought of himself as a scientist, as one for whom truth and fact were not only accessible but ultimate values" (*Literary Impact* 6). I would shift the emphasis from *belief* to *rhetoric* and, at variance with Jarvie, claim that Frazer, when it was strategically advantageous, inscribed himself as a scientist and gained rhetorically from the assertion that "truth" and "fact" were his ultimate values.

That is why his valorization of so-called anthropological facts has such critical import: he needed to demonstrate, or at least persistently assert, that his brand of cultural comparison had a firm empirical foundation. Frazer's "facts," as construed by him, constitute a bedrock of certainty: the palpable, incontrovertible reality of anthropological research. According to Frazer, the process of collecting facts results in a compendium of truths, an open storehouse of cultural nuggets that is destined to stand the test of

time well after the more contrived, and scientifically "softer," theories have
fallen:

> In this as in other branches of study it is the fate of theories to be
> washed away like children's castles of sand by the rising tide of knowl-
> edge, and I am not so presumptuous as to expect or desire for mine
> an exemption from the common lot. I hold them all very lightly and
> have used them chiefly as convenient pegs on which to hang my col-
> lection of facts. For I believe that, while theories are transitory, a record
> of facts has a permanent value, and that as a chronicle of ancient cus-
> toms and beliefs my book may retain its utility when my theories are
> as obsolete as the customs and beliefs deserve to be. (*Balder* xi)

Frazer's rhetorical pose is often that of the scientist who wisely and humbly minimizes the heady, airy role of theorist and sticks instead to the more
enduring nuts-and-bolts activity of collecting and arranging the facts.
When the utter profusion of evidence compels him to step over the inductive line and erect a theory, Frazer's authorial persona is still more than
willing to admit to the possibility of error in judgment. This rhetoric of
humble fact-collector is well illustrated in the preface to *Totemism and Exogamy*: "For though I have never hesitated either to frame theories which
seemed to fit the facts or to throw them away when they ceased to do so,
my aim in this and my other writings has not been to blow bubble hypotheses which glitter for a moment and are gone; it has been by a wide
collection and an exact classification of facts to lay a broad and solid foundation for the inductive study of primitive man" (xvi).

Frazer's pose of humility is carefully calculated to leave room for glory.
Mere fact-collecting, after all, lays the foundation and thus projects the possibility of the future master, a figure who, outside of the framework of
evolutionary comparativism, would not exist.

Frazer's preference for fact is represented by natural figures—"The facts
of nature will always burst the narrow bonds of human theories" (*Spirits
of the Corn* 37)—as well as metaphysical—"For theories are shifting and
transitory, while facts are eternal" (*Man, God, and Immortality* ix). In both
cases, the anthropological "fact" functions as the kernel of culture from
which human interpretation grows, and the figure of the "collection of
facts" serves, in New Critical terms, as the ultimate verbal icon, the culturally wrought material emblem that invites interpretation but is not
bound to it and is, hence, timeless in its shaping.

Frazer's pre–New Critical rhetoric was compelling, repeatable in the
texts of others. In 1918, for example, R. R. Marett duplicated Frazer's rhet-

oric, asserting that "by the magic of his pen [Frazer] has made the myriad facts live, so that they tell their own tale, and we are left free to read their meanings as our own several tastes and temperaments dictate."[12] The "facts" transparently and polyvocally announce themselves, not dependent upon an audience for their existence and yet the center of an audience's attention, totally independent of interpretation and yet the only reliable sites for interpretation. Marett's 1936 review of Frazer's *Fear of the Dead in Primitive Religion* even more strikingly points to the capability of Frazer's storehouse to be both autonomous from interpretation and the plentiful source of its own generation: "despite the mutability of all anthropological interpretation, who would question the permanent value of such a digest of evidence—one so pregnant with suggestion that anyone who takes the trouble to ponder it well can hardly fail to strike out something new" ("De Mortuis" 28).

It is perhaps not surprising that the blurbs to Frazer's books, often printed at the end of a Frazer volume, duplicate his rhetoric. At the end of volume one of *Balder the Beautiful* (part seven of the third edition of *The Golden Bough*), *Outlook* is quoted as claiming: "Whether we disagree or agree with Dr. Frazer's general conclusions [in *Psyche's Task*], he has provided us with a veritable storehouse of correlated facts, for which . . . we can never be sufficiently grateful." Below that blurb the *Times* is reported as asserting that Frazer's *Folk-Lore in the Old Testament* constitutes "a vast and varied store of information . . . a mine of instructive facts for which all future students of the subject will be grateful."

This replication of Frazer's rhetoric of collection surfaces even in texts which are generally critical of his theories and methods. Even Edmund Leach, whose disdain for Frazer is unequaled, claims that though "Frazer's ideas have dated . . . it is the facts themselves that matter, not Frazer's interpretation of the facts."[13] Indeed, Leach goes so far as to suggest that Frazer's collections of fact have a "possible utility . . . for the purposes of structural comparison" (382), and thus holds that "if in his lifetime [Frazer] was credited with undue merit, his collection of facts remain—a quarry for the future rather than a dull record of antiquated ideas" (383).

Though Leach acknowledges here Frazer's "undue" popularity, in other contexts he confirms that in Frazer's own day his theories were severely challenged within anthropological circles ("'Founding Fathers'" 561–62). Some of the main charges against Frazer will be treated below, but more to the point here is that Frazer's "facts" function not only as a powerful positive rhetorical force but also as a fundamental check against the collapse of his theories. Quite simply, Frazer promotes "facts" because he knows his theories are (or will be) considered tenable at best, laughably obsolete at worst. Or put another way, Frazer's persona as *fact-collector* emerges in the rhetoric when his reputation as *theorist* declines.

When, at the end of his career, in the preface to *Aftermath: A Supplement to* The Golden Bough, Frazer writes: "I hold all my theories very lightly," it is important to know that he does so in the knowledge that those theories have for decades been deluged with criticism, indeed challenged to their core.[14] "Sir James Frazer prefers facts to theories," Marett observes late in Frazer's career (1936), and then neatly duplicates Frazer's rhetoric by claiming that "looking to the far future, he can contemplate with equanimity the time when his explanations will have ceased to be in fashion" ("De Mortuis" 27). In effect Marett falls for the Frazerian rhetorical move of projecting his own obsolescence as hypothetical when, in fact, it had been progressing in anthropological circles throughout the second half of his career.

Frazer was often the first to acknowledge the objections to his theories. Indeed, the best source for the challenges to his theories is probably in Frazer's own writings where, with his characteristic rhetorical humility, he constantly shifts his own theories to "fit the facts" and to square with the experts who have disproven his previous ideas. In the preface to the first edition of *The Golden Bough* he skillfully anticipates the later objections to it, stating: "Now that the theory, which necessarily presented itself to me at first in outline, has been worked out in detail, I cannot but feel that in some places I may have pushed it too far. If this should prove to have been the case, I will readily acknowledge my error as soon as it is brought home to me" (ix).

Ackerman rightly points out how Frazer's "willingness to change his mind and his continual emphasis on the provisional nature of his findings combined to produce the most modest of professional personae" (JGF 268), but the biographer does not make explicit that Frazer bolstered his rhetorical authority by professing flexibility and uncertainty; rather, he concludes that Frazer personally was "as far as possible from the dictator laying down the orthodoxy that must be followed at all costs . . . the opposite of prepossessing" (268). I am not asserting that Frazer was necessarily *insincere* in his tentativeness or his willingness to change his theories to "fit the facts"; rather, I wish to focus on the positive rhetorical effects of his hesitancy, uncertainty, and openness of opinion.

There is no decisive point in his corpus where Frazer makes the leap from theorist to humble fact-collector. As we have seen, from as early as the first edition of *The Golden Bough* the role of fact-collector is introduced. But of course other roles are established as well throughout his career; indeed, just as Frazer often takes up the role of fact-collector when advantageous, so at other times he holds himself up as a purveyor of multiple theories or adopts the position of artist (see below). The process involves not a simple diachronic shift from one rhetorical identity to another but rather a complex shuttling between rhetorical identities that serves the broader interest of preserving rhetorical authority.

There is, however, in *The Golden Bough*'s sequence of editions and volumes a generally increasing urgency toward the valorization of fact, a markedly progressive flight from the rhetoric of theorist and toward that of fact-collector. This is most conspicuous in the multivolume third edition. In *Balder the Beautiful*, the last book of the edition, Frazer concedes that the "analogy between the Italian priest and the Norse God [Balder]," the parallel which since the first edition has held the beginning and end of *The Golden Bough* together, has essentially fallen apart. Characteristically, Frazer insists upon accretion rather than deletion of the disproven material. But what *could* justify inclusion, after Frazer's own admission that the entire theory has been disproven? His grounds are that it provides a context in which he may digress on other matters: "I have allowed [the parallel] to stand because it furnishes me a pretext for discussing not only the general questions of the external soul in popular superstition, but also the fire-festivals of Europe" (v). This discussion leads to the most explicit statement of the collapse of his governing theory:

> Thus Balder the Beautiful in my hands is little more than a stalking horse to carry two heavy pack-loads of facts. And what is true applies equally to the priest of Nemi himself, the nominal hero of the long tragedy of human folly and suffering which has unrolled itself before the readers of these volumes, and on which the curtain is about to fall. He, too, for all the quaint garb he wears and the gravity with which he stalks across the stage, is merely a puppet, and it is time to unmask him before laying him up in the box. (v–vi)[15]

Frazer unmasks his theory, and by extension all theory, as merely dramatistic, a shell that, until now, has barely covered the core of fact that justifies the entire enterprise. *The Golden Bough* is revealed, then, as an exercise in the collection of facts. It is true that, as Ackerman notes (JGF 251), Frazer then makes explicit his broader aims in the project: "I have really been discussing questions of more general interest which concern the gradual evolution of human thought from savagery to civilization" (vi), but it is crucial to recognize that Frazer does not acknowledge the assumptions behind those broader aims as theoretical. Evolution for Frazer is not theory but a very important set of facts.

Ackerman views Frazer's journey as circular, beginning as "a digression from a general work on primitive mythology" and ending in the same place, "finally revealed to have been that mysterious general work all along" (JGF 251). So he poses the work as failing in that respect, since the "expectations" set up in the whole work "are completely undercut" in the final book (253). Ackerman thus is surprised when these faults do not ruin the masterwork: "As the volumes appeared, and its immense scope began generally to be appreciated, it was universally acclaimed *despite* its inadequacies as one of the intellectual monuments of the age" (255; italics my own). The italics isolate what I believe is both a duplication and a misinterpretation of Frazer's rhetoric. The clashing theories, the admission of the failure of grand theory, are hardly weaknesses in Frazer's argument, hindrances to Frazer's success. Rather, Frazer succeeds (given the contestatory context in which his work was received) *because* of the rhetorical moves in which he promotes plurality of theory and his own fallibility and humility. Ackerman repeats Frazer's own rhetoric when he heralds the "immense scope" as the saving grace of the project, rather than as an integral rhetorical strategy, inextricably bound to apparently inane digression, theoretical confusion, and illogical transition.

Frazer did not hide the "fact" that his "facts" were essentially observations culled, arranged, and edited by the armchair anthropologist from "sources," primarily fieldworkers such as Spencer and Gillen. Indeed, with his typical pose of modesty, Frazer often acknowledges, profusely thanks, and praises his sources, much to his own denigration. In a letter to his prime fieldworker, Baldwin Spencer, in 1898, Frazer states that "books like mine are merely speculative," and hence "will be superseded sooner or later (the sooner the better for the sake of truth) by better inductions based on fuller knowledge; books like yours, containing records of observation, will never be superseded" (quoted in Hyman, TTB 230).

We can accept Ackerman's claim that Frazer the man "was genuinely humble before his facts and those who supplied them" (JGF 123), but only if we appreciate the rhetorical advantage of that humbling gesture. We must remember that the master's bow of humility was accompanied by an insistence on the separation of fieldwork and theory, the latter of which, Frazer states in a tribute to Spencer, ought "regularly and rightly [to] be left to the comparative ethnologist."[16] And there is no doubt that, despite his disclaimers of the value of theory and his self-promotion as fact-collector, a theorist was what Frazer wanted to be. The reason Ackerman gives for Frazer's refusal to learn any tribal language (he was a proficient linguist and classicist) sheds much light on Frazer's professional and discursive ambitions: "Knowledge of such a language would (or might) imply a specialization that he explicitly rejected. The role he assumed from the start was that of the generalist, one with the entire ethnographic world spread before him" (JGF 122).

Frazer wanted the best of both worlds: the status of the theorist, the controller, the author, but also the humility and reputation of fact-collector. To Spencer, Frazer assumed the role of authorizing and benevolently approving theorist; to his audience he often took refuge as a humble fact-collector: both positions furthered his own rhetorical authority. But it is critical to recognize that Frazer does not simply take advantage of a set of stable, preexistent categories, *fieldwork* and *theory*. Frazer's persistence about the separation of fieldwork and theory obscures the arbitrariness of a distinction that Frazer himself has, at the least, helped to create. In effect Frazer reifies the quite historically and ideologically contingent constructs of *fieldwork* and *theory* in the interests of the comparativist. The separation constitutes one important manifestation of a key Frazerian tactic, in which the comparativist inscribes bifurcations—here, fieldwork and theory—so that his authorial persona is posed as bridging that self-created gap. Frazer demands the separation of fieldwork and theory so that he can gain authority as one who can merge what is torn asunder.

In "The Scope and Method of Mental Anthropology" (1921), a kind of defense in brief for evolutionary comparativism, Frazer characteristically defends what he terms "the division of labour" between the fieldworker and the armchair anthropologist (*Garnered Sheaves* 247). Employing the allegory of salvage, he asserts that what we need now, before it is too late, is the "precise accounts of savages" (244) that only the man in the field can provide. And that is the only thing he *should* provide: "the business of comparison is not for him" (246). The fieldworker should simply "observe" and record, and then ship his "observations" to the anthropologist. The anthropologist, sitting at home amid a literal "heap" of such observations, then "evolves order out of chaos by eliciting the general principles or laws" that animate and unify the multifarious "facts" of culture (247). While Frazer expressly states that the process is ultimately cooperative—the fieldworker and comparative anthropologist "should work into each other's hands"—there can be no doubt that the anthropologist is the controller, the architect and ultimate author of the process, for "everything hinges on the work of comparison" (246).

Frazer is persistently counseling, or better put, lecturing, his fieldworkers to avoid comparative analysis and stick instead to collecting the facts.
In 1887 Frazer put together a pamphlet entitled *Questions on the Manners,
Customs, Religions, Superstitions, &c, of Uncivilized or Semi-Civilized Peoples,*
consisting essentially of a series of questions for those in the field to use.
The preface to the pamphlet indicates the priority of the armchair anthropologist when it notes that the questions "are intended not so much to be
put directly to the savage as to indicate to the civilised inquirer in the field
those subjects on which investigators at home would be glad to have information" (quoted in Hyman, TTB 197). Hyman's commentary on the
pamphlet rightly emphasizes Frazer's insistence upon the division of duties:
"No cross-cultural comparisons are suggested, those being the province
of the library anthropologist like Frazer who has access to materials from
different cultures, and no historical reconstructions are requested, those
being a matter of evolutionary hierarchy better worked out theoretically"
(197).

Yet Frazer is careful not to give the impression that he is forcing a subordinate role upon the fieldworker. In a tribute to fieldworkers Lorimer
Fison and A. W. Howitt (1909), Frazer, "as a warning of permanent importance to anthropologists," quotes Fison himself on the hazards of propounding theories. Theories are "mischievous" and must be avoided, Fison
is quoted as saying, for " 'the pang attending the extraction of an aching
double tooth is sweetest bliss when compared with the tearing up by the
roots of a cherished theory. I speak feelingly here, because I can hold myself
up as an awful warning against theory-making.' "[17] The message, significantly, is tactically delivered as a testimonial from the mouth of the man
in the field.

With his characteristic graciousness, Frazer is also careful not to denigrate the status of the fieldworker. Indeed, his assessment of the career of
Baldwin Spencer refers to the fieldworker's gift of "patient and exact observation unwarped by any theoretical bias," and calls Spencer's work "a
priceless record" (*Garnered Sheaves* 253). What Frazer praises in Spencer's
work is precisely that which Frazer, in other places, states will preserve his
own work: the cleaving to fact and avoidance of theory. When Frazer holds
that Spencer's "facts" will be "variously interpreted," but that their "foundation" will endure, he may as well be talking about his own work and,
indeed, he is: for it is primarily in *Frazer's* pages that Spencer's observations
will survive.[18]

Frazer insists upon the respect that he gives to the autonomy and integrity of the fieldworker's text, and his method of handling his sources at

least in part supports that rhetoric, for we cannot deny that much of Frazer's efforts went simply into recording his sources verbatim. When in the late 1880s zoologist A. C. Haddon agreed to furnish Frazer with his firsthand observations on life in the Torres Straits, Frazer wrote to Haddon to assure him of the care that he would take with Haddon's texts. It is his "rule," Frazer claims, "to publish all first-hand observations exactly as I receive them, except where the rules of grammar require some slight changes (one's correspondents are not always educated men), but even there I touch the MS as sparingly as possible. One cannot be too careful in dealing with descriptions of manners or customs; an apparently insignificant alteration or omission might efface an important piece of evidence" (quoted in Ackerman, JGF 121).

Even if we accept the notion that Frazer revised his sources only for grammar's sake—a dubious claim that Ackerman in part supports, noting that Frazer "did not want 'refined' readers to dismiss, as well they might, the contributions of an unlettered informant" (JGF 121)—we can hardly assume that Frazer does not possess, in a quite proprietary sense, his sources. Frazer makes the fieldworkers' texts his own through simple incorporation. In terms of the bottom line of textual production, Frazer's pose is that of a student gratefully and modestly accruing "facts"; but the result is a mammoth text brimming over with sources, voices, facts, and theories, bearing the signature of the acclaimed author.

In a fundamental respect Frazer appropriates his sources through the tactic of insisting upon their status as "fact-collectors" and his own as theorist, when in fact his fieldwork sources often *do* have their theories. Indeed, as digressive and as lively as the "facts" might be, Frazer ultimately winds back to the theory that his source seems to support and in the process often dismisses the original author's theory in favor of his own. Frazer's use of his source Frank Hamilton Cushing in the first edition of *The Golden Bough* is relevant here. After several pages quoting Cushing's gripping narrative of a turtle ceremony among the Zuni, the text blends into Frazer's generalization: "In this custom we find expressed in the clearest way a belief in the transmigration of human souls into the bodies of turtles" (II 98). A footnote numeral following the theory directs us to the following note: "Mr. Cushing, indeed, while he admits that the ancestors of the Zuni may have believed in transmigration, says, 'Their belief, to-day, however, relative to the future life is spiritualistic.' But the expressions in the text seem to leave no room for doubting that the transmigration into turtles is a living article of Zuni faith" (II 98). Frazer dismisses the interpretation of the man on the spot, which of course he assumes is his privilege as the more "objective" comparativist. Typical of his rhetoric is the counter to the source on the basis of self-evidence, as though the reader will be convinced by just a glance at the text that the comparativist has wisely culled of the rightness of the theory. Once he has presented his source purely and simply, Frazer follows his theorizing in the body of the text with a headlong rush toward more stories, sources, and theories: "the same belief in transmigration is held by the Moqui Indians, who belong to the same race as the Zunis" (II 98–99).

Tentative as he purported to be on theory, Frazer did hold his sources' "facts" very tightly in his fist, not recognizing them, publicly anyway, as the highly skewed representations that they were. Frazer's rhetoric of fact-collection failed to allow for the possibility that his sources would be challenged, not only on the grounds of his use, or misuse, of them, but also on the basis of their very reliability as founts of factual information. The generations of anthropologists after Frazer would roundly criticize him for failing to weigh the integrity of the various sources that reported his supposed facts. Quite typical of a modern anthropological perspective is Leach's criticism that in Frazer's text "the most trivial observation of the most ignorant traveler is given the same weight as the most careful assessment of an experienced ethnographer" (" 'Founding Fathers' " 563). Along the same lines, Alexander Goldenweiser comments that "Frazer displays a curious suggestibility toward the opinions of those who furnish him with facts required by his theories."[19]

In the preface to the second edition of *The Golden Bough*, Frazer typically admits that his cultural interpretations are "light bridges" that "sooner or later break down," but, Frazer insists, he still has faith in the text as "a repository of facts" (xix–xx). Significantly, Frazer did *not* anticipate the criticism that the foundations of "fact" connected to those bridges had already been irrevocably weakened by contact, that the uneven reliability of his sources and his own self-serving manipulations of them might expose their frail underpinnings. Frazer's voice of authority, priding itself on its capacity to gain esteem by a calculated disavowal of its own authority, was in fact in danger of losing a critical defense: its sources. The perpetuation of Frazer's authority, then, required a quite different rhetorical strategy, an alternate mode of authorial projection and defense.

THE FIGURES OF THE "LITERARY"

Stanley Edgar Hyman writes that when Frazer decided in the culminating third edition of *The Golden Bough* that "gods were not the embodiment of fertility rites but deified real men," he "stopped taking any theory seriously" and "went back to being a literary man" (TTB 245). That Frazer presented the third edition as a work of literature finds support in the preface to the first volume which, typically, promotes the work's artistic qualities while at the same time doggedly insisting upon its scientific integrity: "By discarding the austere form, without, I hope, sacrificing the solid substance, of a scientific treatise, I thought to cast my materials in a more artistic mould and so perhaps to attract readers, who might have been repelled by a more strictly logical and systematic arrangement of the facts" (*Magic Art* I: viii).

That the third edition marks the distinct point at which Frazer transformed his persona from anthropologist to author is overstated, but the core of Hyman's point is well-taken: as his work came increasingly under attack, Frazer was performing another shift in authorial perspective: it changed from the gaze of the social scientist to the vision of the creative writer. Ackerman supports this notion of increasing literariness, citing "the increasing attention to the scenic element" in the third edition and in general claiming that "Frazer has now found a justification for enlisting his literary penchant in the service of the immensely enlarged third *Golden Bough,* his *magnum opus*" (JGF 236–37).

Still, it is essential to emphasize that the move to the persona of author was not a simple diachronic shift. Frazer's shuttlings from one mode of authority to another are numerous and difficult to schematize easily: although in the preface to the first volume of the third edition Frazer *does* inscribe a shift away from the form of fact-collection and toward that of art, one page later Frazer moves from theorist to fact-collector, defending the collapse of his theory with the value of his work as a collection of facts. Again, these different rhetorical shifts ultimately work toward the same rhetorical end. For example, in the preface to *Balder the Beautiful* (the last volume of the third edition), the priest of Nemi is unveiled as "a stalking horse" for the carrying of facts, while in the preface to *Magic Art* (the first volume of the third edition) Frazer presents the priest as "the center of a gloomy canvas" (I: viii), the focal point of an aesthetic object, of that "more artistic mould" that organizes the third edition. Ackerman correctly notes that the priest helped clarify "the direction and meaning of the narrative, but he also had his artistic value" (JGF 240). But the point is that Frazer's varying figures for the priest contribute to the same rhetorical function: whether scaffold for facts or artistic focal point, he still serves the purpose of rescuing Frazer from his theories.

The relation between the move from anthropologist to author and Frazer's shift from *theorist* to *collector of facts* is significant in another important respect: both promote at least the illusion of greater latitude on the part of the writer. The move toward *fact-collector* presumably lessens overt authorial control while allowing for the entry of more facts and voices. And the shift to *author* inaugurates the notion that the work is henceforth excused of the need for scientific validation: as a work of literature *The Golden Bough* provides the author room to "play" with possibilities. The following statement from Frazer is a disarming example of this attitude: "I put forward the hypothesis for no more than a web of conjectures woven from gossamer threads of popular superstition" (quoted in Hyman, TTB 244). Textual complexity and ambiguity is foregrounded; verification of theory is shuttled off to the background.[20]

The literary quality of Frazer's text was eminently appealing to a wide readership, and yet the defensive rhetorical tactics behind Frazer's aestheticization were mystified, obscured from that readership. Enthusiastic readers of Frazer tended to describe Frazer's literariness as powerfully augmenting his hard scholarship. Indeed, Ackerman notes that, in 1890 at any rate, Frazer "was hailed as having brought a welcome literary grace to a field not known for that attribute" (JGF 100). And Edward Clodd in his blurb at the end of the third edition states that Frazer in *The Belief in Immortality and the Worship of the Dead* combines "the treasury of his knowledge" with the "consummate art of attractive presentment."

Frazer's figuring of himself as artist, however, and of his work as literature, condemned him in the eyes of subsequent generations of anthropologists. Marty Roth rightly states that "for the commentators who would use the exclusion of Frazer to reconstitute anthropology, Frazer is not an anthropologist but an artist" since "he is a writer; he is a fine writer; his writing is literary" and in that respect "he betrays anthropology, which is opposed to literature more or less as content to form." Similarly, Mary Douglas contends that if Frazer had paid heed to his critics, he would have (*should* have) replied that "above all else, I am writing literature, my work is largely an imaginative effort, my greatest achievement is in the development of a style in which to present my insight."[21] Finally, note Leach's charge that Frazer "thought of himself as writing literature, not history or science; the evidence was simply raw material for fine writing" ("Golden Bough or Gilded Twig" 377).

Clearly Frazer's rhetorical stance of *artist* was used against him. Yet critics like Douglas and Leach oversimplify, for Frazer did think of himself, or more important inscribed himself, as a scientist; unfortunately, that authorial projection was at odds with the emerging paradigm of ethnography, whose proponents were creating their own bifurcation of science versus art, a separation that rejected Frazer's manner of fusion. Malinowski also welded the personae of anthropologist and author, just in a different way, proceeding from different conceptions of science and art. Douglas's insistence that Frazer should have admitted he was writing literature presupposes that *literature* and *science* function as stable categories over the generations, that the concepts mean the same things to Frazer, his opponents of the next generation, and our own generation of readers. The more relevant concern, then, ought to be isolating the literary or more broadly aesthetic properties of Frazer's texts that audiences have found appealing, or unappealing (as the case might be).

Vickery chronicles some of the principle aesthetic qualities emanating from Frazer's writing that readers, and particularly literary Modernists, found attractive: the use of the "grand style," the tendency toward "concreteness," and Frazer's figuring of his book "almost exclusively in pictorial terms" (*Literary Impact* 106–07, 115). But the most important literary quality is the "genre or literary mode" to which *The Golden Bough* belongs. It is a "romance," Vickery claims, "rather than the encyclopedic argument we have always thought it to be" (130); indeed, he asserts that "in essence it is less a compendium of facts than a gigantic romance of quest couched in the form of objective research. It is this basically archetypal consideration that reveals *The Golden Bough*'s impact on literature to be not fortuitous but necessary and inevitable" (128). The reasons for terming Frazer's work a romance are well-taken: the repetition of actions and motifs; "themes" emerging out of "a substratum of Nature myth and fertility rituals" (130); and of course the use of the quest itself. Vickery's insistence on a single genre that archetypally makes the book's influence "necessary and inevitable," however, perhaps tells us more about the assumptions of mid-century myth criticism than about *The Golden Bough* itself. It also tells us something about Frazer's rhetoric: reading Frazer's work as "archetypal" testifies to the capability of his text to replicate itself in the texts of others, regardless of the antipathy Frazer himself might have had to an assumption (the Jungian collective unconscious) that is used to perpetuate his text.

Frazer's text had the impact it did not because it was romance hidden under the guise of objective research, or, conversely, because it was *really* a collection of facts rather than a romance. Rather, it perpetuated itself through the accretion of genres, modes that could then be trotted out at the appropriate defensive moment or could lie dormant in the text, in wait for a critic to raise their particular claim to legitimacy. The best proof of this accretion of genre is in the plurality of interpretations concerning *The*

Golden Bough's proper genre. Vickery's reaction against the work as encyclopedia is clearly a move against the rhetoric of fact-collection inscribed by Frazer and his followers (just as post-Frazerian anthropologists often attacked Frazer's fact-collecting and termed his work, instead, *art*).[22]

Other readers abandon romance entirely. Stanley Edgar Hyman waffles between genres, confused by Frazer's own multiple pronouncements. Hyman first terms the work "an epic of humanity's ascent to rationality," but then compounds his choice of genres: "'Tragic' is the word Frazer frequently uses for his epic of humanity, and in some respects the work seems not so much epic as tragic drama, death and rebirth in the cycle of nature" (TTB 254). He then calls it a "detective story" and even a "comic or ironic mock-epic of human absurdity" (262). Hyman posits the presence of possible alternatives here as emblematic of Frazer's changing moods and personal needs, not in terms of the rhetorical effects of shifting genre.

Marty Roth sees the "model" of *The Golden Bough* as "the oldest moment of epic," isolating the structure of "descent" in the work ("Frazer's *Golden Bough*" 71). And yet his description of Frazer's opening also intimates the genre of detective fiction: "Frazer has had an experience of radical absurdity; he has stumbled upon a clue to a shocking crime both within the past and within the construction of culture" (70). The book is figured in fact as a kind of comparative evolutionary whodunit. Finally, Roth and Leach both suggest the possibility of a genre that Frazer himself would hardly wish to acknowledge: pornography. According to Leach, much of the pleasure of reading Frazer comes from poring over the numerous accounts of "sado-masochistic sexuality" among the savages. Frazer, in his modest Victorian exposure of savage sex, "offers all the delights of polite pornography" ("'Founding Fathers'" 563). Roth concurs in Leach's view but holds that Frazer's text in this case is not the exception but closer to the rule in anthropological writing. Frazer's writing "helped to establish and then threatened to expose [anthropology's] top-secret pornographic agenda. Frazer . . . allows the implicit sexual motive of anthropology to emerge" ("Frazer's *Golden Bough*" 77).

Clearly it is not the case that any one of these readings of genre is right and the others wrong, or even that they are all wrong, or right (all interpretations are equal, and yet some can be more equal, more readable, than others). For example, Frazer either wished to mystify *or* never conceived of pornography as his genre. But just as clearly, he himself inscribed other genres into the text. Frazer characteristically shuttles between multiple genres. While he often refers to his project as "epic," as Hyman notes, tragedy and even comedy are employed. When, for example, Frazer reveals the

priest of Nemi, like Balder, as a mere "stalking horse" for "facts," he presents the fall from theory as a descent from tragedy to comedy, or even to
farce, as "the nominal hero of the long tragedy of human folly and suffering
which has unrolled itself before the readers of these volumes" turns out
after all to be "merely a puppet" (*Balder* vi). Yet several pages later, he teases
us with the possibility of romance: "We have traveled far since we turned
our backs on Nemi, and set forth in quest of the secret of the Golden
Bough" (1).

There are so many renditions of the book's true genre because the text
has made room for so many possibilities, either inscribed and encouraged
by Frazer himself or made possible by the sheer bulk of the gargantuan
work. We return to the notion of *The Golden Bough* as an eminently New
Critical aesthetic object, many-sided and capable of multiple interpretation.
It is, in its sheer massiveness, the shrine around which interpretation gathers. As such it functions as an exercise in literary criticism; in this particular
context Northrop Frye may be right in noting that though "*The Golden
Bough* purports to be a work of anthropology . . . it may yet prove to be
really a work of literary criticism."[23]

Yet stating that Frazer's work is literary or that it works as a piece of
literary criticism requires that we establish what Frazer inscribes as *literary*
or, more broadly, *aesthetic* in his texts. Characteristically, Frazer uses the
rhetoric of bifurcation and opposition, so that isolating what Frazer poses
as literary, metaphorical, or stylized necessarily involves fixing what he sets
off against each of those terms. The very division of the literary from the
nonliterary is significant in that it empowers Frazer to elevate or denigrate
each of those terms, alternating the plus and minus from one side of the
line to the other at his convenience and for his own purposes. Of course
this rhetorical operation is integrally related to Frazer's own authorial projections as "artist," fact-collector, or theorist: when a plus is attached to
"literary," Frazer's status of artist is made to rise; when the "literary" is
assigned a minus, Frazer's status as fact-collector or theorist is elevated.

Given the common categorization of Frazer as "literary," one may find
surprising his persistently pejorative characterizations of literary genres or
properties, as opposed to what is pitted against them. For example, Frazer
often divides "mere fictions" from "facts," as when in *The Dying God* he
insists that "tales of [the type of Beauty and the Beast] might be dismissed
as fictions designed to amuse a leisure hour" when they "really rest on a
basis of facts, however much these facts may have been distorted or mag-
nified in passing through the mind of the story-teller, who is naturally more
concerned to amuse than to instruct his readers" (134). "Fiction" as such

is conceived as the *untruthful* side of narrative, the recreative and hence dangerously lulling half of the story's essence, described in another context in the same volume as the "mere scenic exhibition designed to deceive and impress the beholders" (*Dying God* 165).

That the preceding quotation suggests the dramatic is no accident, for Frazer often uses the figure of drama to oppose what is true, sincere, or factual. In *The Spirits of the Corn and of the Wild,* for example, Frazer states that though certain relevant passages from Plato "are, like all Plato's writings, couched in dramatic form and put into the mouths of others, we need not seriously doubt that they represent the real opinion of the philosopher himself" (II: 308). Dramatic form and sincerity are on opposite sides of a bifurcating line. Poetry is also indicted, as hiding the true nature of a thing. For example, in *Spirits of the Corn* Frazer holds that the "glamour" of "Greek poetry" attempted "to conceal or erase the deep lines of savagery and cruelty imprinted on the features" of Dionysos (I: 34). And near the end of the first edition of *The Golden Bough,* when trying to account for the error of not seeing the Golden Bough for what it really was, Frazer states: "the Golden Bough was nothing but the mistletoe seen through the haze of poetry or of popular superstition" (II: 363). Given the pattern of figuring literary genre as sinister masquerade or, perhaps worse, mere embroidery, it is hardly coincidental that the unveiling of Balder as the "stalking horse" for "facts" is described in terms of the exposure of genre. The markers of "tragedy," the "quaint garb he wears and the gravity with which he stalks across the stage," constitute attempts to conceal Balder's real nature as "puppet." Frazer's satisfying task, then, is to strip off the guise of the tragic, "to unmask him [Balder] before laying him up in the box" (vi), and reveal him as the mere comic or farcical figure that he is.

Neither is the downgrading from one genre to another the end of the story, for the process that leads from tragedy to comedy must end in the abandonment of the dramatistic, indeed, in flight from the literary altogether. To get to his real point, Frazer claims to dispense with figuration completely, as evidenced in the sentence that follows the metaphoric laying up of Balder: "To drop metaphor, while nominally investigating a particular problem of ancient mythology, I have really been discussing questions of more general interest which concern the gradual evolution of human thought from savagery to civilization" (vi). Frazer's abandonment of mere theories is here presented as a defiguring of figuration, the dropping of "metaphor," a peeling away of the dramatistic or literary shell that will reveal the core of "fact" beneath, that "rough and purely provisional classification of facts" that gives value to Frazer's corpus by further illustrating the manifest truth of the evolutionary process.

Frazer's metaphor for metaphor, as embroidery that can be dropped at a moment's notice when truth's beacon brightens, is emblematic of a larger tendency in Frazer's work to reject metaphor as integral to text or to experience and to figure figuring itself as superfluous, ornamental, and even an obstacle to right understanding. In a Platonic sense, figuration is at another remove from reality and hence cannot be trusted or highly valued. It is precisely in this sense that in *Spirits of the Corn* Frazer holds to the primitive conception of the death of animals as "no figurative or allegorical death, no poetical embroidery thrown over the skeleton, but the real death, the naked skeleton, that constantly thrusts itself importunately on [the savage's] attention" (I: vi).

The savage mind according to Frazer is a place from which metaphor cannot be dropped, for it has never been there. Roth, quoting Frazer on how, in the savage mind, trees "'can be married to each other in a real, and not merely a figurative or poetical, sense of the word,'" is right on the mark when asserting that "Frazer's 'primitive man,' . . . knows only the literal. He has not yet fallen into the post-lapsarian world of only metaphor" ("Frazer's *Golden Bough*" 73–74). Frazer is like his savage in the former's resistance to the medium of language as medium, as a construct that is less (or more) than a transparent window to the "real." In this respect Frazer's account in the first edition of the savage killing of the divine king is revealing:

> The divine life, incarnate in a material and mortal body, is liable to be tainted and corrupted by the weakness of the frail medium in which it is for a time enshrined; and if it is to be saved from increasing enfeeblement . . . it must be detached from him [its human incarnation] before, or at least as soon as, he exhibits signs of decay, in order to be transferred to a vigorous successor. This is done by killing the old representative of the god and conveying the divine spirit from him to a new incarnation. (I: 247–48)

Frazer's account of king killing works as a controlling figure for the aesthetics, and more generally the semiotics, at work in Frazer's corpus. Like his savage, Frazer "kills" the medium (language), or rather, the inscribed awareness of a medium, since knowledge of the medium makes problematic that vessel's bearing of the burden of the transcendental signified. More simply and secularly put, the "truth" manifest in Frazer's facts cannot be contained in the material body, that verbal emblem, for "it is liable to be tainted and corrupted by the weakness of the frail medium," the tendency of language to disintegrate, to veer from strict denotative meaning, to be less than utterly referential. Frazer hopes to heal what Roth quite insightfully notes as "that rupture of the lifeline between signifier and signified, sign and referent, which dooms the word to wander restlessly along the paths of improper association" ("Frazer's *Golden Bough*" 73). Hence the "violent death" of the king is emblematic of the slaying of the signifiers, or more accurately put, the slaying of the awareness of the signifying practices of those verbal shells.

Frazer's inscribing of a "plain style" of writing reflects the semiotics at work in the text, in which the word makes the thought manifest and does not chase after extravagant effect. Ackerman makes the sensible point that "most of [Frazer's] work is written in the pellucid Addisonian, or plain, mode, in which his meaning is never in doubt" (JGF 23). The relation between Frazer's rhetoric of fact-collection and his semiotics of transparency inhering in the "plain mode" is significant, for what Frazer calls his "plain record of a curious form of society," that "exact classification of facts" (TE I: xvi), has little room in it for the darkening corners of connotation, the indeterminate spaces between meanings.

Ackerman's reference to Frazer's Addisonian style is no loose association. As Ackerman notes, Frazer "had a lifelong sympathy with the early eighteenth century" (JGF 260), and was particularly enamored of the writings of Joseph Addison, whose letters he edited and whose *Spectator* essays he imitated (see his *Sir Roger de Coverly and Other Literary Pieces,* published in 1920). Frazer's tie to Addison reflects a temperamental affinity; indeed, in the most recent edition of the highly visible *Norton Anthology of English Literature* Addison has been called the "first Victorian," and in this respect the qualities he promulgated, of "moderation, reasonableness, self-control, urbanity, and good taste,"[24] are very much tied to Frazer's brand of commonsensical, gentlemanly rationality. Nowhere is that habit of mind more evident in Frazer than in his often automatically, autocratically (and yet graciously) rational approach to the workings of the "savage" mind.

Frazer's affinities to Addison extend beyond mood or attitude to semiotics and aesthetics. This is especially evident in Addison's belief in the primacy of a "truth" in writing that naturally emerges and makes the medium transparent. Indeed, Frazer's praise of fieldworker Spencer's "verbal descriptions" as "bear[ing] the impress of perfect fidelity to nature" ("Spencer as Anthropologist" 11) echoes Addison's assessment of Boileau in number 62 of *The Spectator*: "This is that natural Way of writing, that beautiful Simplicity, which we so admire in the Compositions of the Ancients; and which no Body deviates from, but those who want Strength of Genius to make a Thought shine in its own natural Beauties."[25]

Addison's discussion of the qualities of "Wit" in writing resonate in Frazer's rhetoric. Addison's comment, "that the Basis of all Wit is Truth; and that no Thought can be valuable, of which good Sense is not the Groundwork," strikes a chord in Frazer's rationalist schema. And Addison's definition of wit as "A Resemblance and Congruity of Ideas" (264) is doubled, interestingly, in Frazer's conception of Sympathetic Magic, which works according to two principles, the Law of Similarity and the Law of Contact (or Contagion). But Addison's conception of wit bears more significant relation to the rhetorical operation of Frazer's comparative method. For the comparative method, like Addison's wit, succeeds in the proportion to which its "Resemblances" can produce "*Delight* and *Surprize* to the Reader." The following quotation from Addison suggests the similarities: "In order therefore that the Resemblance in the Ideas be Wit, it is necessary that the Ideas should not lie too near one another in the Nature of things; for where the Likeness is obvious, it gives no Surprise. To compare one Man's Singing to that of another . . . cannot be called Wit, unless, besides this obvious Resemblance, there be some further Congruity discovered in the two Ideas that is capable of giving the Reader some Surprize" (264).

Like Addison's wit, Frazer's comparative method works by startling its reader into the recognition that apparently dissimilar ideas, peoples, beliefs have a common ground. Frazer's text garners the most attention when it juxtaposes a tribe from the Congo against Irish peasants, not when it compares the trait of a tribe to that of its neighbor or, worse yet, if it compares features within a single tribe. The rhetorical pattern of surprise based upon the congruence of difference is fundamental to Frazerian comparativism.[26] This process is of course essentially metaphoric and imaginative; the former Frazer denied or mystified, the latter he was capable of taking advantage of in other contexts, other turns of his rhetoric.

Frazer was capable of mystifying the essentially metaphorical nature of his comparative method by an act of bifurcation similar to one of Addison's. Addison's insistence that "True Wit" is based on a resemblance of "Ideas" while "False Wit" is based on a similarity of "Letters," "Words," and "Sometimes of Whole Sentences" (265) corresponds to Frazer's division of science from magic, especially in the naive literalism Frazer often attributes to the savage as distinguished from the quality of abstraction that Frazer often holds up as the hallmark of civilized man and science. More pointedly, the Addisonian distinction between similarity of letters or words and ideas underscores the semiotics of transparency at work in Frazer's texts, in which working with real "ideas," with the "facts" of culture, is clearly distinguished from deluding flights of figurative fancy. Frazer in his rhetoric of fact collection aligns himself with Addison's true wit, linked as it is with "Reason," and shuns Addison's false wit, tied to the merely verbal and therefore a party to what Addison terms "Extravagance." To Frazer, in his rush toward the referent, the words and letters themselves are to meld, without fanfare, into the solidity of the ideas.

Though Frazer's plain style, and the semiotics underlying it, are blatantly evident, they tell only half the story. For Frazer has been known from the start as the most "literary" of anthropologists, a "writerly" writer on savage ways. And though the terms for literariness shift in value with each generation, Frazer's prose, with its explicitly dramatic stagings, its gusty ranges of emotion, its vivid and concrete descriptions, its figures of the arts, and what Vickery calls its pervasively "elegiac" tone,[27] does announce itself as "literary." The text, in other words, calls attention to itself, in very conspicuous and period-bound ways, as bearing a *literary* style.

Ackerman correctly notes that Frazer's other prime literary influence, also from the eighteenth century, was Edward Gibbon, and that Gibbon and Addison represent the extremes of his style. Although Addison comes to the fore in Frazer's plain mode, when the rhetoric underscores clarity of "meaning," Ackerman points out that Frazer "tends to affect the Gibbonesque, with its conscious latinity and sententiousness, when he seeks to soar and impress" (JGF 23). Vickery chronicles and defines the accumulating effects of this other Frazerian style: "The Latinate diction, the judicious employment of periodic sentences, the eloquent perorations, the handling of sustained analogies, the apposite allusions, the leisurely development of paragraphs—all stamp *The Golden Bough* as a magnificently sustained example of the grand style" (*Literary Impact* 106). That style, in all its calculatingly broad strokes and wide sweep, permeates the concluding lines of *The Golden Bough,* when Frazer, here the quester come home, returns with densely resonant emotion to Nemi:

> The place has changed but little since Diana received the homage of her worshippers in the sacred grove. The temple of the sylvan goddess, indeed, has vanished and the King of the Wood no longer stands sentinel over the Golden Bough. But Nemi's woods are still green, and as the sunset fades above them in the west, there comes to us, borne

on the swell of the wind, the sound of the church bells of Ariccia ring-
ing the Angelus. *Ave Marie!* Sweet and solemn they chime out from
the distant town and die lingeringly away across the wide Campagnan
marshes. *Le roi et mort, vive le roi! Ave Marie!* (*Balder* II: 309)

The passage, with its massively descriptive swells, purple lingerings, and
richly echoing dyings, constitutes a far cry from Frazer's pose of the text
as a "plain record" of facts. And yet there is sense to the seeming inconsistency, for insisting on a division between plain and "literary" writing,
between a "record" and a work of "art," enables the author to enjoy the
advantages of both: his text is a collection of plain facts, and yet it has the
luxury of also cleaving to its aesthetic superiority; he is a scientist, he is an
artist. Frazer may praise Spencer for avoiding "literary effect by elaborate
word painting" ("Spencer as Anthropologist" 11), but, unlike Spencer, he
can cross to the other side of the line and say on another occasion that his
fieldworkers' accounts "are written for the most part in a plain, straight-
forward way, the authors contenting themselves with describing in simple
language the things which they have seen or had heard reported by com-
petent native informants. Few, if any, possess that magic charm of style
which, by firing the imagination or touching the heart, can alone confer
what we fondly call immortality upon a work of literature."[28]
    The "magic charm of style" is what, according to Frazer, failed Plato in
his later dialogues, where he was "guided by the pale cold light of Reason
instead of by the purple glow of Imagination" (quoted in Hyman, TTB 262).
In this bifurcation of reason from imagination, as in Frazer's description
of the work of literature as opposed to the fieldwork account, we see a
reversal of values, and the role of the author, versus fact-collector, brightens:
facts are facts, but literature is immortal.
    The Frazer who pronounces the virtues of the plain style and the Frazer
who celebrates the "magic charm of style" (and projects it upon himself)
agree on an important issue: literariness is *not* the tropism at the heart of a
text; it is a charm or embroidery, a haze or halo, an irrational force that
enables the author to inspire, transport, or delude. The "charm of style"
is indeed that favorite preoccupation of Frazer the anthropologist, *magic*.
Like the savage's magic, style is, to Frazer's civilized man, superficial, an
almost transparent effort of coercion.[29] Indeed, Frazer's "magic" blatantly
parades itself on the pages, in the form of, for example, extended dramatistic metaphors (the priest as phony tragedian, "stalking across the stage")
that playfully announce themselves as "charms" that can be undone, un-

crossed—embroidery that can be "dropped" when Frazer the idea man means to get down to business.

Frazer forces the text's bracketed literariness upon the reader for ultimately quite defensive reasons. In a short book, first published in 1895, entitled *Passages of the Bible Chosen for Their Literary Beauty and Interest,* Frazer also segregates "literature" from "fact," thus creating an especially useful division across which to shuttle and find rescue from critical attack. Frazer's preface to the volume concludes with the following summation of the Bible: "This may not be science and history, but it is at least an impressive pageant, a stately drama: without metaphor, it is noble literature; and like all noble literature it is fitted to delight, to elevate, and to console."[30]

Typically, Frazer presents access to literature—that which magically transports—to be possible only by dropping metaphor. But perhaps more important, Frazer's equation of the Bible to literature and "pageant" is part of the rhetorical stance, seen in, and upon, *The Golden Bough,* in which the author's failure to substantiate theory with reliable "facts" is read as the triumph of immortal art over perishing "science and history." Frazer's professed purpose as stated in the preface to *Passages,* "that a service might be rendered to lovers of good literature by disengaging these gems from their setting" (vi), becomes an allegory for the anthropologist's antihistorical comparative method that removes "native" customs from their cultural contexts. The blend that results from the culture-welding ethnographer's efforts is not simply a diachronous gallery of voices, but more closely resembles a carefully orchestrated aesthetic suspension, frozen in the present by the author-anthropologist, of the representations of different periods and cultures.[31]

The overt aestheticization of the anthropological work is perhaps Frazer's best defense against critics. The promotion of authority through the welding of literary author to anthropologist is possible only by first marking off the boundaries that separate them. In the case of the Bible, Frazer finds it necessary to disengage aesthetic "gems" from their historical context before they can be appreciated for the "pure literature" that they are. As "stately Drama," the Bible becomes the *representation* of historical process: even Frazer professes that it is *not* "history." The aesthetic "gems" removed from their original settings and glued on garish backboard comprise an odd simulacrum of historical process, a glitzy rendition of the march of ages that resembles a cross between Shakespearean tragedy and vaudeville:

Against this gorgeous background, this ever shifting scenery, now bright with the hues of heaven, now lurid with the glare of hell, we

see mankind strutting and playing their little part on the stage of history. We see them taken from the dust and returning to the dust: we
see the rise and fall of empires: we see great cities, now the hive of
busy multitudes, now silent and desolate, a den of wild beasts. All
life's fever is there—its loves and hopes and joys, its high endeavors,
its suffering and sin and sorrow. (*Passages* vii)

Hyman majestically terms this aestheticization "Frazer's dramatistic vision," repeating Frazer's own strategy of promoting his text as "literary"
and hence "timeless" in its shaping (TTB 200).[32] The Bible, like *The Golden
Bough,* becomes a well-wrought urn that stands outside of process, capturing the necessary spirit of its subjects yet wisely avoiding getting caught
up in the tangle of historical and social particularities. Hyman's need to
rescue Frazer from criticism, to reconcile rampant ethnocentrism and ethnographic unreliability with the majesty and sweep of the work, found its
answer in the "timeless essentializing out of history," the New Critical and
myth critical notion that *The Golden Bough* does not record "a development
in history, but a temporalizing of essence" (246–47).[33] Hyman's attempt
to rescue Frazer is consistent with Frazer's own defense—by claiming that
The Golden Bough is *not* to be taken as an assertion of scientific truth or
ethnographic accuracy, but is *synechdochic* in the most hermetic New Critical
sense, says Hyman: "Frazer knew realistically . . . that primitive tribes did
not evolve from one to the other, but the essence of these modes is that of
a graded series, and their Platonic ideas so evolve. *Man,* not any *men,* had
progressed from magic through religion to science, and *The Golden Bough*
is the epic of that idealized ascent" (247).

Again, Hyman duplicates Frazer's rhetorical tactics, this time by reading
the text as figurative, as epic whole that in time-honored fashion is granted
the privilege of representing any or all cultural "parts." In this respect
Frazer's and Hyman's argument for *literariness* is hardly a harbinger of current writings on anthropology as tropistic, for the former drives a defensive
wedge between the discourses of science and literature. Frazer's strategy
turns the "reality" of native experience into self-promoting fable, and does
so, ironically, by downplaying the role of monologic theorist (whose work
is dependent upon "interpretations") and playing up that of *artist,* whose
well-wrought text gives vent to multiple voices and sources and consequently is capable of emanating a broad spectrum of interpretations (the
"facts" are there, you future students of the savage: do with them what you
will).

The Figures of Anthropology

In a critical rhetorical ploy, Frazer calls attention to his figures so that they can be dismissed and hence not taken seriously as controlling tropes, as shaping ideological forces. The extent to which figuration shapes the anthropological object, idea, or theory is wholly mystified, as Frazer maintains the fiction that style and idea function as superstructure and base, playful form and earnest content. Even critics who have analyzed Frazer's use of metaphors tend to double the mystification of the ideological parameters of his figures. At the same time, those critics illustrate the extent to which Frazer's figures function as eminently interpretable, as objects of hermeneutic contemplation that can be variously read as the times and tastes change.

One such ideologically loaded and highly suggestive figure is Frazer's trope of the "web" of culture, described often by Frazer as "the complex fabric of our society" (*Taboo* v). This figure was powerfully attractive to the practitioners of myth criticism as well as New Criticism, both of which solidified *The Golden Bough*'s reputation as anthropological arche-text. A good example of the critical replication of this figure can be found in *The Tangled Bank,* where Hyman alludes to his own title in his description of Frazer's web: "Frazer's common image for culture is of a great fabric, an orderly tangled bank. He writes of having touched only the fringe, having 'fingered only a few of the countless threads that compose the mighty web'" (248).[34]

Hyman's figure for Frazer's design tells us as much about then-contemporary critical approaches as it does about an anthropological text of a half-century before. An "orderly tangled bank" is, after all, another variant of New Criticism's well-wrought urn: ornate, multi-faceted, highly detailed, eminently ambiguous but ultimately encapsulated.[35] The New Critical ideology of totalization that the orderly bank emplots is explicitly pronounced in Hyman's introduction, where he states that "art" is "the work of the moral imagination, imposing order and form on disorderly and anarchic experience" (x). Clearly, Hyman is using Frazer to promote his own critical ideology, but Hyman's use of Frazer's web is also testimony to the powerful duplicating effects of Frazer's own rhetorical strategies; the variability of Frazer's text, after all, makes possible such a reading.

Hyman's replication of Frazer's "web" is even better illustrated by his reading of an extended example of Frazer's "image for culture" taken from the last pages of the multivolume *Golden Bough*. Frazer writes:

Without dipping so far into the future, we may illustrate the course which thought has hitherto run by likening it to a web woven of three different threads—the black thread of magic, the red thread of religion, and the white thread of science. . . . Could we then survey the web of thought from the beginning, we should probably perceive it to be at first a chequer of black and white, a patchwork of true and false notions, hardly tinged as yet by the red thread of religion. But carry your eye further along the fabric and you will remark that, while the black and the white chequer still runs through it, there rests on the middle portion of the web, where religion has entered most deeply into its texture, a dark crimson stain, which shades off insensibly into a lighter tint as the white thread of science is woven more and more into the tissue. To a web thus chequered and stained, thus shot with threads of diverse hues, but gradually changing colour the farther it is unrolled, the state of modern thought, with all its divergent aims and conflicting tendencies, may be compared. Will the great movement which for centuries has been slowly altering the complexion of thought be continued in the near future? or will a reaction set in which may arrest progress and even undo much that has been done? To keep up our parable, what will be the colour of the web which the Fates are now weaving on the humming loom of time? . . . We cannot tell. A faint glimmering light illuminates the backward portion of the web. Clouds and thick darkness hide the other end. (*Balder* II: 307–08)

Hyman's attitude toward Frazer's trope is basically that of respectful critic paying homage to the literary master: the "web" is one of "several key metaphors" that make up the "imaginative design" of Frazer's masterpiece; Hyman's task as critic is to isolate that metaphor and trace its course in order to deepen our appreciation of Frazer's artistry. As it happens, Hyman's reading is itself a doubling of the rhetorical strategies inhering in Frazer's text, as the critic downplays the significance of Frazer's actual theories and brings to the forefront the "artistic" complexity and ambiguous possibility operating within the text. Hyman does pay attention to rhetorical strategies, but only to the extent that his critical analysis furthers his thesis, stated in the introduction, that "the power and influence of [Frazer, Marx, Freud, and Darwin's] ideas is due to their ability as imaginative writers" (TTB x). Specifically, his principal emphasis on explicating the "web" of "culture" in order to valorize Frazer as an artistic master in effect duplicates Frazer's text by giving the nod to the supposition that culture *is* or *ought to be* just such a "web" or pattern.

But in fact Frazer's rhetorical authority as culture-reader makes that imposing of pattern possible. That the web cannot be read through to the end just further illustrates Frazer's keen rhetorical strategies, for his "culture" matrix is *not* unreadable. Though it is masked in "parable" intended as the thinnest of figurations, Frazer's text encourages us to believe that the pattern *is there*: reading the "web" is merely a matter of degree. Unlike Tiresias, Frazer (at least he tells us) cannot tell the future; but as armchair anthropologist, he functions as reader of past and present, and as such, has the ethnographic edge over other readers. His seeming act of humility ("I can see no further") functions as ploy: his light may not go far into the wilderness of "primitive" voices, but it is the only light that is made available to aid us in our peek into a forest of the author's making.[36]

Frazer's very inscribing of culture as woven "web," as inscrutable, "fragmentary" or "dubious" as the threads of that pattern might be, attempts to give to "culture" a coherence. Frazer urges us to view his staking out of the term as a humble and hopelessly incomplete step toward knowing the unknowable. But reading against the grain of the text (as Clifford tells us we ought), we see not the humility and tentativeness of the anthropologist faced with the profusion of overarching ignorance, but an author whose self-created network, those multiple threads of "unreadable" voices, sources, and causes, makes possible an ideology of containment, in which we are made to feel that the anthropological subject (Frazer's frighteningly elusive "savage") ought to be safely (for us) enclosed, bracketed off within the text. Though we are told that the pattern cannot be deciphered, Frazer's forced identification of, for example, "black" and "red" with "magic" and "religion," attempts to strangle the "savage" in the author's own "orderly tangled bank," a carefully wrought textual jungle of positivist straight lines and right angles. Frazer's web, deftly promoting the notion of the text as artistic, as attractively metaphorical, sanctions the "author" in the act of tenting the anthropological subject. In that respect Frazer's figure functions as both offensive and defensive weapon (here "aesthetics" both kill and protect).

In his very disavowal of figuration Frazer figures concepts of culture into existence. Nowhere is that clearer than in Frazer's figuration of evolution. When in *Balder the Beautiful* at the end of the third edition of *The Golden Bough* he drops theory and "metaphor" he brings his readers round to the real object of his titanic efforts: those "questions of more general interest which concern the gradual evolution of human thought from savagery to civilization" (I: vi). Frazer readily admits to the "difficulties" of such "enquiry," especially compared to analysis of "the record of [man's] physical development" (vi). Adopting the familiar ocular metaphor, Frazer concedes that the "mental development" of man "is harder to read, not only by reason of the incomparably more subtle and complex nature of the subject, but because the reader's eyes are apt to be dimmed by thick mists of passion and prejudice, which cloud in a far less degree the fields of comparative anatomy and geology" (vi).

That Frazer drops metaphor to gain access to the stable truths of his study, that set of facts called mental development, is significant here. Once again, the announced rejection of figure helps conceal the trope disguised as that set of facts. Frazer's humility, again, works as a ploy: defining "mental development" as a document that is hard to "read" assumes that "mental development" is indeed a document, a stable set of significations; and admitting that "mental development" is "harder to read" than the evolution of the "hard sciences" of comparativism plants the ennobling assumption that the study of mental evolution is tied, part and parcel, to those more scientistically authorized fields of comparative study.

Frazer often adopts metaphors that mystify the theoretical nature of evolutionism. For example, in the second volume of *Spirits of the Corn and of the Wild,* in order to account for the "fact" that "the three types of religion" Frazer has delineated are "far from being strictly limited each to its corresponding step in the social ladder," the metaphor of culture as fabric is introduced:

> In short, we cannot really dissect the history of mankind as it were with a knife into a series of neat sections each sharply marked off from all the rest by a texture and colour of its own; we may indeed do so theoretically for the convenience of exposition, but practically the textures interlace, the colours melt and run into each other by insensible gradations that defy the edge of the finest instrument of analysis which we can apply to them. It is a mere truism to say that the abstract generalizations of science can ever adequately comprehend all the particulars of concrete reality. The facts of nature will always burst the narrow bonds of human theories. (II: 37)

In a tactical ploy, Frazer concedes the theoretical nature of the particulars of his theory in order to salvage the idea of evolutionary theory itself as fact. The fabric, introduced as analogy, becomes fact, for we are made to assume that the pattern of textured gradation, of colors running imperceptibly but surely from savagery to civilization, is there, utterly present, and will always defy the niceties of exact analysis. The metaphor of fabric loses its own figural status as the pattern of evolutionism becomes not an analogic "abstract generalization," but a living mosaic of "concrete particulars." Typically, Frazer's tentativeness and humility cloud over the essentialism of his belief in the *theory* of social evolution, the surety of his faith in the supposition that cultures the world over moved from "savagery" to "civilization" if not in identical then in essentially similar steps.

Frazer's inscribed confidence in evolution belies the challenges hurled toward the proponents of evolutionary theory. George Stocking maintains that Frazer's writings largely comprised the third and last major stage of evolutionary anthropology; Frazer's corpus, Stocking reports, brought "a relatively pristine Tylorian [evolutionary] viewpoint well into the century— long after the reaction to it had begun" (VA 287). And Kardiner and Preble significantly note that Frazer lost the battle: once "classical evolutionism in anthropology fell into disrepute," Frazer's corpus, "as a representative of this school . . . suffered a severe criticism from which it has never recovered in official anthropology" (*They Studied Man* 105).

Despite some claims that Frazer was remarkably out of touch with anthropological developments of the second half of his career, he was clearly aware of the shift in paradigm from the evolutionist to functionalist perspectives and the resultant attacks on his own brand of evolutionism. Leach's claim that Frazer "took evolutionist dogma for granted" ("Golden Bough or Gilded Twig" 378) assumes that the absence of a forum on evolution in Frazer's text indicates an ignorance of the issues on Frazer's part. I am not trying to maintain that Frazer rigorously thought through his methodology, but rather that he responded to criticism by refusing in his rhetoric to consider the positions of his adversaries. For if on paper he had entertained those positions at all, he would have been forced to concede the reality that evolution was being challenged precisely on its methodological grounding, thus opening up the very issue of evolution as theory. Frazer was not prepared to open that Pandora's box, for that would mean, ultimately, questioning his "facts" too: since without the evolutionist paradigm, Frazer's facts would become something other. His characteristic response is to restate his own definition of evolution, which, he explains, "assumes that civilization has always and everywhere been evolved out of savagery. The mass of evidence on which this assumption rests is in my opinion so great as to render the induction incontrovertible. At least, if any one disputes it I do not think it worth while to argue with him" (*Man, God, and Immortality* 24).

To Frazer that "mass of evidence," comprising those "facts" from the fieldworkers, was desperately needed to bolster the legitimacy of evolution as theory by disguising evolution's theoretical essence. Frazer needed indisputable "fact" to demonstrate the indisputably nonparadigmatic nature of evolution. And, in a sense, Frazer found that "fact" in the subject of Spencer and Gillen's fieldwork. In the preface to *The Native Tribes of Central Australia,* Frazer states that Spencer and Gillen "found themselves in contact with tribes living in the Stone Age," the Arunta, who are, Frazer pronounces from the armchair, "probably approximating most closely to the type of absolutely primitive humanity" (vii). The discovery of the "type" is presented, then, as the key reconstructionist find, the social-evolutionist equivalent to physical anthropology's piecing together of the missing link. In that respect it is Frazer's utter "fact," the word (ancestor, ur-man) made flesh, the flesh-and-blood map back to the first past, what Frazer in a tribute to Baldwin Spencer called "a mirror in the life of man as it was in ages long before the dawn of history" ("Spencer as Anthropologist" 1). Spencer and Gillen's Australian "savage" is inscribed by Frazer as the utter signifier that, preceding the fall from grace, simply lives the "meaning" of originary experience.

Like evolution, totemism, the relation between the "savage" tribe and its object of worship (plant, animal, thing), was for Frazer a mystified and mystifying article of faith whose legitimacy became dependent upon the "facts" brought back by Spencer and Gillen. The first section of *Totemism and Exogamy* (1910) is composed of his 1887 *Totemism* and essays written since the discoveries of Spencer and Gillen in the 1890s compelled him to reject his original theory of totemism and propose two other theories, the second ultimately rejected in favor of the third. There can be no doubt that after 1887 Frazer quite explicitly projected the role of theorist in his dealings with the issue of totemism, and yet his rhetorical habits remained those of the tentative archivist, the pack rat, the fact-collector. Even though the essays that followed the 1887 volume "revolutionized the whole aspect of the subject" (ix), for example, Frazer never considers the possibility of either omitting the earlier volume or revising substantively; rather, he claims that the "errors . . . are generally not very serious" and are "corrected in the Notes appended to the last volume" (viii).

Natural digressiveness accounts in part for Frazer's seeming inability to discard, and yet there is, again, more to his accretions than meets the eye. Frazer's pages of discussion of his rejected theories makes them something more, or less, than failed theoretical attempts; they become, in their inclusion, part of the historical foundation upon which the study of totemism rests. Robert Alun Jones's comment on the third edition of *The Golden*

Bough as "a history of the development of Frazer's mind" ("Robertson Smith and James Frazer" 38) can be relevantly applied to *Totemism and Exogamy.* Frazer's very chronicling of his shifts of view habituates the reader into perceiving Frazer's mind as the nexus of thinking on the subject.

Indeed, Frazer is rightly seen as a central figure in the nineteenth-century debate on totemism, for, as Ackerman remarks, in the 1887 *Totemism* volume Frazer "virtually creat[ed] and defin[ed] the subject for the earlier generation of fieldworkers" (JGF 217). And, as Stocking reports, when in the late 1890s the fieldwork of Spencer and Gillen gave Frazer evidence of men eating their totems—which gave rise to Frazer's second theory on the origin of totemism—then "the topic [of totemism] became the major focus of anthropological debate until World War I" (VA 297). So when Frazer appended to the original *Totemism* volume the later essays that propounded his later theories in light of Spencer and Gillen and approximately three bulky volumes of an "Ethnographical Survey of Totemism," he was simply solidifying his own role as authority on the burning issue of totemism.

The massiveness of *Totemism and Exogamy,* like *The Golden Bough,* underscores the capacity of an anthropological label, such as *totemism,* to arrange, classify, and hence contain world culture. In the original 1887 volume alone, Frazer's discussion of totemism enables him to report and theorize upon topics as various as birth, death, puberty ceremonies, animal dances, food taboos, ceremonial killings, kinship, descent, and intermarriage. *Totemism* functions as an anthropological magnet around which the filings of cultural "facts" gather, and thus becomes a compelling site of empowerment, a locus from which the comparativist holds sway. In this respect Ackerman's comment that Frazer created the "subject" of totemism has a far-reaching resonance. Frazer did not invent it: in the preface to *Totemism and Exogamy* Frazer, with his characteristic modesty, properly traces its birth to the Scotsman J. F. McLennan (I: vii). But Frazer was more responsible for the spread of totemism as a topic than any other single anthropologist, and was consequently authorized for the role of master of the subject.

But like evolution, totemism as a theoretical model was rejected by later anthropological schools, functionalist as well as structuralist. As Stocking notes, by World War I "Boasian critique had called into question the presumed ethnographic correlation of the various defining features, and 'totemism' as an ethnological category threatened for a time to prove a figment of the later Victorian imagination. When discussion was subsequently resumed by Radcliffe-Brown and Claude Lévi-Strauss, it was on a somewhat different basis" (VA 297).

Later anthropologists did not so much "disprove" totemism as reject this particular conception of totemism as no longer useful within their own theoretical frameworks. But this observation underlines even more the constructed nature of totemism, its essentially figural status and its consequent capability to generate interpretation. Roger Poole in his introduction to Lévi-Strauss's *Totemism* comments on the arbitrariness of the term, and its potential as a site for interpretation, when he notes how "totemism just happens to be the subject" of Lévi-Strauss's study; Lévi-Strauss's book, after all, is nothing if not "an exercise in methodology."[37]

Typically, Frazer obscures totemism's allegorical dimensions, the multiple directions that it can take toward broader ideological commentary. What Frazer calls "the mystic union of the savage with his totem" (TE I: 101) functions, in one of those directions, as a commentary on the pre-symbolic process.[38] The clansman does not "symbolize" the totem animal but rather becomes one with it: the process is simply a matter of unmediated representation. And there are significant spiritual and social corollaries to this semiotic and mystical equivalence. Totemism is defined as "magic" and is decidedly not "religion," for "religion always implies an inequality between the worshipers and the worshiped; it involves an acknowledgment, whether tacit or express, of inferiority on the part of the worshipers; they look up to the object of their worship as to a superior order of beings, whose favour they woo and whose anger they deprecate" (TE IV: 27). And the corollary to this equivalence in totemic cultures is nothing other than the democratic process—"pure totemism is essentially democratic" (28).

The ideological parameters of Frazer's reading of totemism become clearer when, after affiliating totemism, magic, and democracy, he asserts that "primitive society advances simultaneously from democracy and magic towards despotism and religion, and just in proportion as despotism and religion wax, so totemism wanes" (TE IV: 28). Frazer uses his own conception of primitive totemism here to bolster his condemnation of religion; magic, after all, as Frazer points out in other places, is integrally tied to science and opposed to religion, at least to the extent that neither the magician nor the scientist is in a supplicating position to the universe, as is the practitioner of religion. So the association of "religion" to "despotism" is hardly surprising, coming from an author who limns himself as a crusader against the falsehoods of religious worship, as he who works the "battery of the comparative method" that will "breach" the "venerable walls" of superstition and religious belief.[39]

And yet Frazer's position here is not simply to lay praise on totemism (or magic) and blame on religion. He tactically does not isolate religious readers. But more significant, evolution—here, the development from magic to religion to science—is inscribed by Frazer as an ultimate good. Religion is posed as the unfortunate but necessary stepping-stone from the follies of magic to the wisdom of science. When in *Totemism and Exogamy* Frazer sacrifices magic (and with it, the savage) for religion in order to maintain the impetus toward science, totemism's allegorical content becomes blatant, and a map of Frazer's ideological coordinates is revealed:

> Though to many civilised men the personal and intellectual freedom implied by democracy and magic may seem preferable to the personal and intellectual subordination implied by despotism and religion, and though they may accordingly incline to regard the exchange of the former for the latter as rather a retrogression than an advance, yet a broad view of history will probably satisfy us that both despotism and religion have been necessary stages in the education of humanity and that for analogous reasons. Men are not born equal and never can be so; a political constitution which professes their natural equality is a sham. (IV: 28–29)

Frazer's qualification of democracy translates into a barely veiled statement of his elitism. Further, his bifurcation of totemism/magic/democracy as opposed to religion/despotism enables him, once again, to take both sides of a self-inscribed debate, projecting figures that deprecate religion and trumpet science while at the same time killing the savage and his magic in the headlong evolutionary roll toward civilization. The text benefits from heavily elegiac figures recalling primitive democracy, but constructs that "democracy" within a schema that necessitates its destruction. And that is where Frazer's figurations lead us, finally: to the destruction of the savage and his ways. We need to recall that Frazer concludes the massive third edition with the hope that the "white thread of science" will be "woven more and more into the tissue" of the human culture of the future, and the fear that the primitive "black thread of magic" may strengthen and thus "arrest progress and even undo much that has been done" (*Balder* II: 308). Thus, Frazer's search for the proto-Man is ultimately and essentially consolidating, a retrogressive search for the first signifier that, in its figuring, makes inevitable, necessary, and desirable its elimination.

The evolutionary totemic processes, of magic to religion and democracy to despotism, are paralleled in Frazer's figuring of the cyclical appearance and disappearance of totemic objects giving way to hierarchical preservation and gradation: as a tribe develops, evolutionarily that is, "the appearance

of a constantly shifting kaleidoscope of clans . . . has shaken down into a
certain stability and permanence of form" (TE I: 81). For, "with the longer
memory which accompanies an advance in culture," Frazer finds that totems "no longer pass into oblivion, but should retain an elevated rank in
the religious hierarchy" (81). So the disappearance of the object of worship
is replaced by a kind of natural selection, in which certain deities survive
by evolving through the chain of life, from plant to animal to man form,
ultimately becoming anthropomorphic:

> As the attribution of human qualities to the totem is of the essence of
> totemism, it is plain that a deity generalised from or including under
> him a number of distinct animals and plants must, as his animal and
> vegetable attributes contradict and cancel each other, tend more and
> more to throw them off and retain only those human qualities which
> to the savage apprehension are the common element of all the totems
> whereof he is the composite product. In short, the tribal totem tends
> to pass into the anthropomorphic god. (82)

In *The Worship of Nature* Frazer elegiacally refers to this anthropomorphic
evolutionism as "the process of despiritualizing the universe" (*Man, God,
and Immortality* 308). This process is characterized by consolidation, what
Frazer terms "economy of thought," as "the multitude of individual spirits" became "generalized and reduced to a comparatively small number of
deities": thus "animism was replaced by polytheism" (309). Following the
same natural law, "the same desire for simplification and unification," man
then "educed monotheism out of polytheism," as "the many gods . . . were
deposed in favour of one solitary deity, the maker and controller of all
things" (309–10). Frazer then lends to this process of thought an empirical
analogy that attempts to mystify its essence as theory and promote its status as fact: "Thus the spiritualistic theory of the world has undergone a
process of simplification and unification analogous to that undergone by
the materialistic theory: as the materialistic hypothesis has reduced the multitudinous forms of matter to one substance, hydrogen, so the spiritualistic
hypothesis has reduced the multitude of spirits to one God" (310).

Frazer's theories on the origins and purposes of totemism may vary, but
his belief in this evolutionary totemic process is unfailing. Significantly, the
process's theoretical nature is mystified, posed as a fact or set of facts about
totemism: this is simply the way totemism diachronically works. Frazer's
figuring of the "kaleidoscope of [totem] clans" becoming reduced to a
"stability" of totemic formations suggests Nietzsche and Derrida, but with
a critical exception: Frazer does not acknowledge that this process is essen-

tially analogic, metaphoric, that it is he who has inscribed the shifting and freezing of forms, just as it is he who charts the death of primitive democracy and the birth of religious despotism.

When in *Totemism* Frazer criticizes a "generation of mythologists" for aspiring to "patch up the broken chain" of the totemic process by "the cheap method of symbolism" the antitropistic nature of Frazer's rhetoric becomes most explicit: "symbolism," after all, says Frazer, "is only the decorous though transparent veil which a refined age loves to throw over its own ignorance of the past" (I: 82). Frazer's insistence on the cleavage of "symbol" or analogic comparison from the essential "facts" of the totemic process, as incomplete as they might be, functions as an extension of his version of a transparent aesthetics; or, more accurately put, in totemism he has constructed a new space in which to reinscribe his figuration of the strict and superficial limits of figuration. Lévi-Strauss, fully acknowledging the constructed nature of totemism by expanding its boundaries to those of linguistics, provides a telling counterpoint to Frazer: "Metaphor, the role of which in totemism we have repeatedly underlined, is not as a later embellishment of language, but is one of its fundamental modes" (*Totemism* 102).

The distinction between the transparent embodiment of the totem and "cheap symbolism" emerges in *The Golden Bough,* where Frazer charts the evolutionary progress of totems from unmediated animistic presences and identifications to overtly representing or symbolizing anthropomorphic gods. What was a "tree-spirit conceived as incorporate or immanent in the tree" becomes, Frazer claims in *The Magic Art,* "detached from the tree and clothed in human form" (II: 71). Frazer's discussion of the worship of trees, while it ultimately reinforces evolutionary progress, also elegiacally recalls the animistic process; that lament functions as well as an allegorical grieving over the separation of signifier and signified:

> When a tree-spirit comes to be viewed, no longer as the body of the tree-spirit, but simply as its abode which it can quit at pleasure, an important advance has been made in religious thought. Animism is passed into polytheism. In other words, instead of regarding each tree as a living and conscious being, man now sees in it merely a lifeless, inert mass, tenanted for a longer or shorter time by a supernatural being who, as he can pass freely from tree to tree, thereby enjoys a certain right of possession or lordship over the trees, and, ceasing to be a tree-soul, becomes a forest god. (45)

This process of evolutionary totemism, and the aesthetics that accompany it, is anything but incidental to *The Golden Bough*. Indeed, it becomes the answer to the winding argument that began with the riddle of the Arician priesthood. The King of the Wood himself occupies a crucial position precisely because he marks the midpoint between "magic" and "religion"; although he is an anthropomorphic deity, he is considered still "incarnate," for he is "akin to" the people, "not raised to an unapproachable height above them" (*Magic Art* II: 377). In line with totemic evolutionism, Frazer ultimately makes the claim that the King of the Wood (and the priest of Nemi who posed as the King) "personated" either Janus or Jupiter and thereby took on the "essential functions of the god as a power of the sky, the thunder, and the oak" (386). Indeed, Frazer concludes the first edition of *The Golden Bough* with the "result" of the "inquiry" that has driven his Herculean effort: "the primitive worship of the Aryans was maintained nearly in its original form in the sacred grove at Nemi," where "the King of the Wood lived and died as an incarnation of the supreme Aryan god," the god of the oak, "whose life was in the mistletoe or Golden Bough" (370). And in the third edition Frazer reasserts the original totemic (versus religious) powers by declaring that the King "not only served but embodied the great Aryan god of the oak" and that "the original element in his composite nature was the oak."

The Golden Bough becomes, in this respect, a detective story in which we follow the traces back to the original totemic element, in this case the oak, but in other cases fire or thunder. For the ur-totem may change with editions, as the theories Frazer propounds are modified, even rejected. See, for example, the 1922 edition, where he discards the "explanation" that "the oak was worshipped primarily for the many benefits which our rude forefathers derived from the tree, particularly for the fire which they drew by friction from the wood," and offers instead "the present theory," in which the god's link with the oak "was merely an inference based on the frequency with which the oak was seen to be struck by lightning" (709). But the theoretical assumption of a generalized progression from animistic presences to anthropomorphic gods, from a hierarchy of spirituality that extends from the thunder to fire to mistletoe to oak (the order may shift depending upon the newest theory) to oak god to priest remains essentially unchallenged.

The assumption of anthropomorphic evolution from animism to monotheism is shared by the Cambridge Hellenists or ritualists (Jane Harrison, Gilbert Murray, F. M. Cornford, and others). Indeed, Harrison's *Themis*, first published in 1912 and perhaps the central volume of the ritualist school, essentially repeats Frazer's contention that savage and relatively amorphous spiritual power is progressively frozen into a civilized hierarchy of anthropomorphism, especially as typified in the gallery of Olympian gods. Harrison's distinction between the "Olympian," such as Zeus, and the "mystery-god," such as Dionysos, provides but one illustration of her assumption of Frazer's rhetoric: "The mystery-god is the life of the whole of things, he can only be felt—as soon as he is thought and individualized he passes, as Dionysos had to pass, into the thin, rare ether of the Olympian. The Olympians are of conscious thinking, divided, distinct, departmental; the mystery-god is the impulse of life through all things, perennial, invisible."[40]

When Frazer states in *Spirits of the Corn* that "the old savage theory" is "masquerading under a flowing drapery of morality and sparkling with the gems of Attic eloquence" (II: 308), we see a virtual blueprint for the Cambridge Hellenist program. And tied to the Cambridge Hellenists as well is the conclusion to that volume, where Frazer applies his notion of the survival of the fundamental forms of primitive spirituality to contemporary society: the "elaborate theologies" and "solemn rites" of civilized religion are destined "to pass away like 'all Olympus' faded hierarchy,'" while the "simple folk . . . will still mumble the old spells and make the old magic passes" (II: 335).

But Ackerman is correct in pointing out that Frazer was not a Cambridge ritualist pure and simple; for one thing, Frazer held three different theories on ritual, only the first of which maintained the primacy of ritual performance over myth, the cornerstone of Cambridge ritualist belief. Indeed, fairly late in his career Frazer, as Ackerman also points out, took pains to dissociate himself from the ritualist position, stating that "by a curious limitation of view, some modern writers would restrict the scope of myths to ritual, as if nothing but ritual were fitted to set men wondering and meditating on the causes of things."[41] Yet it is also true that the first edition, the book which primarily influenced the Cambridge Hellenists, was decidedly ritualistic. There Frazer points to the "extensive class of myths which are invented to explain ritual" and asserts that "ritual may be the parent of myth, but can never be its child" (II: 246).[42]

But the persistent identification of Frazer as a Cambridge Hellenist is due more to his rhetorical habits of accretion, his refusal to throw anything away. Both Jones and Ackerman do well to stress that Frazer's accretive habits encouraged adoption of him as a forefather of ritualism, but both also hold that at bottom Frazer's orientation as a spokesman for "Reason" separates him from a ritualist perspective.[43] Ackerman asserts that Frazer's ritualism "was fundamentally inimical to [his] thoroughgoing, eighteenth-century-style rationalism" ("Frazer on Myth" 133). And Jones claims that Frazer's baseline belief in the savage's essentially logical thinking prevents Frazer from embracing ritualism ("Robertson Smith and James Frazer" 39).

But these positions do not recognize that Frazer's accumulation of ritual belief and, more specifically, his assumed theory of totemic evolutionism so important to the ritualists, need not be considered separate from his rationalist perspective. Indeed, the separation of the two perspectives— Frazer was not a ritualist but a rationalist—tends to reinscribe Frazer's characteristic bifurcations. His conception of the animistic becoming anthropomorphic is essentially rationalistic in conception and yet, importantly, exudes a heavy nostalgia for the prelapsarian savage cohesion with the spirit; similarly, the reason that enables Frazer to follow the traces back to the originary past of the proto-Man also compels a retracing, through religion, that murders the savage. Ultimately both reason and ritual work in the construction of a logocentric urge, a rationalist funneling toward irrational origin that, in the effort to build a civilizing civilization, powerfully animates the Frazerian text.

The logocentric urge is at the core of Frazer's other incontrovertible anthropological assumption, the validity of the comparative method itself. While it is true that Frazer's comparative method, according to Marcus and Fischer, "played a profound role" in the attempt "to establish a secular-scientific outlook" and "to initiate the modern sense of tolerant pluralism" (*Anthropology as Cultural Critique* 128), it is more significant that the method gathered and arranged its "facts" from the vantage point of a rational search for the lost key to the civilized mind. Despite Frazer's own advertisement that the comparative method "guards us from narrowness and illiberality in our moral judgements" (*Taboo* viii), "the subliminal message," Marcus and Fischer warn, "tends to be affirming of the basic superiority of modern European or American society" (129).

Typically, Frazer's comparative method operates by creating a bottom ground of similarity that is made possible only by bifurcation. In other words, the distinction between civilized and savage, essential to Frazerian comparativism, becomes necessary if Frazer is to establish the savage continuity of mind, that "essential similarity in the working of the less developed human mind among all races" (*Balder* I: vi). In his tribute to William Robertson Smith, Frazer insists on the unifying impulse in the comparative method, the process of reducing difference and promoting similarity: when "we examine side by side the religions of different races and ages, we find that, while they differ from each other in many particulars, the resemblances between them are numerous and fundamental" (*Gorgon's Head* 282). And yet, again, this is a similarity made possible by the inscription of difference, for those "resemblances" are only resemblances in the context of an evolutionary paradigm, in which the grid of distinct diachronic and hierarchical stages is superimposed upon the various cultures, past and present.

Frazer mystifies the essentially analogic nature of his comparison, driving a wedge between figuration and scientism, by, typically, equating an anthropological conception of sameness with that of the "harder" sciences. Referring to those "well-meaning but injudicious friends of anthropology" who "would limit the application of the method," Frazer in 1922 defends the reduction of human difference by stating:

> They would apparently refuse to allow us to compare the thoughts and institutions, the arts and crafts, of distant races with each other, and would only allow us to compare those of neighbouring races. A little reflexion may convince us that any such restriction, even if it were practicable, would be unwise; nay, that, were it enforced, it would be disastrous. We compare things on the ground of their similarity, and similarity is not affected by distance. Radium is alike on earth and in the sun; it would be absurd to refuse to compare them on the ground that they are separated by many millions of miles. What would be thought of any other science which imposed on itself the restriction which some of our friends would inflict on anthropology? Would geology prosper if it confined its investigation, say, of sedimentary rocks to those of England and refused to compare those of Asia and America? (*Garnered Sheaves* 240)

Frazer's analogic use of radium is an attempt to mystify analogy; words such as *similarity* and *distance* function as transdiscursive signifiers, leaping from discipline to discipline and retaining their unshakably stable significations. Frazer's use of "any other science" is itself a sly appeal to scientism, a farfetched analogy that masquerades as hard truth, as though anthropology were any other science. And of course the ultimate disguised analogy at work concerns the objects of study themselves, humanity on the one hand easily equated to rocks and radium on the other.

In Enlightenment style, Frazer's argument for the comparative search for similarities mystifies the distinctions between types of "differences" and blatantly denies that "differences" of any kind matter. That denial in itself is a mystification of the rhetorical effect of his own brand of comparativism, in which Addisonian surprise arises from the comparison of cultures most unlike. The rhetorical effect of the congruence of radical difference can be powerful, and as such has much to do with the attention that Frazer, as opposed to other, more erudite scholars and anthropologists, garnered. It is no surprise that Frazer eclipsed Robertson Smith as the forefather of Cambridge Hellenism, given that, according to Jones, the latter's comparative method was "more cautious and historical" than Frazer's, "generally avoiding comparisons between Semitic and non-Semitic cultures, or between Semitic societies representing different evolutionary stages" ("Robertson Smith and James Frazer" 36).

Hyman earlier made much the same point when stating that "more boldly than Smith, Frazer delights in parallels as far apart as possible" (TTB 237). And in this context Hyman is correct when stating that "*The Golden Bough* is a vast argument from analogy" (237); but, significantly, he does not acknowledge the crucial act of mystification that Frazer performs, the denial that the comparison is metaphoric. The model inscribed by Frazer is one of extreme differences bound within a sphere of similarity, the differing traits inside the border of the circle but pressed to opposing sides. In fact, much of Frazer's rhetorical power has to do with the delicate balance of inward and outward tensions, as the centrifugal force that expands his field of inquiry, digressively expanding to the furthest reaches of the globe and thus enlarging his compass, negotiates with the centripetal force that narrows the difference between those items, demonstrating their essential oneness, and thus strengthening the border, the integrity, of the circle.[44]

The reduction of distracting difference to sameness is portrayed as the learned skill of the comparative anthropologist, without which the "accumulated observations" of the fieldworkers "would remain an undigested and disorderly heap"; for, according to Frazer, "it is the application of the comparative method to the heap which evolves order out of chaos by eliciting the general principles or laws which underlie the mass of particulars" (*Garnered Sheaves* 246). Frazer's choice of signifiers such as *heap* and *mass* underscores his conception of humanity as a terrifyingly sprawling mess of diversity that must be reduced to its containable, controllable unifying principles. And, significantly, this is done through a process that, though it is reserved for the elite comparativist, simply *happens* (as in a chemical experiment) when the "facts" are appropriately pigeon-holed: "If only our comparisons are just—in other words, if we have correctly sorted out the facts into their proper compartments according to their real similarities—

the colligation of the similars in a general truth or law follows almost automatically" (24).

Frazer's call for the future master, the great synthesizer, functions as another ploy of humility that valorizes the process of "automatically" reducing cultural material to utter similarity by creating a realm in which such winnowing has reached its perfection: collect your facts now, Frazer announces in *The Magical Origin of Kings,* "in order that when, in the fullness of time, the master-mind shall arise and survey them, he may be able to detect at once that unity in multiplicity, that universal in the particulars, that has escaped us" (quoted in *Man, God, and Immortality* 31). Frazer's looking forward to a time when the Master shall make the order of all things "magically" manifest itself among the mere particulars is a doubling of his prelapsarian aesthetics, in which the transcendental signified message, the incarnate god-word, shall reveal itself. What James Boon conceives as pre-Enlightenment biblical method (*Other Tribes* 30–31) underscores the essentially logocentric impulse of Frazer's rhetoric, the drive toward that ur-moment when the messy bits of variegated races, cultures, and words shall coalesce into the great principle that manifests the one message.[45]

But Frazer the Enlightenment rationalist gives to an essentially religious (or, more precisely, transcendental) semiotic a secular, materialistic, even deterministic figuring. For throughout history, Frazer tells us in *The Worship of Nature,* "the mind, in obedience to a fundamental law, seeks to form a conception which will simplify, and if possible unify, the multitudinous and seemingly heterogeneous phenomenon of nature" (quoted in *Man, God, and Immortality* 420). As proof Frazer provides the example of science, specifically chemistry, in which eighty-eight elements have been reduced to "the single element of hydrogen, of which the rest would appear to be only multiples." Biology as well illustrates the process, as "the theory of evolution reduces the innumerable species of plants and animals to unity by deriving them all from a single type of living organism" (420). Both of these physical sciences thus demonstrate that "unity and simplicity of conception which the human intellect imperiously demands if it is to comprehend in some measure the infinite complexity of the universe" (420).

However humbly Frazer may pose human effort—and Frazer does note that "as that complexity is infinite, so the search for the ultimate unity is probably endless also" (*Man, God, and Immortality* 420–21)—his comparative method, given the inscribed limits of the human mind, is seen to be most capable of proceeding with the task, since it can best comprehend and gather "infinite complexity" while at the same time containing it through the reduction of "difference." Frazer once again figures into existence an arduous task, this time couched in the form of quest, whose progress is assessed as tentative at best: "For we may suspect that the finality, which seems to crown the vast generalizations of science, is after all only illusory, and that the tempting unity and simplicity which they offer to the weary mind are not the goal but only halting-places in the unending march" (421).

One could pose Frazer in this context as a kind of harbinger of post-modern incompleteness, a prophet of the provisionality of cultural reading. But to do so ignores the rhetorical ploy of constructing the unending march and, more specifically, obscures the figure Frazer has chosen for himself. For the "halting-places" underscore not the uselessness of the journey but the determined heroism of the culture-reader as quester: "For the thinker there is no permanent place of rest. He must move for ever forward, a pil-grim of the night eternally pressing towards the faint and glimmering il-lumination that eternally retreats before him" (421). That his figure of the pilgrim is followed by a reference to Tennyson's Ulysses—"experience is an arch . . . whose margin fades / For ever and ever when I move"—does not underline the tentativeness of attainment so much as it trumpets the exertions of the quester, who, though he can never reach the arch, is rep-resented at the center of a dramatic canvas, forever bound in a beeline to-ward the arch that frames the infinite complexities of the "untravelled world." The whole of Frazer's corpus funnels toward that arch, toward that as-yet untravelled world which holds, incarnate, the ur-moment when word and thing, figure and fact, spirit and vessel coalesce.

Frazer's tactics, to be fully understood, must ultimately be read in terms of a consolidating rhetorical power. His moves toward fact-collector and artist, which appear to be an abandonment of the privileged position of armchair theorist, in fact represent a power play on his part to wrest control of the campaign from his aggressors. That tactical maneuver toward greater authority had significant attractions for readers and writers of the twentieth century, whose texts were catalyzed by what is perhaps the essence of *The Golden Bough*: the capability of its sheer mass to exude variabilities, ambiguities, multiple motives, sources, voices, meanings, theories, facts, and figures that can then be appropriated by the author-authoritarian in the event of threat. Frazer's bifurcations, of theory from fact, fact from literature, therefore provide him (and those who followed him) with the opportunity to play both sides of the imaginary line, thus insuring the dominance of the open, shifting text. Under threat, the text's value as theory is subsumed under its contribution to "fact"; when "fact" is called into question, the halo of authorship brightens. What survives, in the end, is the text itself, that many-headed author.

2

T. S. Eliot:
Figuring the Unfigurable

> Frazer's eminence is not merely a matter of superior erudition among writers whose standard of learning is prodigious; nor does it depend, like that of two writers who are more distinctly *sociologists,* MM. Durkheim and Lévy-Bruhl, upon brilliant theories of human behavior. On the contrary, with every fresh volume of his stupendous compendium of human superstition and folly, Frazer has withdrawn in more and more cautious abstention from the attempt to explain. The first edition of *The Golden Bough,* in two volumes, was an attempt to explain the Priest of Nemi. It led to allied investigations, so that another and larger edition was required.
>
> —T. S. Eliot, 1924

FACTS AND FRAGMENTS

In 1924, flushed from the triumph of the publication of *The Waste Land* and his subsequent accession to the editorship of *The Criterion,* T. S. Eliot wagered that Frazer, with Henry James and F. H. Bradley, would exert unrivaled influence among men of learning "upon the sensibility of one or two or more literary generations."[1] Eliot's justifications for Frazer's claim to literary fame, in this instance, duplicate Frazer's own defensive rhetorical tactics, especially as articulated in his prefaces: *The Golden Bough,* claims Eliot, constitutes a storehouse of knowledge to be of use to further generations; its massiveness coupled with the authorial refusal to be pegged to any one position insures its survival. Clearly, Eliot's account of the genealogy of Frazer's magnum opus is a doubling of Frazer's authorial justifications: the refusal, or inability, to interpret—to tie "facts" neatly to theories—generating a succession of words/works that progressively trim the hopes for the ultimate signification of explanation.

Interpretation in *The Golden Bough* functions, according to Eliot, in inverse proportion to textual mass: the diminution of theory, what Eliot calls "a conscious and deliberate scrupulousness" ("Prediction" 29), corresponds to an ever-enlarging corpus, a "stupendous compendium" of multiple sources and voices. Eliot ranks Frazer as the greatest anthropologist for precisely the reasons that Frazer, in his rhetoric of fact-collection, projected: because he is essentially a noninterpretive reporter. His gargantuan text, Eliot claims, has "perhaps greater permanence" than Freud's corpus "because it is a statement of fact which is not involved in the maintenance or fall of any theory of the author's" (29).

Eliot's public acknowledgment of the heterogeneity of Frazer's text is not an unwitting emulation of Frazerian tactics. In 1922 Eliot's praise of Joyce's "mythical method" that, through the comparative juxtaposition of varying periods and cultures would "make the modern world possible for art," appeared tailor-made to Eliot's own efforts in *The Waste Land,* published the same year. Two years later, Eliot's celebration of *The Golden Bough* as a storehouse of voices and sources resisting the yoke of singular interpretation reads like a promotional trailer to *The Waste Land,* a tag announcing that the accretion and organization of pure description or "fact" (in this case, the authentic images and voices of culture) amount to an elasticity of interpretation, insuring the "greater permanence" of art.

Frazer's comparativist text furnished Eliot with a valuable rhetorical model that, as we have seen, was at odds with the anthropological paradigm just emerging and about to become dominant. Typical of the lag between social-scientific production and aesthetic appreciation and appropriation, *The Waste Land*'s appearance coincided with the publication of Malinowski's *Argonauts of the Western Pacific,* the dramatic model for the functionalist monograph that depended upon the rhetoric of participant observation and thus had little use for Frazer's textual dependence. Ironically, Eliot's "Burial of the Dead" (part one of *The Waste Land*) brought the rhetoric of Frazerian comparativism to the height of its literary exposure and usefulness at just the moment when anthropology was burying that comparativist corpus. In a sense what died within the discipline of anthropology was a textual dependence that encouraged the profusion of myriad voices, sources, cultures, epochs: what sprouted was an emphasis upon the single culture as mediated by the single voice of the ethnographer.

What *The Waste Land* attempted to extend was a comparativist profusion of voice and source. The original working title of the poem, "He Do the Police in Different Voices," testifies to the poem's ventriloqual qualities, as the speaker, persona, poet, whoever, mimics the ancient and the modern, the high and the low. No matter who precisely is speaking (much recent critical debate has centered on that question), versions of other voices break forth, unrestricted by an ethnographic authority that would limit the range of voice to what is within earshot of the ethnographer (though certainly restricted in other ways, as this chapter will make evident). *The Golden*

Bough gave "voice" to then-contemporary Esthonians, ancient mourners of Dionysos, Kafirs of Zululand, and the Incan Sun-God, as chronicled by authors as diverse as Plutarch, Leviticus, Aeneas Sylvius, Adolph Bastian, and Captain John Moresby; *The Waste Land* projects the shouts and murmurs of the Sibyl, Bill and Lou, the young man carbuncular, Queen Elizabeth, Phloebus, and Thunder, and in the process registers sources as various as Ezekiel, Baudelaire, the *Handbook of Birds of Eastern North America,* the Upanishads, and Thomas Kyd's *Spanish Tragedy.*

But of course the magisterial sweep made possible by the comparativist's position in the armchair was challenged by more scrupulous field-based anthropologists and, later, ethnographers. And Frazer's cleaving to the "facts" of his borrowed accounts constituted a full-fledged attempt at disarming criticisms that his comparativist appropriation of materials had less than the grit of the scientific. Eliot was clearly engaged by Frazer's empiricist rhetoric, especially the dichotomy Frazer figured as fact versus theory. In the "Prediction" piece of 1924 Eliot uses the distinction to construct a dichotomization of social science (anthropology versus sociology) and in the process to valorize Frazer. In the same year Eliot echoes this tactic in a review of two books by W. J. Perry: "Evidently, Mr. Perry's work is as much sociology as it is anthropology. That is to say, his work is not so much the accumulation and collocation of material, such as is found in *The Golden Bough,* as it is the construction of this material into a single edifice: he may be classified with Durkheim and Lévy-Bruhl rather than with Sir James Frazer."[2]

The distinction Eliot adopted at least in part from Frazer, between the accumulation of fact and the construction of interpretation, was not new-formed in 1924. Indeed, Eliot's early reading of anthropology, dating back to 1910, catalyzed what became a persistent deliberation upon the value and nature of "fact." In a graduate-student paper entitled "The Interpretation of Primitive Ritual," composed 1912–13, Eliot establishes a distinction between fact and interpretation, only to conclude that pure description of the primitive is impossible since interpretation invariably enters into that description. He proceeds from the early comparative evolutionism of Tylor, on to Frazer, Harrison, Lévy-Bruhl, and Durkheim and in the end asserts that no single anthropologist is capable of establishing the "fact" of ritual with adequate clarity. Eliot does praise Frazer for sticking to the facts of ritual, but criticizes him for occasional lapses into "interpretation" (namely, the explanation Frazer gives for the magical rites of spring festivals at the end of his volume on the Dying God). That Eliot did not declare Frazer the master of "fact" in this early paper hardly diminishes the centrality of Frazer to Eliot's contemplation on fact: the terms by which Eliot framed his rhetoric were Frazer's; and by 1924 Eliot had clarified, or more accurately, simplified, his own position by declaring Frazer's work as having "greater permanence" than that of other anthropologists since it constituted no less than "a statement of fact."[3]

Eliot's emergent literary criticism owes much to this contemplation on "fact" and "interpretation." Indeed, the figuration of the Frazerian fact-collector significantly contributes to Eliot's formation of the figure of the modern literary critic. In the influential "Function of Criticism," first published in 1923, Eliot holds that "the critic must have a very highly developed sense of fact. This is by no means a trifling or frequent gift." Clearly Eliot is promoting the notion, described by Jacob Korg, that "the sense of fact [is] a civilizing asset for critics."[4] Eliot's elaboration upon this sense in the literary critic resonates with the authorial rhetoric of Frazer the master accumulator:

> The sense of fact is something very slow to develop, and its complete development means perhaps the very pinnacle of civilisation. For there are so many spheres of fact to be mastered, and our outermost sphere of fact, of knowledge, will be ringed with the narcotic fancies in the sphere beyond. To the members of the Browning Study Circle, the discussion of poets about poetry may seem arid, technical, and limited. It is merely that the practitioners have clarified and reduced to a state of fact all the feelings that the member can only enjoy in the most nebulous form; the dry technique implies, for those who have mastered it, all that the member thrills to; only that has been made into something precise, tractable, under control. That, at all events, is the reason for the value of the practitioner's criticism—he is dealing with his facts, and he can help us to do the same. (SE 19–20)

As Frazer does with his rhetoric of the anthropologist-as-collector, Eliot looks forward to the prospect of a stone-by-stone accumulation of small certainties toward what amounts to a futurist "pinnacle" of achievement. It is significant that this must be the work of specialists, of technical experts set apart from the common breed of appreciators. Just as the armchair anthropologist's distance from the field supposedly imparts to him the capability to distinguish between the "fact" and the "fancy" of the field-worker, so the literary critic's ability to distill the feelings of the mere appreciator into a state of fact makes the object of study—for the armchair anthropologist, the native; for the literary critic, the poetry—"into something precise, tractable, under control," possessed, in other words, by the scientistic, empirical authority of the professional gatherer.

The essentially "critical labour" of artist and critic alike is seen much as both Frazer and Eliot describe the activity of the Frazerian comparativist: as "the labour of sifting, combining, constructing, expunging, correcting, testing" (SE 18). Relevant here is Michael Levenson's claim that Eliot's version of art "involves selection, suppression, control, and order," as opposed to the romantic notion of art as "mirroring the soul."[5] And, indeed, what Eliot is trying to deemphasize through his catalogue of critical labors is the romantic conception of the spontaneous inspiration of the personal artist, a sense of individualism which significantly corresponds to the literary critic's subjective act of interpretation. Echoing Frazer and his own critical commentary on Frazer, Eliot proclaims that "it is fairly certain that 'interpretation' . . . is only legitimate when it is not interpretation at all, but merely putting the reader in possession of facts which he would otherwise have missed" (SE 20). This statement brings to mind Eliot's praise of Frazer, in the 1924 "Prediction" piece, for his "more and more cautious abstention from the attempt to explain" (29) and the paramount importance Eliot gives to description over interpretation in his paper on primitive ritual (where, again, he lauds Frazer).

Eliot's caveat against "interpretation" is followed by the promotion of the two activities, "comparison and analysis" (SE 21), that constitute the Frazerian comparativist. These activities, though Eliot does not rigorously define them here, are opposed to "interpretation" in their sticking to the "facts" of the case, producing the evidence and judiciously comparing and analyzing on the basis of that evidence. But Eliot's metaphor for the method is medical rather than juridical: "Comparison and analysis need only the cadavers on the table; but interpretation is always producing parts of the body from its pockets, and fixing them in place" (21). Ironically, this metaphor uses the same figure that Benedict will to condemn Frazer's methodological practices: in the place of Frazer as Frankenstein, Eliot puts the interpreter, who inserts various opinions willy-nilly into the corpus. Perhaps more significant, Eliot's figure of the correct surgeon, who needs only the body and the tools of comparison and analysis, lends a scientific legitimacy, and biological urgency, to the activities of the literary critic.

Criticism, however humble, is useful, even permanent, to the extent to which it cleaves to the bedrock of "fact" and avoids the imprecise, airy heights of interpretation. In this belief Eliot echoes Frazer's claim that "while theories are transitory, a record of facts has a permanent value" (*Balder* I: xi). "Any book, any essay, any note in *Notes and Queries*," Eliot claims, "which produces a fact even of the lowest order about a work of art is a better piece of work than nine-tenths of the most pretentious critical journalism, in journals or in books" (SE 21). Eliot's rhetoric on the modest, even pedestrian, but essential collection of fact echoes Frazer's own shrewd defense of himself as humble fact-collector and replicates Eliot's assessment of Frazer as more permanent than those "other scholars of equal erudition and perhaps greater ingenuity" ("Prediction" 29). It does not seem that "the discovery of Shakespeare's laundry bills would be of much use to us," Eliot states, "but we must always reserve final judgment as to the futility of the research which has discovered them, in the possibility that some genius will appear who will know of a use to which to put them" (SE 21). Eliot's rhetoric here startlingly duplicates Frazer's, making the importance of seemingly humble fact-collecting dependent upon the projection, into the future, of a supreme interpreter. For Frazer depicts his humble "facts" as "materials for a future science of Comparative Ethics . . . rough stones which await the master-builder, rude sketches which more cunning hands than mine may hereafter work up into a finished picture" (*Taboo* II: viii).

Richard Shusterman makes the point that the critical perception of Eliot as a "naive and unequivocal objectivist" is "falsely simplistic and unfair to the complexity of Eliot's thought."[6] Shusterman holds that Eliot's early critical writings are indeed "clearly and avidly objectivist" (44) but that Eliot "could find no philosophically adequate solution to this complex problem of objectivity, and came increasingly to affirm and emphasize the subjective and personal in his critical theorizing" (72). Clearly Shusterman is correct about the complex nature of Eliot's musings upon objectivity. As early as 1913, in the student paper on primitive ritual, Eliot's contemplation on objectivity waffles in philosophical complexity, staking out certain possibilities for pure "fact" or description that are then pulled out (or at the least, loosened). But more to the point here is the desire on Eliot's part, admittedly at times not achievable, to isolate the ground of "fact" and more pertinent, the persistent rhetorical *effect* to which Eliot put that aspiration, an effect that increased the status of Eliot the critic and poet. In this respect Shusterman perceptively states that "one could interpret [Eliot's] early objectivist critical theory as an ingenious method to disguise the essentially subjective and self-seeking character of his early criticism" (48).

The objectivism operating in Eliot's early criticism was but one facet of his attempt to broaden rhetorical authority by incorporating useful aspects of other, stricter, more legitimated disciplines. This effort toward appropriation and control is not simply personal, though it is certainly ultimately self-seeking. For this drive did not merely promote Eliot as author, but successfully chiseled out definitions of modern criticism and Modernism that would then necessitate viewing him as central to those movements. Michael Levenson's remark that 1922 was more important as the founding year of the *Criterion* than as the publication date of *The Waste Land* (*Genealogy of Modernism* 218) underlines Eliot's importance in institutionalizing Modernism while elevating his own cultural status to a new level.[7]

Eliot makes one thing clear in his early criticism: as a literary figure he (and modern criticism as a whole) needed to have a significantly wider intellectual grasp than was available. And Eliot eagerly pursued the social sciences toward that end. Levenson notes that anthropology's significance for Eliot is that the discipline "offers the broadest view," and the comparative method, in this respect, helps "to bring pattern into the heterogeneity of human culture" (*Genealogy of Modernism* 196). In 1929 Eliot indicates that literary criticism has been able to ingest both English and French social-scientific developments, especially in anthropology, in ways that have furthered the field's assimilative grasp. In "Experiment in Criticism" Eliot underlines the importance of interdisciplinary activity in criticism, noting that "it is by no means irrelevant" that Sainte-Beuve, "the first interesting historian in criticism . . . began his career with the study of medicine; he is not only an historian but a biologist in criticism."[8] Here, again, Eliot stresses the importance of aligning the critic to a more legitimated field (here he reaches as far as a hard science). He turns to a "good recent piece of literary criticism," Herbert Read's *Phases of English Poetry,* to illustrate "some of the assumptions of knowledge and theory which you would not find in criticism of two hundred years ago." Eliot's discussion of Read's book highlights the advances made in criticism owing to the importation of anthropological theory:

> On the second page [Read] tells us that his is an inquiry into the evolution of poetry, and speaks presently of English poetry as a "living and developing organism." Even these few words should give a hint of the extent to which the critical apparatus has changed with the general changes in scientific and historical conceptions, when a literary critic can treat his audience to terms like "evolution" and "living organism" with the assurance of being immediately apprehended. He is taking for granted certain vague but universal biological ideas. A little later he informs us that "the beginning of this study belongs to anthropology." Now, a great deal of work has to be done by a great many people, and already more or less popularized, before a critic of liter-

ature can talk in this way. The work of Bastian, Tylor, Mannhardt, Durkheim, Lévy-Bruhl, Frazer, Miss Harrison, and a great many others has gone before. (228)

Eliot hardly promoted a faith in a simple evolutionist approach to art. Indeed, in "Tradition and the Individual Talent" he takes pains to point out that European art's "development, refinement perhaps, complication certainly, is not, from the point of view of the artist, any improvement"; but his point that "the conscious present is an awareness of the past" greater than "the past's awareness of itself" (SE 6) suggests the value for literary theory of a social-scientific methodology that can diachronically gather artistic "facts" and thereby widen the historical and cultural perspective of the gatherer. It is *not* that anthropology makes literature or literary criticism improve, but Eliot's essay does suggest that literary critics have a much larger arsenal of cultural "facts" at their disposal than ever before.

Though Eliot often questions the possibility of realizing the purely objective, one assertion that sticks with a fair degree of firmness, first appearing in the primitive-ritual paper and replayed in later writings, is the notion of the permanence or reality of the "rite" itself. As Piers Gray notes, "Eliot concludes that the only *fact* to be found in any past social behavior is 'the actual ritual.'" Eliot's assertion of rite's empirical primacy in the paper is somewhat undercut by the example chosen for the treatment of rite: the work of Harrison. According to Eliot, though Harrison's books are fascinating, the bare fact of rite as treated in her work becomes interpretation—that is, her own explanations of the rite do creep in. Eliot nonetheless still maintains that the ritual itself, because it is a tangible entity, can be contemplated as fact and be considered in lieu of intention, purpose, or meaning.[9]

The Frazerian fact that Eliot longs for, and the rite that represents to him (for the time being) the only ethnographic site of that fact, have significant repercussions in his later rhetoric. In 1926 Eliot recalls his graduate-student paper in terms that look to his own critical interests: "Some years ago, in a paper on *The Interpretation of Primitive Ritual,* I made an humble attempt to show that in many cases *no* interpretation of a rite could explain its origin. For the meaning of the series of acts is to the performers themselves an interpretation; the same ritual remaining practically unchanged may assume different meanings for different generations of performers; and the rite may even have originated before 'meaning' meant anything at all."[10]

The meaning of the rite becomes caught in an interpretive quagmire; but the rite itself, as object, as bare "fact," stands free of meaning or the lack of it and in a more critical sense incorporates all possible interpretations. The implications of Eliot's point for his literary criticism are great: for example, the "objective correlative" functions as a version of that rite, one response to the need for the actual object standing not as "meaning" or "interpretation" but as the scaffolding upon which to hang interpretation. It is significant in this respect that Eliot, in the essay "Hamlet," pronounces as a premise to his discussion of objective correlative that "the work of art cannot be interpreted; there is nothing to interpret; we can only criticise it according to standards, in comparison to other works of art; and for 'interpretation' the chief task is the presentation of relevant historical facts which the reader is not assumed to know" (SE 122). The critic, again, is posed as the Frazerian fact-collector whose responsibility and claim to fame lie not in "interpretation" proper but in the correct collection, classification, and presentation of the facts. And in this regard Eliot's "mythical method" shares much with the notion of objective correlative, for in his famous review of *Ulysses,* Eliot states that the "mythical method" does not interpret but, like Frazer's textual strategies, collects and organizes: "it is simply a way of controlling, of ordering, of giving a shape and a significance to the immense panorama of futility and anarchy which is contemporary history."[11] Eliot names *The Golden Bough* (along with the fields of psychology and ethnology) as a crucial model for the method.

Sanford Schwartz's *Matrix of Modernism,* which investigates the Modernist "use of constructs that integrate abstraction and sensation," emphasizes Eliot's imperative that "emotions . . . can and should be rendered precisely through their correlative objects," and in this context quotes Eliot's statement that "language in a healthy state presents the object, is so close to the object that the two are identified."[12] Now the interpenetration between emotion, sensation or experience, and object in Eliot's rhetoric is quite complex (as Schwartz, Walter Benn Michaels, and Richard Shusterman all demonstrate), but clearly there persists the need to isolate the object, rite, or "fact" that would concretize, organize, dispense of—but *not* interpret—subjective speculation.

Frazer's activity as fact-collector served as an especially appropriate figure for Eliot's efforts, since it lent them a scientistic authority. The objective correlative, after all, operates by ordering, by making empirical sense of, the monads of disparate experience, just as Frazer's collocation of "facts" in *The Golden Bough* brings to light the layers of information gathered from numerous sources: neither constitutes an interpretation (at least, according to Frazer and Eliot). The link to the Frazerian rhetoric of the primacy of fact is made evident in Eliot's famous definition of the objective correlative:

"a set of objects, a situation, a chain of events which shall be the formula of that *particular* emotion; such that when the external facts, which must terminate in sensory experience, are given, the emotion is immediately evoked" (SE 124–25). And remember that the reason for *Hamlet*'s failure, according to Eliot, is that "Hamlet (the man) is dominated by an emotion which is inexpressible, because it is in *excess* of the facts as they appear" (125).

Eliot's figures for objective reference (objective correlative, mythical method) found another anthropological model in the totem. Frazerian and Durkheimian conceptions of the totem clearly fascinated Eliot, for he discusses them in several reviews and essays. In line with his skepticism concerning interpretation, Eliot, in a review of the English translation of Durkheim's *Elementary Forms of the Religious Life,* considers the French sociologist's account of totemism as "the best because it is the nearest to being no theory at all." By 1924 Eliot would shift this favored status from Durkheim to Frazer, but the criterion, the absence of "theory" or interpretation, remained the same. In this regard, Eliot here and in other reviews dismisses the possibility of arriving at the "meaning" of totemism; instead, he stresses the *function* (not purpose or meaning) of the "real" totem object as a magnet around which the filings of a society, for whatever reason, group themselves. The following quotation, taken from a review of Durkheim's book ascribed to Eliot in the August 1916 *Westminster Gazette,* points up the totem object's social significance: "Totemism is the organisation of the group, and the religious festival is its expression. 'By uttering the same cry, pronouncing the same word, or performing the same gesture in regard to some object individuals become and feel themselves to be in unison.' Collective sentiments find expression spontaneously in a material emblem."[13]

In a striking sense, Eliot's objective correlative functions as the totem object, as the "material emblem" through which "collective sentiments find expression." For the correlative is constituted of that set of external facts which, when made evident, immediately evoke the emotion (SE 125). And, like the totem, the objective correlative becomes the site for gathering, the occasion at which popular audiences, and critics, convene. Shusterman holds that Eliot in the early criticism moved toward the notion of "objectivity simply resid[ing] in the consensus of a cooperative community maintaining a common tradition" (*Eliot and Philosophy of Criticism* 70). Indeed, in "The Function of Criticism" Eliot maintains that "for the kinds of critical activity which we have admitted, there is the possibility of cooperative activity, with the further possibility of arriving at something outside of ourselves, which may provisionally be called the truth" (SE 22). In this respect Eliot's articulation of totemic experience as tribal members finding common voice and truth in the face of the totem object significantly parallels the grouping of critics around the correlative, the set of "facts," that upon contact triggers group emotion.

But Eliot's figures for objective reference, and their anthropological models, are even more useful in understanding the rhetorical power behind his creative corpus. In a crucial respect, Eliot promotes *The Waste Land* as a kind of sacred-secular rite (and site) for collective interpretation; a "fact" in the midst of, and bearing witness to, the ruin of civilization: a totemic object pouring forth the voices of our tribe and in turn evoking the tribe's interpretations, yet refusing to be denoted, identified, as any of those voices. The poem's massive urge toward elusiveness, as with the rite and the totem, is grounded in its powerful sense of *presence* as cultural fact. Eliot knew, from Frazer, of the authority inherent in that sense of presence, the scientistic aura produced by a fist fat with "facts." That aura is built by Eliot from the ground up, from the pebbles that make up the mighty earth at the base of its shifting structure. At first glance, Eliot's praise of Frazer as reporter of facts juxtaposes oddly with the verbal and cultural "ruins" of *The Waste Land*. But those "facts" make a certain sense (and certain sense) as the "fragments" that the poem's persona (Eliot, Tiresias, or a projection of the author) has "shored against [his] ruins,"[14] nuggets of cultural verities representing the minimal stand of certitude against the onslaught of cultural, and interpretive, chaos.

Eliot, following Frazer, marched out the pure minimal authentic, the cultural "facts" ("despite their fragmentary character," Frazer tells us) which apparently first emerged from the cultural fount and are just now receding from our grasp into extinction. Those cultural nuggets—myths, poems, gods, holy books, cathedrals—accumulate to form a last-chance purview of World Culture, just as Frazer's persistent gathering of anthropological "fact" ultimately produced, according to Eliot, a "stupendous compendium" of "superstitions" that are daily disappearing from our lives. But this parting glance at culture functions as ploy. In *Writing Culture* James Clifford writes of the allegory of salvage at work in ethnography, "the persistent and repetitious 'disappearance' of social forms at the moment of their ethnographic representation." Clifford feels that this pattern "demands analysis as a narrative structure" and acknowledges that it is part of a larger Western tradition tied to impulses toward the ultimately Edenic (112–13). Critics often claim that Eliot's poem is a response to the disillusioning experience of World War I, and the poem itself alludes to war as a central figure for civilization's collapse. That the Great War brought the notion of catastrophe to a new level is undeniable, but this is not the same as saying that Western civilization is literally disappearing. Eliot's figuring of "hooded hordes swarming / Over endless plains," of the "falling towers" (ll. 369–70) of the major cities in the history of Western civilization— "Jerusalem Athens Alexandria / Vienna London" (ll. 375–76)—are deliberately funneled into a fall of the West, feeding fuel to a readership already tending, understandably, toward the Apocalyptic.

Richard Poirier warns against "the tendency to believe in the wasteland as an historic fact," noting that "it has to be remembered that the fragmentariness which is its principal characteristic is a condition of Eliot's mind even when he is not addressing cultural issues." And Perry Meisel asserts the self-serving function of Eliot's depiction of civilization's collapse, claiming that Eliot, "in order to insure his own apparent originality," invents "the most influential Modern myth of all—that modern life is itself a wasteland, projecting onto the world a state that really inheres largely in the history of imagination alone." Indeed, the rhetorical question near the poem's end, "Shall I at least set my lands in order?" operates as an after-the-fact self-invitation to fabricate, out of a fabricated incoherence, a brilliant configuration of culture. The mosaic that results is comprised of the fragments, figured as facts turned to barely recognizable debris, that are shored against the ruins of culture in a last-ditch attempt at preservation. The method, in the end, pays tribute to the genius of the arranger: "making the modern world possible for art" becomes, in practice, the artist making the modern world in his own image.[15]

The appropriative nature of Eliot's rhetoric is muffled but present in the pyramidal structure of influence depicted in "Tradition and the Individual Talent," in which the "ideal order" of literary classics is "modified by the introduction of the new (the really new) work of art" (SE 5).[16] That the "awareness of the past" possessed by the modern poet is greater than "the past's awareness of itself" (6) provides the poet (here Eliot) the license not only to readjust the canon and misread its contents but to take possession of the ideal order: Baudelaire is no longer Baudelaire, Shakespeare no longer Shakespeare. Eliot, as the good comparativist, tears the texts of the ideal order from their original cultural and authorial contexts, so that they lose their old "meanings" as they are fitted into the pyramid whose eye, at top, is Eliot.[17] In one sense Eliot is playing out what he himself observed in his paper on primitive ritual: he is letting stand—and in the process helping to preserve—the old rites that now evoke new interpretations. But the architecture surrounding the collection of the rites is his: the massive edifice of cultural facts displays the signature of the compiler.

Eliot's brand of the multivocal, like Frazer's system of classification, gives an appearance of transparent representation, to the limited extent, anyway, that the author appears to clip out voices and let them stand in odd but interesting juxtaposition: Marie's voice breaks into that of the quester-figure, which breaks into that of Madame Sosostris. What we are given is the impression of real voices, nuggets of real life, that are, as in *The Golden Bough,* obsessively rehearsed. Those voices amount in the end, however, to a cultural mosaic that is decidedly of the author's own making. Frazer's purpose in his book on the Bible, to disengage the literary "gems" of the Bible from their mere religious and historical contexts, proves allegorical of Eliot's comparativism, for Eliot too removes "native" material from its local, culture-specific context. The culture-blending product is hardly the spontaneous and untampered gallery of voices but, rather, is a precisely sculpted and highly skewed representation of different cultures and epochs. Relevant here is Philip Rahv's startingly early perception (1953) that the writings of Eliot (and Pound) are "not the workings of the mythic imagination but an aesthetic simulacrum of it, a learned illusion of timelessness" ("Myth and Powerhouse" 115).

Important recent criticism on *The Waste Land* revolves around the issue of the freedom of its voices, with some conflicting but useful responses. Calvin Bedient's *He Do the Police in Different Voices* sees *The Waste Land* as essentially polyphonic, but interprets the voices at work in the poem as babble that transcends signification and aspires toward the ineffable absolute. Bedient opposes Terry Eagleton's view that the obstruction to meaning in the poem, the apparent difficulty of linking the "signifying codes" to "their signifieds," is actually a way to preserve surreptitiously the poem's "meaning." That meaning is a contradiction, Eagleton says, in that the poem tells us that cultures "collapse" while simultaneously preserving and valorizing "Culture" in the form of the poem itself. Bedient strenuously disagrees with Eagleton, claiming that the poem's voices point not to "an ideology of cultural knowledge" but to the otherworldly, the "Unsignifiable." One view sees in the multiple voices an escape from cultural experience; the other insists upon an ideological, and ultimately monologic, underpinning.[18]

Fundamental to this chapter is the assertion that the voices of Eliot's poem *do* map out an ideology, their inscriptions marking the margins of a determined and culturally specific definition of culture. The crazed sequence of voices in the poem form a network that, like Frazer's inscribing of culture as woven web, attempts to give to *culture* an ultimate coherence. As in *The Golden Bough,* the multiple threads of voices figured as "unreadable" (presented as they are in juxtaposed, erratic manner) make necessary an impulse toward containment, through which we are to feel that the anthropological subjects of the poem ought to be bracketed off. That enclosure in *The Waste Land* often takes the form of cultural preservation: hold to these values, these peoples, these texts, Eliot tells us in between the lines. But containment also threatens elimination: like Frazer's darkly painted savage, the hordes, infidels, and most of the women in *The Waste Land* are given voice in a chaos that propels their elimination.

But it is equally undeniable that the voices of Eliot's poem are directed toward something, somewhere, not of this world. The erratic chain of obsessive signifiers, the various evocations of man, woman, god, saint, tenuously link in an urge toward the transcendental: the poem's concluding lines, a mad flurry of signifiers, seem held together only to the extent that they are, collectively, about to fly apart into the Great DA of the other world, that open space at the poem's end given shape only in a voice that demands a renunciation into bodilessness. Eagleton's observation on the ideology underlying the poem is important, but does not address what has made *The Waste Land* a poem to return to. Indeed, what makes much of Eliot's poetry, and especially *The Waste Land,* so compelling is the textual, and densely textured, momentum toward what is not of the text, and the necessary circling back to what is. This in itself is not a wholly original observation. But what has not been discussed is how the complex rhetoric of the shuttling between the figurable and the nonfigurable contributes ultimately toward Eliot's authorial authority, and does so in ways that are distinctly anthropological in origin and nature.

TOTEMS, ANDROGYNES, AND POET-PRIESTS

The complex relation in Eliot's poetry between the sayable and unsayable, figurable and nonfigurable, profane and sacred can be illuminated by recourse to anthropological texts, familiar to Eliot, that commented upon "primitive" semiotics, the primal relation of name to thing, signifier to signified. For example, Lévy-Bruhl, Durkheim, and Sigmund Freud in *Totem and Taboo* all comment on the sacred nature of primitive names and the consequent need to protect or conceal them.[19] Frazer in *Taboo and the Perils of the Soul* holds that to the primitive person the personal name is a "vital part of the self" through which one can be injured: thus it is important to keep that name secret. Frazer gives a whole catalogue of tabooed names and stresses the precautions against uttering the names of the dead (318–34, 349–91). In all cases the name is represented as a metaphor operating upon nonlogical or "prelogical" processes (to borrow Lévy-Bruhl's term), embodying a person's primal spiritual identity and thus recovering the plenitude of the person's sacred ancestral past. It is not symbolic in the modern, Saussurean context, for the connection between signifier and signified is anything but arbitrary.

We find a conspicuous use of the taboo upon names in Eliot's *Old Possum's Book of Practical Cats*. In "The Naming of Cats" Eliot tells us that a cat has three names: an everyday name, a "particular" and "dignified" name, and a name that only "THE CAT HIMSELF KNOWS, and will never confess." That third name owes much to the social-scientific conceptions of the sacred and secret name that is revealed only at the peril of its bearer. It is a name that "you never will guess," "that no human research will discover" because it represents, or rather embodies, the sacred totem animal. Because it is thus separated from the profane, it is unutterable, as Eliot proclaims in the poem's conclusion:

> When you notice a cat in profound meditation,
>   The reason, I tell you, is always the same:
> His mind is engaged in a rapt contemplation
>   Of the thought, of the thought, of the thought of
>   his name:
>   His ineffable effable
>   Effanineffable
> Deep and inscrutable singular name.[20]

The cat's third name is not the only name in Eliot's canon that is figured as so sacred that it is "ineffable," so "deep" that it is "inscrutable." The *verbum infans,* though it is an explicitly Christian concept, is a central figure in Eliot's poetry from 1918 to 1942. It is itself the ultimate ineffable, the "word within a word, unable to speak a word" ("Gerontion," 1. 18), the *mana* ("primitive" spiritual essence discussed in evolutionary comparativist writings) that, like the holy thunder discussed in numerous anthropological texts, is at the source of sacredness and thus inexpressible.

Indeed, both thunder and the infant word are versions of the sanctity that has no verbal equivalent, as William Harmon implies when referring to the thunder utterance "DA" that appears in the last section of *The Waste Land*— "Then spoke the thunder / DA"—as a "heavenly voice" that "expresses something prior to itself, some unutterable and unuttering principle that, inscrutable, has no names and no qualities."[21] Now the thunder's voice does signify in the most basic sense: after the initial "DA" is pronounced, three critical words in Hindu follow: *Datta, Dayadhvan, Damyata,* translated by Eliot in the notes to the poem as "give, sympathize, control," respectively (*Collected Poems* 75). But what those words mean, and even whether they operate as injunctions, commands, questions, or perhaps even sheer phatic utterances, is not clear. In any case, the persona of the poem's last section responds, at least indirectly, elliptically, to each of the thunder's signifiers, and critical commentary since 1922 registers a profound variation of interpretation as to the meaning of those responses. For example, does the response to "*Datta*: what have we given?" (l. 402), beginning as it does with "My friend, blood shaking the heart / The awful daring of a moment's surrender" (ll. 403–04), signify liberation of body or a *giving in* to mere passion, or something else entirely? More important, do the collective responses at end signify the success or the failure of the poem's quester?

In any event, the voice of thunder stands as utterly present and eminently capable of interpretation, and yet essentially transcendent, referring to, if anything, its own heavenly and crucially nameless origin. Relevant here is Bedient's claim that Eliot speaks of the "Absolute" as "the pre-nominal," and that names in Eliot's work divide into those of the "supernatural and the superhuman" versus those of the "natural and the human" (*He Do the Police* 53). In fact, Bedient's bifurcation is another version of the split between the sacred and the profane, a notion first coming into prominence in social-scientific circles in Eliot's day.

Without denying the essentially Hindu and Christian origins of the Thunder utterance DA and the verbum infans, respectively, it is not too much to say that the "primitive" equivalents to those concepts encouraged Eliot to put them into play as figures expressing not only the relation between word and spirit but also between the poet who wields that powerful word and the members of the tribe who stand dumb before its pregnant presence. He might have found an interesting parallel between the verbum infans and Freud's theory, in *Totem and Taboo,* of the "antithetical primal word." Like "the word within a word," the "antithetical primal word" is the prototype of verbal expression, the original word that encompasses all meaning and thus contains contraries. Freud provides "taboo" as an example of a "primitive" word that gave verbal expression to two contrary ideas, "that which is holy" and "that which is unclean" (67).[22]

In "Mr. Eliot's Sunday Morning Service" we find just such a process at work. The "Word" that was there from the "beginning" was the primal antithetical word. It was a "Superfetation" (l. 6) in the sense that it contained the embryos or sources for two different ideas. "At the mensual turn of time" the primal Word "Produced enervate Origen" (ll. 7–8), passed from the One to the Many, or, in another sense, gave birth to multiple expression. In theological terms Origen represents a weakening of doctrine; in anthropological terms he represents the fall from a state of indivisible mana to the anthropomorphic; in linguistic terms he represents a loss of the all-encompassing power to contain contraries.

The anthropologically motivated process of linguistic fall that Eliot narrates looks forward strikingly to contemporary theory's contemplations on the original word. In his seminal essay "Structure, Sign, and Play in the Discourse of the Human Sciences" Jacques Derrida cites Lévi-Strauss's discussion of mana as the ultimate "floating signifier," what Lévi-Strauss calls the "valeur symbolique zéro," a "symbol in the pure state . . . capable of becoming charged with any sort of symbolic content whatever." It is that power to contain meaning, "without entailing by itself any particular signification," Lévi-Strauss notes,[23] that the totem and the rite exhibit. Each is an anthropological signpost evoking multiple interpretations and yet refusing to be held to any. And it is precisely that power which gives Eliot's thunder and verbum infans, as the vessels of mana, such resonance.

This is not to say that the efficacy of the myth of primal word gives that word truth value. Eric Gould's statement on the nature of the sacred inexpressible in linguistic mythic structures is relevant here: "The fact that classical and totemistic myths have to refer to some version of translinguistic fact—to the Gods and Nature—proves not that there are Gods, but that our talents for interpreting our place in the world may be distinctly limited by the place of language."[24] But Gould's structuralist analysis does not consider the rhetorical power gained by the artist who wields the sacred words. For it is critical that, in spite, or more pointedly, because of the sacredness and ineffability of the sacred words, the poet *does* spell out, or at the least draws a circle around, what cannot be expressed, does give voice to the secret and sacred names, or at the least gives the strong impression that he holds the power to do so.

Eliot's figuring the sacred words does, by Frazerian contagion at the least, attribute to the poet a "magical" or "mythic" power. For in an age of dissociation, when sacred and profane emerge as distinctly divided, and signifier and signified are forever separate though chained, the poet-magician at least gives the powerfully nostalgic illusion of return to that seamless whole that is the first word. J. Hillis Miller, in words strongly reminiscent of Freud's antithetical primal word, speaks of the "intuition of unitary origin" that makes the reader search for that "original state of unity" of the word before "primal division" occurred.[25] *The Waste Land* is a perfect example of a text that invites such a search and gives the illusion of being near, or in, the presence of that origin. Using a Frazerian tactic, Eliot makes desirable and necessary the entry of the indivisible primal word—here, the DA of thunder—by creating, through a complex network of signifiers that reach back before *The Waste Land,* a vast allegory of post-lapsarian fall. Like the thunder, the Holy Grail functions as a correlative of that primal word, a sacred thing that engenders searches and interpretations that seek to weld what has been torn asunder. And yet while Eliot begins his notes to the poem stating that "not only the title, but the plan and a good deal of the incidental symbolism of the poem were suggested by Jessie L. Weston's book on the Grail legend" (*Collected Poems* 70), in the poem itself the Grail functions implicitly, unimaged but ever-present, its power grouping the poem's figures like filings around a magnet, as its absence makes redolent that state of indivisible grace before the fall.

In "Mr. Eliot's Sunday Morning Service," the weakening of spiritual power exemplified in the move from Word to Origen is figured in sexual terms as "Superfetation," the production of two different embryos in the same uterus. The Word's power to contain contraries and the falling off from that unitary origin is further represented in terms of gender near the poem's end, when the bees that pass from staminate to pistillate—images suggesting presbyters collecting money from the male and female parishioners—are contrasted to Christ himself, the "Blest office of the epicene," here by definition of either sex, or partaking of both sexes.

The power of the Word to contain opposites is thus tied to a prelapsarian vision of androgyny or double-sexedness. Of course Eliot was quite familiar with contemporary conceptions of the god as androgynous: see especially Eliot's own 1918 review of James Rendel-Harris's *Ascent of Olympus* (1917), which focuses on the animistic Dionysos, who has evolved, in Frazerian–Cambridge Hellenist fashion, from the worship of thunder (pure mana) to plant to goat to the androgyne, god of either sex.[26] In *The Waste Land* sacredness is tied significantly to androgyny: when Christ (the Word in flesh) finally appears in the poem's last section, he is described as "Gliding wrapt in a brown mantle, hooded / I do not know whether as man or a woman" (ll. 365–66).

More important, Tiresias, described by Eliot in the Notes as "the most important character in the poem, uniting all the rest" (*Collected Poems* 72), has the power to prophesy and the vision to encompass all characters because he is a hermaphrodite, an "Old man with wrinkled breasts" who is "throbbing between two lives" (61). Indeed, in the Notes Eliot intimates that Tiresias owes to that androgyny the power that he possesses: "Just as the one-eyed merchant, seller of currants, melts into the Phoenician Sailor, and the latter is not wholly divorced from Ferdinand Prince of Naples, so all the women are one woman, and the two sexes meet in Tiresias. What Tiresias *sees,* in fact, is the substance of the poem" (72).

Tiresias is not a god, but he is a dimmed representative of one. It is worth noting here that Tiresias in *The Bacchae* is a devoted follower of the primitive goat-god Dionysos, an integral figure in the revival of the old totemistic religion. Eliot, in the note on Tiresias in *The Waste Land,* cites as his ostensible source a passage from Ovid's *Metamorphosis,* claiming it to be of "great anthropological interest" (*Collected Poems* 172). The lines he goes on to quote, in the original Latin, tell of the argument between Juno and Jupiter over who enjoys the sexual act more, the male or the female. They have chosen Tiresias as judge since he has experienced love as both man and woman. Years before, Ovid explains, Tiresias saw two snakes mating in the forest and, hitting them with his staff, was changed into a woman. Seven years later the same series of actions occurred and he was changed back into a man. Thus he is qualified to give a decision on the debate between the gods and agrees with Jupiter that women enjoy sex more and hence is blinded for his insolence by Juno. Jupiter, feeling responsible for the maiming of Tiresias, gives him the power to tell the future.

The passage does have "anthropological interest" in part because it narrates, and thus appears to legitimize, the pervasive evolutionary interpretation by which spiritual power (or mana) operates. This becomes strikingly clear when one looks to Eliot's review of Rendel-Harris, where Eliot, paraphrasing, states: "The appearance of an androgynous Dionysos is due to his identification with *both* firesticks, and the firesticks are made out of ivy because there is thunder in the ivy" (640). The ivy is sacred because the mana embodied in the thunder has entered it, a contention that has significant parallels to both Frazer's theorizing on the sacredness of the mistletoe in *The Golden Bough*[27] and the mystical dynamics at work in "What the Thunder Said," the last part of *The Waste Land.* But more specifically, the contours of the mythic tale of Tiresias as told by Ovid exactly trace the lines of Rendel-Harris's schema. The following overlay of Eliot's own paraphrase of Rendel-Harris's schema illustrates their fit: "The appearance of an androgynous Dionysos [read, Tiresias] is due to his identification [meeting] with two firesticks [snakes], the 'male' and the 'female.'"

Eliot also commented in the review on "the animistic belief" that "makes everything that thunder touches into thunder." It is that very dynamic, as figured in the mythic tale and Rendel-Harris's account, that transmits androgyny both to Tiresias and to Dionysos upon contact with the male and female sticks (snakes). In both cases each stick, the male and female, must derive from the sacred plant (ivy) or animal (snake). For Rendel-Harris, the conjunction of the male and female sacred sticks produces the holy fire, the "thunder," that is "androgynous Dionysos," just as the coupling of the scared snakes, when "touched" by Tiresias, transmits the mana that changes sex and ultimately leads to the power of prophecy. The point here is not to demonstrate precise anthropological influence but to note a confluence of sources and *uses*. The progression we find in *The Waste Land* need not be Rendel-Harris's—that is, from thunder to oak/vine to goat to Dionysos. But the Frazerian–Cambridge Hellenist reading of the approach to the Thunder through the mediation of the androgyne approximates an important structural and ideological sequence in *The Waste Land,* as Tiresias the androgyne anticipates the (possible) coming of the androgyne man-god (Dionysos/Adonis/Christ), who is foreshadowed by the (possible) coming of the more primal and less anthropomorphic Thunder.

The Waste Land narrates the approach to a purer form of spiritual energy, but that movement by the poem's end does not crystallize to a pure and distinct image of spiritual power, a firm focal point of spiritual figuring. In linguistic terms, though the scattered signifiers move toward the transcendental signified, they do not compress into a final, integrated meaning; rather, they fan out, toward the DA, the thunder, the mana (like the characters in "Gerontion" who are "whirled / Beyond the circuit of the shuddering Bear / In fractured atoms," ll. 69–70), and they do so precisely because the transcendent is represented, in Frazerian totemistic terms, as furthest from the anthropomorphic and hence shapeless.

But, to recall Derrida, "the praise of silence" that leads to "the myth of a full presence"[28] functions as ploy, for the Absolute in its seeming nonfigurability *is* framed, is figured. Though Bedient is keen on the ideological underpinnings of the voices at work in *The Waste Land,* his insistence on the poem's ultimate superiority over signification and escape from cultural experience falls victim to Eliot's tactic of divorcing the transcendent from "meaning," garnering authority from the approach to the sacred ineffable. This is not a criticism of the quality of Eliot's belief, but a questioning of the rhetorical tactic that posits absence as nonfigurable and hence removed from the representational hold of the author. It is in this respect that Eliot's poem, like Frazer's masterwork, opens in order to close, proliferating voices that move outward toward the ineffable in order to control both and in the process protect and privilege the comparativist author. The multiple voices and points of view aired in Eliot's poetry seem to move, in a Frazerian feint of humility, toward the admission of the mighty inexplicable. Eliot's various statements on the inadequacy of language—"I gotta use words when I talk to you" ("Sweeney Agonistes"), or "Words strain, / Crack and sometimes break, under the burden" ("Burnt Norton")— though perhaps honest admissions of language's failings, mask the rhetorical authority that is gained from wielding the only medium available. [29]

The voice of Tiresias is the most predominant in *The Waste Land* simply because he is the most androgynous, all-inclusive persona, and hence is most capable of sustaining an archetypical aura that closes off alternative voices and world views. As Gregory Jay indicates, Tiresias does not restore us to the wholeness before dissociation, but he does function as a trace of that quest for the ultimate signified, a logos that is only fully felt by absence. Tiresias marks that absence, marks the way back to the mana, and thus his presence resounds with an archetypical tenor. And yet the androgyny that suggests a prelapsarian wholeness functions precisely to delimit. Sandra Gilbert, noting Tiresias as example, claims that the male Modernists habitually reenacted the "ritual sexual inversion" whose "primary purpose was usually to reinforce the sexual social hierarchy." In an appropriative manner, the male "assimilates femaleness into his maleness . . . so that he mysteriously owns the power of both sexes in a covertly but thrilling male body." [30]

Tiresias does indeed function as a striking example of this assimilative sexual doubling, for he has experienced woman's way and returned *as man* to judge the woman as inferior (as enjoying sex more than the man). The impetus to deemphasize, or even eliminate, gender distinctions strips away our outer gender coverings to reveal a sexual amorphousness that is figured by a peculiarly male consciousness. This rhetorical move is justified, given a kind of anthropological legitimacy, through the archetypally resonating figure of the androgyne. Gilbert comments that what "Tiresias sees" is not so much "the substance of the poem," as Eliot says in his Notes, but, rather, a "comment on that consciousness" that limits, confines gender roles. Indeed, the androgyny that in the poem represents a state of all-encompassing, prelapsarian wholeness in fact helps to map a strategy of containment in which women are conflated, squeezed against the periphery, rendered useful only as aids toward male-centered regeneration (the Grail Bearer for the poem's knight-quester) or ascetic flight (the hysterical woman for the beleaguered husband in part two).

Tiresias cannot provide the way out of the worldly tangle simply because he is all too human. His androgyny becomes, in the living world, often parodic or grotesque—note Gilbert's claim that Tiresias evokes "the fever dream of the Hermaphrodite, the nightmare of gender disorder" ("Costumes of the Mind" 403)—and thus justifies a move back to a hierarchical (male) system of dominance. Eliot's urge toward the transcendent required a voice less human. The Thunder at the poem's end becomes that voice because it is voice without human form. The invisibility of the thunder, its very physical amorphousness, promotes the notion of the transcendent as beyond language; and yet the powerful impression of something not of this world is only achieved through the presence of the "voice" of thunder.

Bedient's celebration of the poem's push toward the transcendent falls for the Eliotic rhetorical move that announces the beyond as beyond language, and in effect validates Eliot's tactic of pointing to what is not there. The effects of the misogyny and ethnocentrism inscribed in the poem, though well noted by Bedient, are dimmed as the poem flies into that other, nonfigurable world. But it is crucial here to recognize that this disavowal of signification itself is inscribed and, further, its figuration is integrally related to the poem's exclusionary and delimiting tactics. The textual pointing to what is not there amounts to a selective rejection of what is. The thunder that propels outward at the poem's end ought to be considered an ideologically motivated simulacrum, a resonance-gathering figure that justifies, in the name of cosmic-comparativist inclusiveness, the power subversively to exclude: the "hooded hordes" of Eastern Europeans (in "What the Thunder Said"), hysterical and ravenous women (in "A Game of Chess"), homosexuals (Mr. Eugenides in "The Fire Sermon") are shunted aside in the beeline to a perfect realm. The politics barely implicit in Eliot's retreat from the signified world in *The Waste Land* become explicit in Eliot's later social criticism; there he makes only too clear what kind of world we ought to have (see below).

At the poem's end words attempt to rush back to the primacy of the sacred thunder.[31] Jay appropriately refers to the thunder as "a primal image of voice that might resolve the cacophony of belated and mutilated tongues by returning to the originating Word" (*Poetics of Literary History* 191). In this instance the verbum infans takes the form of DA, the utterance which signifies the ancient Hindu holy word but also evokes the primal and, implicitly, paternal DA-DA. Bedient is referring to this backward spin to the originating Father tongue when he notes that "the last words of the poem borrow from the oldest surviving scripture, as if endeavoring to go back to language at its pristine source, prior to its degeneration into babble" (*He*

Do the Police 221). In the tradition of evolutionist comparativism, Eliot's foray through world cultures ultimately takes the form of the search for the protolanguage.

That first word, the voice of thunder, reverberates, then disappears into anonymity: we are left with the empty space signifying an authorless and impeccable absence. But, as Menand notes in *Discovering Modernism,* "Eliot appears nowhere, but his fingerprints are on everything" (91). What remains in the air is the authority of the one who has the reach back to the earliest words, who has guided us to the brink of the nonfigurable. Levenson in this respect refers to Eliot's primitivist "search for origins" as "not atavistic but assimilative" (*Genealogy of Modernism* 22). Certainly the wide angle made possible by the comparativist lens enables Eliot to take in the largest amount of cultural material and put his stamp on it. The comparativist perspective gives to Eliot's efforts a diachronic capacity largely forsaken by Malinowskian ethnography: Eliot's grandly resonant search for the lost first chord clearly would not have been possible without the freewheeling evolutionism of the Frazerian text.

But more generally, Frazer's rhetorical tactics of encyclopedic inclusion, and the apparent refusal to implement an interpretive frame that would limit that input of cultural material, provided Eliot with a rhetorical blueprint for anthropological dominance. Eliot learned the lesson only too well, for in exercising that authority the poet out-Frazered Frazer, making use of the rhetorical framework while feeling free, in *bricoleur* fashion, to pick up and discard the anthropological voices, sources, "facts," and interpretations that Frazer, among a good number of others, put forth. Eliot in *The Waste Land* ultimately did to Frazer what he did to all of his sources: he incorporated him to widen his own perspective.

The Waste Land implied in its performance what Eliot's literary and social criticism made explicit: that the poet does or can or should have a heightened social status. We already have seen how Eliot attempted to raise the status of the critic through alignment to the figure of the Frazerian fact-collector. As critic Eliot took on the authority of the Frazerian anthropologist by trotting out the anthropological "facts" that were at his disposal and were of use in his own construction of the literary artist. He borrowed significantly from anthropology certain notions about "primitive mentality" in order to widen the compass of the Modernist artist's reach. In 1919, in a review entitled "War-Paint and Feathers," Eliot wrote that "primitive art and poetry can even, through the studies and experiments of the artist or poet, revivify the contemporary activities."[32] In that review Eliot persistently reminds the reader of the uses the modern poets can make of "savage" mind and culture:

> And as it is certain that some study of primitive man furthers our understanding of civilized man, so it is certain that primitive art and poetry help our understanding of civilized art and poetry. . . . The maxim, Return to the sources, is a good one. More intelligibly put, it is that the poet should know everything that has been accomplished in poetry (accomplished, not merely produced) since its beginnings— in order to know what he is doing himself. He should be aware of all the metamorphoses of poetry that illustrate the stratifications of history that cover savagery. (1036)

Clearly the poet is meant to appropriate the "savage" (in this case, the "savage bard") for use in the contemporary artistic program. The ethnocentrism of Eliot's position is undeniable and is reinforced in numerous reviews and essays that emphasize the evolutionary appropriation of the "primitive" by the modern artist. And yet Eliot's ethnographic abuse of the "primitive" is somewhat abstract, for the "savage" portrayed by Eliot is a highly skewed representation designed by the poet-critic to meet his own poetic and critical needs. Indeed, we ought to consider Eliot's "primitive" as precisely that: as *his,* a figure (to borrow again from Benedict's metaphor for Frazer) assembled in his own mind out of the parts of "savages" pulled from the Frazerian storehouse of anthropological "fact." That Frankensteinlike figure emerges in Eliot's work as it becomes useful to Eliot the literary and social critic.

From the beginning of his career, Eliot adumbrates the tie between artist and "primitive." In the September 1918 issue of *The Egoist,* the young poet and critic concludes his review of Wyndham Lewis's novel *Tarr* with the following observation: "The artist, I believe, is more *primitive,* as well as more civilized, than his contemporaries, his experience is deeper than civilization, and he only uses the phenomena of civilization in expressing it. Primitive instincts and the acquired habits of ages are confounded in the ordinary man."[33] The notion that "primitive instincts" are destroyed or at least muddled in modern man likely derives from Eliot's reading of Lévy-Bruhl, who believed that primitive mentality, which he calls "pre-logical" or "mystical," is absent from the civilized mind, which operates according to the rules of Aristotelian logic.[34] The prelogical mind through the mystical "law of participation" fuses the physical and spiritual, human and non-human realms. Fifteen years after the publication of the *Tarr* review, in *The Use of Poetry and the Use of Criticism,* Eliot refers to an essay by two Frenchmen, E. Cailliet and J. A. Bédé, and makes the following summation: "The authors, who have done field work in Madagascar, apply the theories of Lévy-Bruhl: the pre-logical mentality persists in civilized man, but becomes available only to or through the poet."[35]

In Frazerian fashion Eliot introduces bifurcations, like *primitive* versus *civilized,* so that he as author may step in and fill the gap: the primitive's "prelogical" mentality survives in civilized man, after all, "only to or through the poet." It is revealing that Lévy-Bruhl himself does not deal with the relation between poet and primitive medicine man: that connection is left to Cailliet and Bédé, Eliot himself, and other early social scientists. In this respect Eliot's drive to valorize the Modern poet found support in the numerous anthropological discussions of the social status accorded to the wielder of magic words in "primitive" societies. According to the social scientists, some words are so powerful that their meanings remain secret, known if at all to a select few medicine men. The native often is affected not on the basis of the "meaning" of the words but out of a faith in collective representations, those mystical perceptions of reality inherited from the society in which he is reared.[36] Lévy-Bruhl, for example, holds that to the primitive tribesman, "what we call the meaning of the words or the form matters little. The people remain indefinably attracted by them, because their mystic virtue and magic efficacy have been known from time immemorial" (HNT 157).

The notion of avoidance or unimportance of "meaning" looks forward to the call in Eliot's later criticism for an aesthetic stance that depends upon a faith in extrasemantic (or presemantic) factors. In this respect Eliot vividly recalls Lévy-Bruhl:

> The more seasoned reader, he who has reached, in these matters, a state of greater *purity,* does not bother about understanding; not, at least, at first. I know that some of the poetry to which I am most devoted is poetry which I did not understand at first reading; some is poetry which I am not sure I understand yet: for instance, Shakespeare's. And finally, there is the difficulty caused by the author's having left out something which the reader is used to finding; so that the reader, bewildered, gropes about for what is absent, and puzzles his head for a kind of 'meaning' which is not there, and is not meant to be there. (UPUC 144)

Here Eliot resembles one of the Klamath Indian "conjurers" who, according to Lévy-Bruhl, "are generally loth to give [the ritual songs'] meaning, even if they should understand them" (HNT 157). Indeed, Eliot's reluctance to deal with semantics and his willingness to communicate with his readers on a "primitive" level helps to account for the statement that "I myself should like an audience which could neither read nor write" (UPUC 146). By avoiding meaning the poet is said to be able to focus upon the preservation of that supposed primitive mentality that operates according to mystical laws and eschews Aristotelian logic. And yet keeping an audience ignorant of "meaning" is insuring that the power in a society is held by the artist, just as the medicine man, according to Lévy-Bruhl, held an exalted position in the tribe by virtue of the words to which only he was privy.

Eliot is clearly fascinated by the notion of a mystical mentality, be it "primitive," Christian, or Hindu, that establishes links between physical and spiritual realms. This way of perception involves states of feeling that, like the mana behind *The Waste Land,* are figured as nonfigurable and point toward absence. But this urge toward transcendence should not be divorced from Eliot's ideology, which became increasingly clear in later years. It is, after all, scarcely a comma that separates "Royalist in politics" from "Anglo-Catholic in religion,"[37] and Eliot after all would hope to be of the caste of Donne, whose experiences, according to "The Metaphysical Poets," are not dissociated from each other but "are always forming new wholes" (SE 247). Lévy-Bruhl's medicine man serves as a perfect example of a figure uniting social power and transcendence or, more simply put, politics and religion, as his channeling of mystical participations is instrumental to the social formation and maintenance of the tribe and to the expanded authority of the medicine man himself.

The point, again, is not to prove the influence of a particular anthropologist (here, Lévy-Bruhl) upon Eliot, but rather to demonstrate how the rhetoric of comparativism enabled Eliot persistently to appropriate anthropological materials in order to further his status as poet and critic. In this case the role of the poet as unifier, bringing together not only *civilized* and *primitive* but social power and transcendence, masks the rhetoric that has created those bifurcations. Eliot's poet requires the division of ritual and "meaning" in order to function as the bridge between them, just as Frazer's armchair anthropologist insists upon the separation of fieldwork and theory in order to serve as the conduit connecting them.

Eliot shares with Lévy-Bruhl not only the notion that the participants in primitive ritual (excepting the medicine man) need not involve themselves with "meaning," but also that those present will be satisfied, indeed, captivated, by what Eliot calls "the auditory imagination," a prelogical instinct which he defines as

the feeling for syllable and rhythm, penetrating far below the conscious
levels of thought and feeling, invigorating every word; sinking to the
most primitive and forgotten, returning to the origin and bringing
something back, seeking the beginning and the end. It works through
meanings, certainly, or not without meanings in the ordinary sense,
and fuses the old and obliterated and the trite, the current, and the new
and surprising, the most ancient and the most civilised mentality.
(UPUC 111)[38]

Again, Eliot creates the bifurcation of "ancient" and "civilised" in order
that the poet may step in and fuse them, here through the formulation of
the sound of verse. This process, characteristically, is conceived in evolutionist terms as a return to "primitive" origins. Eliot denotes the primitive
nature of the poetic vocation when he makes the following assertion: "Poetry begins, I dare say, with a savage beating a drum in a jungle, and it
retains that essential of percussion and rhythm; hyperbolically, one might
say that the poet is *older* than other human beings" (148).

As in Frazer's later authorial figuration (and to an extent, Eliot's early
construction of the literary critic), Eliot downplays the role of "meaning,"
interpretation, or theory in the workings of the poet and plays up that of
pure aesthetics, typified by the resonant sound that resists singular signification and hence is not held to one meaning but is capable of multiple
interpretation. Eliot's rhetoric on the primitive sound of poetry is thus integrally related to his rhetoric on the rite: both are inscribed as powerful
sites around which "meanings" may gather but which defy attachment to
any one interpretation. But, according to Eliot, in the modern age the pre-
logical aesthetic is threatened. Like Lévy-Bruhl, Eliot posits "civilized"
man as radically different from the "savage," for in the modern age the
primacy of rhythm over meaning has been reversed: "meaning" has become a premium for the individual listener or reader, so that the artist must
attempt to satisfy the logical urge for signification while somehow passing
along to his audience, sub rosa, the essentially primitive *sound* of poetry.

Eliot makes this surreptitious method only too clear when he states that
"the chief use of the 'meaning' of a poem, in the ordinary sense, may be
. . . to satisfy one habit of the reader, to keep [the reader's] mind diverted
and quiet, while the poem does its work upon him: much as the imaginary
burglar is always provided with a bit of meat for the house-dog" (UPUC
151). Meaning, then, works on a superficial level, not to clarify the author's
intents or purposes but rather to lull the reader into a ritualistic trance controlled by the poet as medicine man.

Not surprisingly, Eliot follows this observation by concluding that the "ideal medium for poetry" is "the theatre." Drama provides optimal conditions for the poet mainly because it can "cut across all the present stratifications of taste," providing meaning or "plot" to "the simplest auditors" and giving to others, "the more literary" and "the more musically sensitive," the "words and phrasing" and "rhythm" (UPUC 153). Verse drama is, after all, only poetry in a disguise that will make it acceptable to the masses, the most fundamental of schemes used, as Eliot wrote in a letter to Pound, to keep "the bloody audience's attention engaged" so that the poet "may pull off 'monkey tricks' behind the audience's back."[39]

"Meaning" then becomes subterfuge by which the author engages in "monkey tricks," those ideological meanings, purposes, intents that are cloaked in turn by the alluringly reverberating rhythms of verse. As in Frazer's brand of comparativism, the sheer variety of responses possible obscures the divisions that are created—here, between plot and rhythm, simple and sophisticated auditor—and then dissolved by the author-controller. The socially hierarchical value attached, from "meaning" to "sound," insures that the less intelligent and educated will receive the wrong "meaning" whereas the more cultivated will receive all "sound" and no meaning (or a vague multiplicity of meanings): in any case, the author, like Frazer's armchair comparativist and Eliot's early conception of the critic, avoids getting pinned down to, or held responsible for, any interpretation, theory, or intention.

Eliot found that the multivoiced and multidimensional effects of the stage, like Frazer's dramatistic prose style and metaphors, drew a crowd. And through his plays Eliot increasingly sought the crowd, sought to fuse his powers to those popularizing elements and thus bring poetry back as a "social" event and, even more important, bring back to the poet a central social function. His criticism registers that desire. In "The Social Function of Poetry," published in 1945, Eliot discusses the "deliberate conscious social purpose" of poetry in "its more primitive forms, . . . some of which had very practical magical purposes—to avert the evil eye, to cure some disease, or to propitiate some demon."[40]

Eliot did not literally wish his art to regress (as he would see it) to the level of witchery (note his criticism of Yeats's occultist tendencies), but he did want to return to the poet the power to persuade society, and in his plays he used incantations, cures, and propitiations as seductive rhetorical vehicles toward that end. The Guardians of Eliot's dramas call into play mystical forces in order to bring about beneficial changes for characters:

Agatha in *The Family Reunion* works a spell to uncross the bones and reverse the family curse; Julia, Alex, and Reilly in *The Cocktail Party* speak "the words for the building of the hearth" and the "words for those who go upon a journey" (*Poems and Plays* 368–69).[41]

Eliot, then, saw in the dramatist an opportunity for the poet to function as a powerful crowd pleaser, and his later criticism often calls attention to modern artists as entertainers. For example, in his essay "Rudyard Kipling," Eliot claims that even though Kipling may not have reached certain aesthetic heights, he "had at least the inspiration and refreshment of the living music hall" (PP 231). This salute to the artist as veritable song-and-dance man brings to mind earlier criticism in which he cried out for the return of the poet as public entertainer and placed that call in a primitivist context. For example, Eliot's 1923 essay "Marie Lloyd" uses the occasion of the death of a music-hall performer to launch into an elegy for the loss of live entertainment, a lament which leads him to recall how, according to anthropologist W. H. R. Rivers, "the 'Civilization' forced upon [the Melanesian natives] has deprived them of all interest in life." If we trade in our theaters, music halls, and musical instruments for cinemas and gramophones, Eliot concludes, "it will not be surprising if the population of the entire civilized world rapidly follows the fate of the Melanesians" (SE 407–08). Eliot's implications are quite clear: to keep our culture alive we must retain those more "primitive" forms of art and popular entertainment that require spontaneous communication between performer and audience.

The tie between social bonding to an audience and the author's extended authority is strongly suggested when Eliot asserts that "poetry is not a career, but a mug's game," and that the poet, then, might at the least have "the satisfaction of having a part to play in society as worthy as that of the music-hall comedian" (UPUC 147). This says much on what led Eliot out of the private sphere of the poet and into the public ring of the dramatist. As a genre, poetry no longer serves a serious and powerful social function in our society. To bring about a practical change in a group, the author must keep the group's attention, keep it mesmerized, which is only possible today in the theater. The call for drama is, in the broadest sense, a call for ritual expression that, in primitivist fashion, can sway the group toward certain "practical," or magical, ends.

Anthropology, Social Planning, and Sacred Sites

After the experiment that constituted *The Waste Land* Eliot saw the need to move more fully into the public sphere. The poem did not fail (and obviously Eliot did not give up writing poetry) but poetry as a genre was alone unable to hold the interest of the public and thus unable to furnish a site from which the author could hold comprehensive sway. Indeed, the move to drama (in 1935, with the staging of *Murder in the Cathedral*) accompanied Eliot's increasing importance as literary critic and editor and coincided with his emergence as a social critic (*After Strange Gods,* his first work of social criticism broadly conceived, was published in 1934). The move from drama to social criticism represents a shift in genre, and yet the rhetorical authority remains essentially the same. The divisions formulated in his literary criticism between sophisticated and simple audiences, and the bridge then built by the dramatist, coincide with the bifurcations created in the social criticism between the simple populace and the Elites of a society, that are bridged according to Eliot's theories. What Eliot does in effect is apply his blueprint of social dynamics in the literary-dramatic arena to society at large.

In *After Strange Gods* Eliot calls for the preservation of "Tradition," which he defines as "all those habitual actions, habits and customs . . . which represent the blood kinship" of "the same people living in the same place." The anthropological purport of the passage becomes explicit when (in the sentence following) Eliot states that tradition "involves a good deal which can be called *taboo*: that this word is used in our time in an exclusively derogatory sense is to me a curiosity of some significance."[42] Clearly the "habitual" behavior of the populace equals the instinctive, "pre-logical," ritualistic patterning of the savage of the anthropology to which Eliot was exposed. Those "habits" proceed from the collective representations that, by the supervision of the witch doctors–chiefs, guide the members of the tribe, the "primitive" audience.

The activity of the witch doctor, who channels the collective representations to the tribe, is parallel in Eliot's conception of societal structure to the task of the elite, who consciously supervise the unconscious religious habits of the populace. Indeed, in *After Strange Gods,* Eliot distinguishes between "Tradition," which is "unconscious," and "Orthodoxy," that which guides the group and is handed down from the leaders of the religious-social complex, "a matter which calls for the exercise of all our conscious intelligence" (31). In *The Idea of a Christian Society* (1940), as well, Eliot states that although the practice of religious belief would be "unconscious," that belief would be created and maintained by "the Religious Elite," "the consciously and thoughtfully practicing Christians."[43] In both cases Eliot creates divisions, between the unconscious/habitual and conscious/intelligent, that necessitate a merger and promote the authority of the author.

As in other places in Eliot's work, the rhetorical strategy of integration is basically nostalgic, as the author strives to reunite what an overdeveloped civilization has torn asunder. This is especially true in *The Idea of a Christian Society*, where Eliot constructs a primitivist community at odds with modern liberalism: "By destroying the traditional social habits of the people, by dissolving their natural collective consciousness into individual constituents, by licensing the opinions of the most foolish, by substituting instruction for education, . . . by fostering a notion of *getting on* to which the alternative is a hopeless apathy, Liberalism can prepare the way for that which is its own negation: the artificial, mechanised or brutalized control which is a desperate remedy for chaos" (13).

Eliot sets against modern industrial society the "community unit," and gives as an example the country parish. His description of this unit makes clear its primitivist nature: "this unit must not be solely religious, and not solely social; nor should the individual be a member of two separate, or even overlapping units, one religious and the other social. The unitary community must be religious-social, and it must be one in which all classes, if you have classes, have their centre of interest. That is a state of affairs which is no longer wholly realized except in very primitive tribes indeed" (ICS 28).

Nowhere does Eliot advocate a simple return to "savagery"; again, he takes pains to point out that mere regression is not desirable. But, he claims, the primitive "model" can be of use to the civilized one: "And without sentimentalizing the life of the savage, we might practice the humility to observe, in some of the societies upon which we look down as primitive or backward, the operation of a social-religious-artistic complex which we should emulate upon a higher plane" (63).[44]

At first glance, Eliot's use of the "primitive" seems enlightened and might suggest a kind of cultural relativism on his part: he rejects the simple evolutionism that condemns the "savage" as aberrant other. And yet Eliot's very construction of a unitary primitive community that is at odds with the more differentiated modern society presupposes an evolutionary framework. By returning to the "savage" Eliot is only, to use Levenson's words, widening his "assimilative grasp," making use of materials from the extreme end of his broadly comparativist field of vision. Like the advanced modern literary critic, the modern social planner is at an advantage to those who came before because he has more cultural material at his disposal; he has a wider vision because he sits on a "higher plane," and that plane is high because it is built upon the layers of cultural facts, now mostly turned to debris, that the social sciences have helped to amass.

Again, Eliot's abuse of the "savage" is in some respects rather abstract. One could say that Eliot is at three removes from the authentic "native" when he makes use of Durkheim, Frazer, and Lévy-Bruhl, who all interpret Spencer and Gillen's field observations on the Arunta. The filtering process that leads from an authentic Arunta ceremony to Eliot's generalizations on a "primitive" mystical mentality and unitary religious-social system is of course ethnographically outrageous. Nonetheless, the Arunta do exist, and Eliot's representation of them and others as falling within the marginal class of "savage" further delimits them. Just as important, the model for society that Eliot erects with the unwitting and thrice removed assistance of these very real tribes sets off chain reactions, multiple divisions of culture versus culture, culture versus subculture. Eliot's support of local subculture, like the community parish, sets that unit in opposition to homogenizing culturism, a tactic that pits traditionalists against liberals. More infamous, his argument in favor of local subculture in *After Strange Gods* necessitates an oppositional other whose articulation would have frightening repercussions in later years: in this case, organic local communities, like those in the southern United States, are threatened by the presence of "any large number of free-thinking Jews" (ASG 20).

Eliot's figuration of local Southern agrarian society, coupled with the denigration of the mobile Jew, functions simply as another articulation of what he termed, in *The Idea of a Christian Society,* that "unitary community," vitally bound to tradition and religion. Again, paradoxically, the beneficial aspects arising from such a "unified community" require strict bifurcations. For example, Eliot claims that "you cannot expect continuity and coherence in literature and the arts, unless you have a certain uniformity of culture, expressed in education by a . . . positive distinction between the educated and the uneducated" (41). It is the "duty" of the "Community of Christians," that collection of elites, "collectively to form the conscious mind and the conscience" of that community (43).

In *Notes toward the Definition of Culture* (1948) Eliot expands upon his figure of the unitary-bifurcated community. His view of education becomes, if anything, more stringent, as he severely criticizes what he calls "the equality of opportunity dogma" applied to the education of a citizenry. Characteristically, Eliot calls to the floor several quite differing figures of the "savage" in order to defend his views on education. On the one hand, primitive society is trotted out as the ultimate example of *right-minded* (in terms of both correctness and political affiliation) traditionalism that is at variance with current, declining culture: "But what is important is to remember that 'half-education' is a modern phenomenon. In earlier ages the majority could not be said to be 'half-educated' or less: people had the education necessary for the functions they were called upon to perform. It would be incorrect to refer to a member of a primitive society, or to a skilled agricultural labourer in any age, as half-educated or quarter-educated. . . . *Education* in the modern sense implies a disintegrating society."[45] In primitivistic fashion Eliot hearkens back to the good old days when members of a society knew their right and natural places in society: he does not mention *who* calls upon that mass stratum of society to perform those hallowed functions.

But *Notes toward the Definition of Culture* problematizes the relation between the primitive/unitary and modern/complex. Eliot begins the volume by attempting to define *culture* using Edmund Tylor's classic anthropological definition (from *Primitive Culture*), and yet insists upon enlarging its ramifications to include highly developed societies as well. Eliot demonstrates that in an "advanced" society, *culture* has various meanings and functions; however, he recalls the "primitive" unitary community of evolutionary anthropology when he disputes the claim that "in a society, of whatever grade of culture, the groups concerned with each activity of culture will be distinctive and exclusive." In fact, Eliot claims, "it is only by an overlapping and sharing of interests, by participation and mutual appreciation, that the cohesion necessary for culture can contain" (24). He then goes on to make explicit the most pronounced form of this social fusion:

> It is obvious that among the more primitive communities the several activities of culture are inextricably woven. The Dyak who spends the better part of a season in shaping, carving and painting his barque of the peculiar design required for the annual head-hunting, is exercising several cultural activities at once—of art and religion, as well as amphibious warfare. As civilisation becomes more complex, greater occupational specialisation evinces itself: in the 'stone age' New Hebrides, Mr. John Layard says [in *Stone Men of Malekula*], certain islands specialise in particular arts and crafts, exchanging their wares and displaying their accomplishments to the reciprocal satisfaction of the members of the archipelago. (24)

Now Eliot as sociologist here is not simply saying that civilized man must return to the unitary society of the Dyak. But while he posits a society's development toward "functional complexity and differentiation" as an inevitable and complex process that can produce both good and bad, clearly Eliot points admiringly at the fusion of societal functions into single activities, as evidenced by the Dyak, and, in Frazerian and Cambridge-Hellenist fashion, denigrates the late evolutionary stage at which various activities "become abstractly conceived apart from each other" (NDC 24), much as he downgraded modern education as an overly differentiated, dissociated abstraction. We cannot and should not return to the living conditions of the Dyak, Eliot states, and there are advantages to "a very advanced stage of civilisation"; we only know for certain, however, that "as new values appear, and as thought, sensibility, and expression become more elaborate, some earlier values vanish" (25). The nostalgic current that flows through this passage is tempered only to be ultimately strengthened in the passage that follows: "That is only to say that you cannot expect to have all stages at once; that a civilisation cannot simultaneously produce great folk poetry at one cultural level and *Paradise Lost* at another. Indeed, the only thing that time is ever sure to bring about is the loss: gain or compensation is almost always conceivable but never certain" (25).

The passage opens with an air of detachment but turns firmly toward the expression of a deep nostalgic impulse. Obviously the loss felt transcends merely personal expression on Eliot's part. Relevant here is James Longenbach's notion, in "Matthew Arnold and the Modern Apocalypse," that Eliot participates in a tradition of apocalypse, but perhaps it is more accurately articulated as a culturally bound and influenced allegory of, if not quite apocalypse, steady loss, in which the author is always at the horizon of cultural disintegration and ruin. What is left implicit here, but significantly at work, is the culture reader's claim upon arriving at the scene that he can piece together that always-and-already vanishing culture. The figures of damage make the rhetorical moves toward assimilative salvage necessary. Significant here is Eliot's stance, in the social criticism, of comprehensive and objective (to the degree that he admits possible) culture reader, a figuration that places him squarely in the armchair, surveying his various sources, anthropological and otherwise, by name or through loose association: Tylor, Layard, Lévy-Bruhl, Durkheim, and others.

While Eliot traverses the domain of sociological and anthropological fact and speculation, he also glides easily into the territory of the literary: anthropologists and witch doctors jostle shoulders with Milton and the anonymous minstrel-scop. The similarity here to the comprehensiveness of source material in *The Waste Land* is not fortuitous. In both cases cultural loss is evoked through a rich profusion of various and varying figments of culture. But a more fundamental observation is the seeming aplomb with which Eliot as culture reader fuses the activities of social critic, literary critic, and literary artist, and how that coherence of activity functions rhetorically against the authorially conceived backdrop of increasing specialization. Eliot's rhetoric announces that his very articulation of society's outward movement, "in fractured atoms" ("Gerontion"), toward "cultural disintegration" (NDC 26), is itself supreme testimony to his own abilities to reign in culture and provide, for now, a comprehensive demonstration of cultural coherence.

Eliot's contemplations in *Notes* on the nature and limitations of anthropological activity also, ultimately, work in the interest of fusing social functions into his authorial self. His caveats on applying evolutionary and other empirical frameworks to social phenomena seem to presage current anthropological writing that warns of the provisional nature of the cultural accounts of others. He cautions, for example, that "I am anxious to avoid speaking as if the evolution of primitive culture to higher forms was a process which we knew from observation" (NDC 35), a hesitancy that echoes his graduate-student paper "The Interpretation of Primitive Ritual," in which, with the support of Lévy-Bruhl, Eliot attacks Tylor's claim of modern man's unqualified and schematic improvements over the savage. More significant, *Notes* echoes the graduate paper's real concerns with what Eliot saw as the bounded limits of social-scientific methodology:

> The anthropologist may study the social system, the economics, the arts, and the religion of a particular tribe, he may even study their psychological peculiarities: but it is not merely by observing in detail all these manifestations, and grasping them together, that he will approach an understanding of the culture. For to understand culture is to understand the people, and this means an imaginative understanding. Such understanding can never be complete: either it is abstract—and the essence escapes—or else it is *lived*; and in so far as it is *lived*, the student will tend to identify himself so completely with the people whom he studies, that he will lose the point of view from which it was worth while and possible to study it. Understanding involves an area more extensive than that of which one can be conscious; one cannot be outside and inside at the same time. (NDC 41)

Here Eliot's hermeneutic dilemma (which, in turn, essentially restates his deliberations in the graduate-student paper) in some respects resoundingly presages current anthropological speculation on the nature of anthropological perception: how can one communicate through discourse the "essence" of an "other" culture, given that one cannot be both "outside" and "inside" simultaneously? Eliot's deliberations, however, are affiliated with biases and fears that are at odds with most recent interpretive anthropological writing. Namely, most current inquiry hardly subscribes to the notion that the account is worthwhile only if told from our point of view. In *Notes,* the student, to grasp the ways of the tribe, must "*live*" the life of the tribe. Yet Eliot, maintaining that the student should not enter too far into the life of his subjects, assumes the necessity for cultural distancing: "What we ordinarily mean by understanding of another people, of course, is an approximation towards understanding which stops short at the point at which the student would begin to lose some essential of his own culture" (NDC 41).

The need for an objectifying gap is figured in familiar primitive-as-boogie-man fashion: "The man who, in order to understand the inner world of a cannibal tribe, has partaken of the practice of cannibalism, has probably gone too far: he can never quite be of his own folk again" (NDC 41). And Eliot's note to that comment, "Joseph Conrad's *Heart of Darkness* gives a hint of something similar," reinforces the notion that this interpretive dilemma is fueled in part by a fear of savage alterity. That fear, what Eliot in "The Dry Salvages" calls "the backward look behind the assurance / Of recorded history, the backward half-look / Over the shoulder, towards the primitive terror" (ll. 106–08), confirms what is an evolutionary affiliation in Eliot's writing between the prehistoric and the contemporary "primitive," the mutual darkness and ignorance of the pre- and nonliterate.

In general, Eliot's rumination on the problematics of anthropological interpretation functions as another rhetorical act of bifurcation, in which two seemingly irreconcilable polarities are posed: the "abstract," empirical approach through which the "essence" escapes but the student remains in the realm of communicability, and the "*lived*" approach, through which the student enters into that "essence" but cannot return, in Lazarus-Prufrockian fashion, "to tell you all." This is another version of Eliot's rhetorical shift into the ineffable, in which what is articulated as shapeless ("living" the culture and returning to tell; spelling out the Absolute) is in effect framed and hence contained, possessed, by the author. In this case Eliot makes clear that what is needed, however incomplete it might be, is an "imaginative understanding." As with Frazer, Eliot's ties to the literary-imaginative confer on him a special capability unavailable to the mere empirical social scientist, who can only "study the social system, the economics, the arts," in hopelessly piecemeal fashion.

A critical dichotomy at work in *Notes* that is integrally related to the distinctions posed between the "lived" and the "abstract" is the one posited between "the religious and the sociological point of view" (68). Eliot claims to approach the relation of religion to culture "from the point of view of the sociologist, and not from that of the Christian apologist" (68). To distance himself from the position of "apologist," he claims that his conclusions have "applicability to all religion," and that he mentions Christianity most *only* because of the preponderating influence of Christianity upon Western culture. Clearly this rhetorical posturing is meant to lend to the author the authority of scientistic objectivity while deflating any notions of him as a prejudiced or impassioned believer. In his discussion of religious belief, Eliot claims that "from the sociological point of view, the truth or falsity [of that belief] is irrelevant; we are concerned only with the comparative effects of different religious structures upon culture" (69). Here Eliot's position from the armchair lifts him above the position of mere believer, elevating him to a perspective from which he, like the comparative anthropologist far from the field, can discern social causes from effects and draw lines of similarity from one culture to another.

But Eliot's insistence on a dichotomy between believer and sociologist contains its own internal critique. Eliot is quick to note: "I do not think that the difference between the religious and the sociological point of view is so easily maintained as the difference between a couple of adjectives might lead us to suppose" (NDC 69). *Notes,* like Eliot's paper on ritual, expresses skepticism over the capability of one point of view to enter into another and to articulate that other point of view while not dissolving its own integrity (and of course Eliot's dissertation on F. H. Bradley deals with much the same basic question). In *Notes* the articulation of the dichotomy between the "sociological" and the "religious" restates his dilemma: "But, for one thing, no religion can be wholly 'understood' from the outside—even for the sociologist's purposes. For another, no one can wholly escape the religious point of view, because in the end one either believes or disbelieves. Therefore, no one can be as wholly detached and disinterested as the ideal sociologist should be" (69).

Once again, Eliot isolates an interpretive quagmire, a site of hermeneutic indeterminacy; the dichotomy he has inscribed, however, enables a detour around that difficult spot. In this case, in a note to the above passage Eliot cites "a valuable article" by anthropologist Edward Evans-Pritchard, and provides from that essay the following quotation: "The answer would seem to be that the sociologist should also be a moral philosopher and that, as such, he should have a set of definite beliefs and values in terms of which he evaluates the facts he studies as a sociologist" (NDC 69). Eliot's own reasoning for citing the Evans-Pritchard piece as a possible answer to the dilemma seems circular, reinstating the polarities—"beliefs and values" versus "facts"—that were just put into question. Eliot has also just stated that he does *not* function as believer here but as "sociologist."

But in fact Eliot's pointing to Evans-Pritchard's remark is an attempt at effecting a middle ground between "belief" and "fact," and in that light it is not surprising that Eliot contradictorily employs his authority as both believer and scientist to promote his final point on the unity of European culture. And that final point is a profoundly and simply partisan one: "if Christianity goes, then the whole culture goes," after which "you" (the reader) "must pass through centuries of barbarism" (NDC 122). Eliot's argument is based upon the critical premise that the "unifying factor" and "germ" of European culture is Christianity (122), but more telling is the authority with which he vests himself to make such a statement: "And I am convinced of that, not merely because I am a Christian myself, but as a student of social biology" (122).

As did Frazer, Eliot promotes a dichotomy (believer/social scientist) in order to step in and become the middle term that unites them. Since Eliot is a Christian and since he has the tools of social-scientific analysis at his disposal, the statements he makes about Christianity are arguments that faithfully (in the empirical sense) isolate the "facts" of the faith. The author is presented as Evans-Pritchard's "sociologist"/"moral philosopher," who holds a "set of definite beliefs" through which he judges "the facts he studies as a sociologist."[46] In this respect, Frazer's insistence that his value lies not in his theories but in his amassing of facts strongly parallels Eliot's claim that he functions not as an apologist propounding arguments but as a sociologist gathering facts.

The dichotomy between believer and sociologist recalls an earlier Eliotic bifurcation, that between tradition and orthodoxy. According to *Notes,* the "student of anthropology" or "sociologist" (equal terms in Eliot's vocabulary in this volume) is a representative of the elite who possesses a "more conscious culture" than the mass of society (48). The elite is comparable to the same orthodoxy defined in *After Strange Gods,* while "unconscious" culture represents tradition. Neither tradition nor orthodoxy is described as inherently positive or negative: what determines the health of a culture is whether the "blood" (the source of tradition) and the "brain" (the source of orthodoxy) can strike an even balance (Eliot's notion of what came before the "dissociation of sensibility" comes to mind). If the "blood" of the society dominates, then the society becomes unitary, group-oriented, and overly primitive; if the "brain" takes greater control, the result is a segmented, individualistic, and overcivilized society. In *Notes* Eliot, discussing the analogous relation between *religion* and *culture,* comes to terms with this dynamic in a way that helps to expose his authorial tactics:

> The contrast between religion and culture imposes a strain: we escape from this strain by attempting to revert to an identity of religion and culture which prevailed at a more primitive stage. . . . It is only by unremitting effort that we can persist in being individuals in a society, instead of merely members of a disciplined crowd. Yet we remain members of the crowd. . . . Hence, for the purposes of this essay, I am obliged to maintain two contradictory propositions: that religion and culture are aspects of one unity, and that they are two different and contrasted things. (68)

The "two contradictory propositions" are in essence the opposition between the primitive and civilized versions of society: in the primitive society, religion is indistinguishable from culture; in civilized society, religion has become a separate function. For Eliot the sociologist, Guardian, member of the elite, directed by "intelligence" in his striving toward orthodoxy, this opposition is expressed as a logical "contradiction." But to the poet, who by nature operates more through tradition than orthodoxy, more through the blood than through the brain, that opposition can be expressed as paradox, which in the "primitive mentality" of Lévy-Bruhl's savage is believed to be a legitimate way of knowing. In this light, it is hardly insurmountable to the mentality behind "Burnt Norton" that "the way up and the way down are the same." Eliot can make some sense out of the interpretive quagmire but only through appeal to a sense that is non-sense.

The point is not that Eliot works logically in his prose and nonlogically in his poetry. Rather, as with Frazer, Eliot's collective assimilation of sources and points of view enables him to shuttle between and amalgamate varying kinds of authority: as the poet of *The Waste Land* and *Four Quartets,* he borrows the cultural materials and some of the methodologies of the anthropologist in order to erect poems of seemingly unsurpassed breadth; as social critic, he both draws from anthropological materials and methods and appeals to an aesthetically oriented way of perception that is posed as antithetical to the ways of the social scientist. In each case the author, to his own tactical advantage, draws authority from both sides of a self-created dichotomy (art/social science, imagination/reason, blood/brain).

This strategy has significant repercussions in the relation between Eliot's main volumes of social criticism, published between 1934 and 1948, and *Four Quartets,* the poetic masterwork of the latter half of his career, published between 1935 and 1942. After all, the reader's perception of Eliot as social critic must be affected by the resonance of that mystical quartet. For example, when encountering a self-confessed "logical contradiction" in *Notes,* how unwilling would readers be to suspend their disbelief, when the signature identifies the author of poetic paradoxes such as "Here, the intersection of the timeless moment / Is England and nowhere. Never and always" ("Little Gidding," ll. 54–55)?

At the same time, Eliot's poetic masterwork draws ideas, and hence authority, from his social-scientific arsenal. Clearly his own sustained deliberation on interpreting the "primitive," and his questioning of evolutionary interpretive frameworks, is reflected in the following passage from "The Dry Salvages":

> It seems, as one becomes older,
> That the past has another pattern, and ceases to be a mere
>   sequence—
> Or even development: the latter a partial fallacy
> Encouraged by superficial notions of evolution,
> Which becomes, in the popular mind, a means of disowning
>   the past.   (ll. 87–90)

Eliot implements the authority of the anthropologist to distance himself from the populace who take in simplified evolutionary views thirdhand. Eliot follows the passage with the resounding line, "We had the experience but missed the meaning," which moves us from the realm of the scholarly, the theoretical, or the "sociological" into the realm of the "lived" and the "imaginative": we feel the poet's rightness here because of his human directness, his simplicity.

In *Four Quartets* Eliot effectively fuses his humanness, his "lived" quality as a poet, to his more abstract and philosophical concerns as a "social biologist," as a reader of culture. Sometimes, however, the "human" and "felt" gives way to the "abstract" or theoretical. For example, in "East Coker" the author claims that there exists "only a limited value / In the knowledge derived from experience. / The knowledge imposes a pattern, and falsifies" (ll. 84–86). Here Eliot adopts the vantage of the "social biologist" who from the distance of the armchair can isolate the "facts" of experience that disguise the cultural subject. The facts, in this case, are Eliot's knowledge of the provisional nature of interpretation, an issue that returns us to "The Interpretation of Primitive Ritual" and other essays. In the 1924 review essay entitled "The Beating of a Drum," in fact, Eliot faults Dr. O. E. W. Oesterley, the author of a book on primitive religious dance, for "fall[ing] into the common trap of interpretation, by formulating intelligible reasons for the primitive dancer's dancing." According to Eliot, "it is equally possible to assert that primitive man acted in a certain way and then found a reason for it."[47] In both the 1924 review and "East Coker" Eliot makes the point that firsthand "experience," or direct contact with the cultural subject, is not an accurate gauge to meaning, for all of us unwittingly "falsify" our own experience.

The only "meaning" in the dance, Eliot tells us in both "The Interpretation of Primitive Ritual" and "The Beating of a Drum," is in the *dance itself* as rite. In the latter piece Eliot makes the Cambridge-Hellenist assumption that "drama was originally ritual; and ritual, consisting of a set of repeated movements, is essentially a dance" (12). As in Eliot's early criticism as well as *The Waste Land,* the rite functions as the sustained object of attention whose interpretations may vary but whose presence remains undeniable. And, Eliot importantly comments in his graduate-student paper, the rite is the only thing we can faithfully observe with sufficient clearness. It is in this respect that Eliot praises Frazer for simply recording the "facts" of ritual and refraining from entering too far into interpretation.

The significance, sacred in the "primitive" context, of the ritual object correlates with Eliot's postconversion figurations of sacred places, activities, or things around which the collective group gathers and generates interpretations. The very titles of the quartets signify those sacred gathering places: Burnt Norton, East Coker, Dry Salvages, Little Gidding. These sites are pregnant with a significance that defies attachment to a particular meaning or interpretation; like the "illegible stone" at the conclusion of "Little Gidding," the sacred site functions as a totemic object that is simply there, utterly present, a fact in the midst of dubious, ambiguous, and conflicting motives, upright but unable to be definitively read. The post-conversion poetry, particularly *Four Quartets,* revolves around such signposts of certainty: ritual markers where time intersects with the transcendent, reassuring "facts" amid the hosts of dubious interpretations, totemic places or objects that gather the folk, evoke multiple significations but are not accountable to or explained away by any specific meaning. Little Gidding serves as just such a sacred site that, as an empirical site for collective interpretation, refuses to be explained:

> If you came this way,
> Taking any route, starting from anywhere,
> At any time or at any season,
> It would always be the same: you would have to put off

> Sense and notion. You are not here to verify,
> Instruct yourself, or inform curiosity
> Or carry report. You are here to kneel
> Where prayer has been valid.   (ll. 41–48)

The function of the figurations of these sacred sites as linguistic markers for the inarticulate, indeterminable, or transcendent links the poem significantly to *The Waste Land* and to Frazer. Like Frazer's facts, these sites are presented as sources for speculation and interpretation that cannot simply be explained away. Hence Eliot's admissions of the failure of language—it is "a raid on the inarticulate / With shabby equipment always deteriorating" ("East Coker," ll. 182–83)—doubles Frazer's humbling gesture of insufficiency; we, after all, can only *provide* the sacred sites, narrate those moments where the timeless intersects with time.

But of course the rhetoric of the pure presence of sacred site or "fact" is accompanied by much commentary and abstraction. As in *The Golden Bough,* where the rhetoric of the virtue of pure "fact" stands alongside reams of interpretation, in *Four Quartets* the social scientist rubs shoulders with the visionary collector, for beneath the pregnant silence of sacred site (and rite) there can be heard the persistent murmurings of speculation. The shuttlings between pure fact and interpretation perhaps ought to invalidate one or the other, or both, but in his final poetic masterwork the rhetoric promotes what long before, as a student of social science, Eliot had concluded: that the two cannot so easily be separated, that interpretation always finds a way in. Perhaps Eliot's most significant rhetorical discovery is that each can be used to the mutual benefit of the other—and to that of the author.

In a Frazerian manner, the movement between "fact" and interpretation becomes an empowering process. Eliot's refusal to attach theories definitively to the sacred site or fact generates an interpretive chain reaction that is promoted as a failure of ultimate signification. And yet that site, that terminal marker of the indeterminate, is so compelling precisely because it forever eludes firm signification; it becomes, to borrow Lévi-Strauss's term, an almost perfect embodiment of the "valeur symbolique zéro" or "zero phoneme," "capable of becoming charged with any sort of symbolic content whatever" (*Structuralist Controversy* 261). It is in this crucial respect that the posed inability to signify leads to the use of those sites to consolidate authority. The *absence* of meaning invites the author, and he responds by filling the emptiness of signification with power.

Recalling Frazer, Eliot's anthropological authority, in a twofold process, welds the most efficacious of both sides of a self-constructed dichotomy, what Eliot himself referred to in the *Tarr* review as the "thought of the modern" and "the energy of the cave-man" (106). The believer, the "pre-logical" poet, embodying tradition, works through "primordial" channels that, like the thunder of *The Waste Land*, broaden persuasively toward a nameless origin; on the other hand, the social scientist, maintainer of orthodoxy, has a directed, "conscious intelligence" that organizes, brackets, the text for social utility and makes explicit the place of the author in the social arena. What these rhetorical constructions have in common is the symbiosis that has created them, and that finds its middle term in the all-encompassing figure of the comparativist author.

3

Northrop Frye:
Ritual, Science, and "Literary Anthropology"

THE AUTONOMOUS SCIENCE OF LITERARY CRITICISM

In the conclusion to his first book, the groundbreaking study of Blake entitled *Fearful Symmetry,* Northrop Frye asserts that "a study of comparative religion, a morphology of myths, rituals and theologies, will lead us to a single visionary conception which the mind of man is trying to express."[1] Frye then claims that anthropology and psychology have recently made significant strides toward realizing Blake's version of that unified vision and extending its usefulness to literary study: "many of the symbols studied in the subconscious, the primitive and hieratic minds are expanding into patterns of great comprehensiveness, the relevance of which to literary symbolism is not open to question" (424). These icons of supremely expansive significance, rooted in the elementary mind and excavated through "the study of ritual" and "mythopoeic dreams," constitute Frye's central conception of the "archetype." Frye then makes clear the importance of the analysis of this form for literary study:

> But if we can find such impressive archetypal forms emerging from sleeping or savage minds, it is surely possible that they would emerge more clearly from the concentrated visions of genius. These myths and dreams are crude art-forms, blurred and dim visions, rough drafts of the more accurate work of the artist. . . . A comparative study of dreams and rituals can lead us only to a vague and intuitive sense of the unity of the human mind; a comparative study of works of art should demonstrate it beyond conjecture. (424)

Though Frye in later writings would vigorously pose himself as at odds with Frazerian evolutionary assumptions, here his hierarchy of figures, of the "crude art forms" of the savage leading inexorably toward "the more accurate work" of the civilized artist, are distinctly Frazerian, particularly in their evocation of the future Master-artist whose work is foreseen in those "rough drafts" of the primitive imagination. But perhaps more significant here, the evolutionary rhetoric is extended to the institutional applications of the comparative method itself: the real future Master is the literary critic who clarifies "beyond conjecture" the unity of human mind that is only so hazily suggested, in rough draft form, by the comparative anthropologist and psychologist.

Frye makes clear in his early writings that the possibilities for archetypal criticism are indeed found in draft form in comparative anthropology and, conversely, are found wanting in the more limited, and limiting, studies of post-Frazerian, field-based ethnography. In a review published in the same year as *Fearful Symmetry,* of *Eranos Yearbooks* (edited by Joseph Campbell) and selected works by Mircea Eliade, Frye echoes Eliade in making the claim that "it is possible to revert to nineteenth-century comparative methods now that anthropology and psychology have developed their own structures and are less in danger of being twisted out of shape by an alien interest." And in a review of works by Jung, first published in 1953, Frye claims *The Golden Bough* to be "a book on literary criticism" rather than "a book on anthropology" (as "intended") because "in extracting a single type of ritual from a great variety of cultures, Frazer has done what the [functional] anthropologist, with his primary interest in cultural patterns, cannot do . . . but he has also done precisely what the literary critic, with *his* interest in ritual pattern, wants to see done."[2]

In the previous passage—only slightly reworded in its later inclusion in *Anatomy of Criticism*—Frye displaces Frazer's masterwork from anthropology to literary criticism on account of its out-of-phase relation to then-current functional anthropology. Frazer, emblem of an out-of-sync anthropological past, is of no use to present anthropology but of great import to future literary criticism, which rejects the anthropological focus upon the multiple traits of the single culture. In the literary sphere that shift translates into a deemphasis upon explications of single literary works and an emphasis upon the commonalities between literary works of often radically differing periods and cultures.

Robert Denham, Frye's most assiduous critic, comments that Frye "characteristically moves away from, rather than into, the literary work, and thus he emphasizes the thematic, narrative, and archetypal similarities among literary works rather than the explication of single texts."[3] If we replace, in this passage, the terms *literary work* and *text* with *native culture* or *local culture,* a description quite fitting to Frazer's comparativist practices emerges, one which certainly helps to account for Frazer's appeal to literary Modernists and Frye. So we are hardly surprised to find Frye noting, in his review of Eliade, that "*The Golden Bough*'s main influence was in literature" primarily, since, according to functional anthropologists, Frazer's

use of the comparative method "was overenthusiastic and premature, because they [the functional anthropologists] were trying to relate such phenomena as vegetation myths to the cultures which produced them, instead
of comparing them" (NFCL 100). Therefore, Frye's celebration of Frazer in
one respect serves as a press release for his own emergent literary criticism,
which promoted ultimate unity of human consciousness by disregarding
the boundaries between literary traditions, periods, and particular literary
texts, much as Frazer argued for unity of mind by traversing the lines between specific native cultures.

The archetypal criticism presaged in Frye's early reviews and in *Fearful
Symmetry* came to light, of course, in *Anatomy of Criticism,* published in
1957. The reading public was swept away by Frye's tour de force, much as
Frazer's audience was bowled over by the monumentality of *The Golden
Bough* over half-a-century before: in both cases the massiveness foregrounded the author's genius at massive arrangement. Frank Mc'Connell's
remembrance of his first impressions of *Anatomy,* as a graduate student in
the Yale English department in the early 1960s, could easily apply to Frazer's reception: it was "the exhilaration of the enterprise, more than the
specific details of the system, that made Frye so intoxicating and . . . so
suggestive"; and, perhaps an even more telling remark, "Where, you had
to ask yourself, had you seen an imaginative scope like this? Where had
you come across such a breadth of allusion?"[4]

It is crucial to remember, as Mc'Connell does, that the revolutionary
nature of Frye's project can best be appreciated by recalling the preeminent
position of New Criticism in that period (622). And yet Frank Lentricchia
rightfully emphasizes that "by about 1957 the moribund condition of the
New Criticism and the literary needs it left unfulfilled placed us in a critical
void" and that myth criticism for years had prepared an alternative that
triumphantly culminated in Frye's *Anatomy* (*After the New Criticism* 4).

Although there are significant filiations between Frye's method and New
Critical method, Frye himself and his critics of the time usually described
Anatomy as a full-frontal assault against the cause of New Criticism, particularly in its resolute break away from the orthodox method of close reading of single texts and its turn instead to a more multidimensional approach
of reading "between" texts. In this respect New Criticism, with its self-
promoting myth of careful, limited, intensive, scientific prodding, and its
general refusal to extend beyond the particular literary text, clearly approximates the modern monograph, with its emphasis upon the particular
culture and its hesitancy to pluck examples of cultural traits or types willy-
nilly from multiple and sundry cultures. Frye's portrait of the unusability

of contemporary anthropology for modern literary study, then, functions as an important harbinger of, and allegory for, the necessary supplanting of the New Critical doctrine of limited close reading.

And yet critical to Frye's rhetoric, and fundamentally Frazerian, is the notion that the method of *Anatomy* constitutes not simply an alternative to New Criticism (or traditional historical criticism, for that matter) but rather that the critical method governing *Anatomy* represents the sum of *all* critical methods, the ultimate accretion of all critical approaches, what in his introduction to *Anatomy* Frye calls "a synoptic view" and in his "Tentative Conclusion" he refers to as "a comprehensive view of criticism."[5] In fact, this rhetorical move is crucial to Frye's rank as the greatest myth critic: Frye is foremost in that school precisely because he resists its label, striving instead for the overarching range of a master comparativist.

Characteristic of Frazer's habit of collecting multiple and even contradictory sources and points of view (as well as his professed reluctance to engage in debate), is Frye's claim that *Anatomy* "attacks no methods of criticism . . . what it attacks are the barriers between the methods" (AC 341). And in the explicit discussions of his theoretical aims in his introduction and conclusion, Frye, like Frazer, takes on the rhetorical tack of humbly minimizing his own role as creator of such a compendious system and stressing instead his function as collector, classifier, and synthesizer of those observations garnered from the various readers at work in the field: "The gaps in the subject as treated here are too enormous for the book ever to be regarded as presenting *my* system, or even my theory. It is to be regarded rather as an interconnected group of suggestions which it is hoped will be of some use to critics and students of literature" (3).

Frye's representation of a broad spectrum of literary critics with limited views approximates Frazer's description of fieldworkers whose critical acumen is realized only when their observations are brought together by a great comparative synthesis. But like Frazer, Frye comes to admit that though all methods are equal, some are more equal than others. In the Tentative Conclusion he concedes that "in this process of breaking down barriers I think archetypal criticism has a central role, and I have given it a prominent place" (341). Importantly, archetypal criticism is prominent precisely because it concerns the interconnection of varying methods, the potential for synthesis, and as such it is an important correlate of that fundamental synthetic mechanism, the comparative method.

Frye's determined rhetorical pattern of narrowing a profusion of materials and methods to singular principles strikingly resembles his own description of the prose genre of anatomy, as Denham rightfully points out

(NFCM 117). The anatomist, Frye notes, "dealing with intellectual themes and attitudes, shows his exuberance in intellectual ways, by piling up an enormous mass of erudition about his theme" (AC 311; NFCM 117). And yet what Frye calls this "encyclopaedic farrago," this "creative treatment of exhaustive erudition," constitutes "the organizing principle" of *Anatomy,* and indeed Frye notes that anatomy "presents us with a vision of the world in terms of a single intellectual pattern" (AC 310). In his essay "The Instruments of Mental Production," first published in 1967, Frye refers to this steady funneling of sweeping vista in terms of the disciplinary shift from comparativist activity to more limited, field-based social-scientific researches. Frye's description reads as a best-case scenario of his own profile as much as a restatement of the superior position of past comparativists:

> Subjects regroup themselves and other subjects take shape from the shifting relations of existing ones. . . . . It is in these moments of regrouping that the great genius, with his colossal simplifying vision, gets his best chance to emerge. I wonder if anyone of Freud's stature could emerge from psychology right now: there might be a feeling that he was an armchair theorist who had not served enough time in laboratory routine to be a professional psychologist. The Freuds of the future are more likely to emerge, as Freud himself did, from a point of mutation at which psychology begins to turn into something unrecognizable to its scholarly establishment.[6]

Like Freud, and like Frazer, who helped to found a social science on the basis of a merger of classical scholarship and folklore studies, Frye himself is the armchair architect of a virtually new discipline, the "science" of criticism. Frye's figure of the "great genius, with his colossal simplifying vision," strikingly recalls Frazer's evocation of the "master-mind" who "shall arise and survey" the records we have collected and classified and "may be able to detect at once that unity in multiplicity, that universal in the particulars, that has escaped us" (*Man, God, and Immortality* 31). And it is precisely that quality of simplification and unification that ties Frye most integrally to Frazer.

Frye's rhetoric indicates a disposition fundamental to Frazerian comparativism: commonalities matter more than differences. As early as *Fearful Symmetry* Frye asserts that "the similarities in ritual, myth, and doctrine among all religions are more significant than their differences" (424), a priority ultimately based on a most Frazerian (as well as Jungian) assumption, what Frye calls "the unity of the human mind" (FS 424). So when Frye in 1953 applauds Frazer's "extracting a single type of ritual from a great variety of cultures," he believes that the extraction gives proof of the aim of archetypal criticism, the "single visionary conception" of man. And that is why Frye in his review of Jung calls *The Golden Bough* "a cornerstone of archetypal criticism" (NFCL 123).

Like Frazer's method, Frye's comparativism operates precisely by shocking the reader into the perception of the sameness of seeming difference. This is also articulated as a key aesthetic principle. Indeed, in his book on Eliot, Frye approvingly paraphrases the critic on the capability of melding diverse figures as a principle of art: "In great poetry we are aware of the variety of experiences that can be fused together, and great poetry differs from lesser poetry not by an ethical quality like 'sublimity' but by an intensity of combination."[7]

Frye's method, like Eliot's and Frazer's, succeeds because of its practice of casting the net wider. That net, Frye's system or "code," works, like Frazer's web, as an ambitious strategy of containment that purports, because of its sheer dimensions, to do anything but contain. This combination of centrifugal (comprehensive, universal) and centripetal (narrowing, containing) tendencies is what, according to M. H. Abrams, makes Frye's method "not science" but "wit." Frye's inheritance of the essentially Addisonian tendency of Frazerian comparativism is made clear by Abrams when, for his definition of "wit," he quotes Addison: "'A combination of dissimilar images, or discovery of occult resemblances in things apparently unlike.'"[8] Abrams's description of Frye's "Wit-criticism" in action functions precisely as a synonym for Frazer's use of the comparative method; in fact, with the substitution of a few of Frye's more modern literary subjects, the method as articulated by Abrams is indistinguishable from Frazer's:

> When we are shown that the circumstances of Pope's giddy and glittering Augustan belle have something in common with the ritual assault on a nature goddess, that Henry James's most elaborate and sophisticated social novels share attributes with barbaric folk tales, and that the ritual expulsion of the *pharmakos,* or scapegoat, is manifested alike in Plato's *Apology,* in *The Mikado,* and in the treatment of the umpire in a baseball game, we feel that shock of delighted surprise which is the effect and index of wit. Such criticism is animating. . . . An intuitive perception of similarity in dissimilars, Aristotle noted, is a sign of genius and cannot be learned from others. Wit-criticism, like poetic wit, is dangerous, because to fall short of the highest is to fail dismally, and to succeed, it must be managed by a Truewit and not a Witwoud. (196)

The point that gets obscured in Abrams's closing praise of Frye's dizzying effects is not that wit can fail or that wit is equal in value to science, but that wit can be confused with science. Indeed, a key to Frye's success is that, like Frazer, he mystifies the essentially tropological powers of comparativism, whose effects add tremendously to its reception, while garnering the authority of a scientism that promises the foundation for a hard and clear truth.

Like Frazer, Frye realized that the time was ripe for a welding of scientistic authority to a field that lacked the appearance of having a firmly empirical system. Frye's *Anatomy* was so appealing precisely because it articulated the feeling, as paraphrased by Terry Eagleton, that "criticism was in a sorry unscientific mess and needed to be smartly tidied up,"[9] and then proposed a system, both comprehensive and scientistic, that filled that need. This becomes especially important in assessing Frye's place as the predominant myth critic: far more than Hyman, Chase, Campbell, and others, he studiously avoids dependency upon the "fuzziness" of Jungian mythical thinking and proposes instead a hard system that sticks to the "facts" and methods of science.

In the "Polemical Introduction" to *Anatomy* Frye begins his treatment of the scientific nature of literary criticism by insisting that pure criticism be defined only by the progression of data to theoretical system that characterizes science: "if criticism exists, it must be an examination of literature in terms of a conceptual framework derivable from an inductive survey of the literary field. The word 'inductive' suggests some kind of scientific procedure. What if criticism is a science as well as an art?" (7). He goes on to state that "if criticism is a science, it is clearly a social science, and if it is developing only in our day, the fact is at least not an anachronism" (16). This categorization is not meant, however, to decrease criticism's potential to be an accurate and disinterested tool of research, for Frye elsewhere in his criticism accepts the late nineteenth-century assumption (via Herbert Spencer, Tylor, and Frazer) that with the social sciences "we have developed the ability to study our own civilized institutions in the same detached and objective spirit with which we study nature."[10]

Frye's assertion of the essentially inductive nature of arriving at criticism's first principles recalls Frazer's defense of his own method of the reliable collecting of anthropological "facts" leading inexorably to comparative principles. "The first thing the literary critic needs to do," claims Frye, "is to read literature, to make an inductive survey of his own field and let his critical principles shape themselves solely out of his knowledge of that field" (AC 6–7). Literature becomes, in a sense, Frye's collection of facts, the raw material, the crosscultural data garnered from the field, that enables the comparativist's generalizations.

Frye also insists upon the "progressive element" of the sciences in literature, the notion that continued study results in a steady accumulation of knowledge. In *Anatomy* he bemoans the seeming lack of a building-block model for literary criticism and sees in the growing diversity and complexity of literary criticism a failure to move forward: "In the growing complication of secondary sources one misses that sense of consolidating progress which belongs to a science" (8). In this regard Denham notes that Frye works under the influence of "the textbook tradition," which "represents scientists as having worked on the same set of problems with the same set of fixed canons and as contributing to a cumulative understanding of the order of nature" (NFCM 199). Denham, drawing on Thomas Kuhn, notes that the scientific community works not according to "fixed canons" but rather with "competing paradigms" that conceive of "facts" in new ways (199).

But we should not rush to brand Frye's scientistic conceptions as naive and mistaken. While it is true that Frye in *Anatomy* assumes that there are knowable "facts" or data of literature that the disinterested critic can draw out and base theories upon, Frye's rhetorical positionings on "facts" are more complex, more movable and interpenetrating, than they might at first appear. For example, in *The Stubborn Structure* Frye writes of "the sense of facts as given, as irreducible data to be studied in their inherent arrangements instead of being arranged. There may actually be no facts of this kind, but it is important to pretend that there are, that facts lie around immovably where they have been thrown, like rocks carried down by a glacier" (40–41).

Frye's notion of the willed illusion of fact suggests Eliot, who in at least one of his rhetorical turns removes "fact" from strict objectification and views it as the correspondence between members of a community or a communally recognized phenomenon. More significant, this notion of "facts" as necessary angels, that we believe in because we convince ourselves we must, represents in one sense a complexification of Frazer's conception of fact, which insists that facts *do* lie where they are thrown. And yet clearly Frye wishes to suspend our disbelief and will us back into the belief that Frazer inscribed: that anthropological "facts" not only lie where they have been thrown, but that there is a pattern to their positions, and discerning that pattern can enable us to trace whence they, and we, came.

That is why Frye, with Frazer, must cleave to the necessity of fact collecting while also asserting that what he is after is not merely a collection of literary facts, what he disparagingly refers to as "a huge aggregate or miscellaneous pile of discrete 'works'" (AC 16). Rather, comparative analysis of the placement of the rocks set down by the glacier of literary tradition reveals a simplified evolutionary pattern: for when we analyze the patterns of "total literary history" we are afforded "a glimpse of the possibility of seeing literature as a complication of a relatively restricted and simple group of formulas that can be studied in primitive culture" (16–17). Reduction to primitivist sameness is Frye's way of revealing a design that, in this turn of his rhetoric, he opposes to mere agglomeration, and he does so by an appeal to the activities of physical science: "We have to adopt the hypothesis, then, that just as there is an order of nature behind the natural sciences, so literature is not a piled aggregate of 'works,' but an order of words" (17).

Again, however, we simplify Frye's position if we claim that he believes in a natural order of literature that criticism traces. For Frye also claims that what unites literature is not so much the principles inherent in itself but "a conceptual framework which criticism alone possesses" (AC 15–16). Indeed, he insists that criticism move beyond the "state of naive induction as we find in a primitive science," in which the discipline studies the actual, physical attributes of nature (such sciences "take the phenomena they are supposed to interpret as data") and become more like a modern science, which analyzes the external world according to the terms of the discipline's own conceptual framework. The principle of evolution in science Frye provides as one example of a move beyond induction: "As long as biology thought of animal and vegetable forms of life as constituting its subject, the different branches of biology were largely efforts of cataloguing. As soon as it was the existence of forms of life themselves that had to be explained, the theory of evolution and the conceptions of protoplasm and the cell poured into biology and completely revitalized it" (15).

In one sense Frye exposes the naïveté of Frazerian fact-collecting here, although Frazer also admitted that the "facts" he collected would lie in wait for the genius who would synthesize them. More important, Frazer himself, as we have seen, tore cultural subjects from local contexts, reading the forms of life in evolutionary terms. Indeed, Frye recalls not only the example of Darwinian evolutionary biology but also that of Frazerian evolutionary anthropology (remember that Frye specifies criticism as a "social science") when he asserts that "criticism seems badly in need of a coordinating principle, a central hypothesis which, like the theory of evolution in biology, will see the phenomenon it deals with as parts of a whole" (AC 16).

Like Frazer's disregard of the phenomena under study, those actual groups of people termed *primitive,* Frye's concern is not with the truth value that criticism can derive from literature, what criticism can tell us about literature. He bluntly states that "at no point" in this systematic criticism "is there any direct learning of literature itself" (AC 11). Again, he draws his illustration from the hard sciences: "Physics is an organized body of knowledge about nature, and a student says he is learning physics, not nature" (11). What he is primarily interested in is the potential for his principle to systematize on a large scale. The point, ultimately, is not to explain the phenomena (for that would be naive) but rather to use the phenomena as further proof of the viability of the system: "Literature is not a subject of study," Frye reminds us, "but an object of study" (11).

Central to Frye's method is what he termed the assimilating of the work into the system. In the Tentative Conclusion to *Anatomy,* Frye keys in on the "analogy" between mathematics and literature. Math for Frye represents the epitome of the move beyond "naive induction" because it "appears to begin in the counting and measuring of objects" but in reality, in practice, it is "an autonomous language, and there is a point at which it becomes in measure independent of that common field of experience which we call the objective world" (350). What excites Frye about the analogy to math is the autonomous and thus appropriative relation of math to its supposed phenomena, the outside world: "Mathematics relates itself indirectly to the common field of experience, then, not to avoid it, but with the ultimate design of swallowing it. It appears to be a kind of informing or constructive principle in the natural sciences: it continually gives shape and coherence to them without being itself dependent on external proof of evidence, and yet finally the physical or quantitative universe appears to be contained by mathematics" (352).

The ramifications of literature's autonomy are extensive, but more to the point here is the elision of the more fitting analogy, math to criticism (rather than math to literature). Criticism, after all, needs to move beyond "naive induction," according to Frye, and criticism, not literature, Frye labels a science. And it is criticism that, like math, avoids direct identification with its phenomena (its data, literary texts) in order to swallow them. Criticism draws from its data (its texts) for its existence and yet is not dependent upon them and finally gives the impression that it shapes, gives coherence to, those works of literature. Criticism, then, shapes the texts to which it appeals.

Thus Frye is able to draw on science in two ways, each to his advantage. On the one hand, the "facts" of science, even if we tacitly recognize them as fictional constructs, provide the authority of dealing with the rock-hard certainty, with the irreducible. On the other hand, science functions as conceptual, abstract, and thus able to avoid dependence on fact. In a series of rhetorical turns Frye is able to draw from "facts" for support, remove himself from the responsibility of being dependent upon them for evidence, and finally contain them.

In *Anatomy* Frye establishes the primacy of critical autonomy. In the first place, he defines a dichotomy between "literature" and "criticism" in which, surprisingly, literature appears more dependent upon criticism than the other way around: while "criticism can talk . . . all the arts are dumb" (4). The critic becomes the ultimate, and indeed only genuine, interpreter, who "must be" the "final judge" of a poem's "meaning" (5). Frye's insistence here clearly is aligned with the New Critical notion of the intentional fallacy: see, for example, where he notes that an interpretation of *Hamlet* by Shakespeare himself would not constitute a "definitive criticism" (6). And yet Frye takes a twist beyond New Critical dictum to assert that "what is true of the poet in relation to his own work is still more true of his opinion of other poets. It is hardly possible for the critical poet to avoid expanding his own tastes, which are intimately linked to his own practice, into a general law of literature" (6). In a harsh bifurcatory move, in which the figures of Eliot as dominant poet-critic and himself as emergent professional critic are thinly veiled, Frye charts the necessary avenue by which the former must submit his critical speculations to the latter: "The poet speaking as critic produces, not criticism, but documents to be examined by critics" (6).

What comes through persistently in Frye's Polemical Introduction to *Anatomy* is not what we can learn from or about literature but how important it is for criticism to legitimate itself as a field. Frye laments the "absence of systematic criticism" not because its presence would give us a fuller understanding of the workings of literary texts but because that lack "has created a power vacuum, and all the neighboring disciplines have moved in" (12). The urgency in Frye's tone comes primarily out of the concern over institutional power brokering, just as the language brings to mind the rhetoric of corporate takeover.

One of Frye's arguments for autonomy is that relying on an "externally derived critical attitude" tends to "exaggerate the values in literature that can be related to the external source, whatever it is" (AC 7). When a critic adopts a method or attitude originating from another discipline, Frye claims, "it is all too easy to impose on literature an extra-literary schematism, a sort of religio-political coloration, which makes some poets leap into prominence and others show up as dark and faulty" (7). Frye assumes here that while other fields are integrally connected to ideological positions (a reasonable supposition, on its own), criticism must float free of such "coloration" by virtue of its autonomy.

Of course we question from the start why criticism's autonomy guarantees freedom from bias while psychology's or anthropology's autonomy does not. Actually, Frye holds that fields of study, particularly literary criticism, take the scientistic impulse beyond induction and toward the "coordinating principle." This progressive scientistic leap is potentially pandisciplinary and hence not an intrusive element from another field, as Frye makes clear when he states that "the presence of science in any field" in effect is "safeguarding the integrity of that subject from external invasions" (AC 7). It is hard to say whether Frye's assumption here, on the extrainstitutional nature of pure scientific principle, is naive or deliberately mystified, but in either case it enables Frye both to invoke the authority of science and to retain his own field's autonomy from scientific disciplines.

Frye proposes, as a necessary first step toward attaining this autonomy, that we "recognize and get rid of meaningless criticism, or talking about literature in a way that cannot help to build up a systematic structure of knowledge" (AC 18). Such a revamping includes ridding ourselves not only of "all lists of the 'best' novels or poems or writers" but also of

> all casual, sentimental, and prejudiced value-judgements, and all the literary chit-chat which makes the reputations of poets boom and crash in an imaginary stock exchange. That wealthy investor Mr. Eliot, after dumping Milton on the market, is now buying him again; Donne has probably reached his peak and will begin to taper off. . . . This sort of thing cannot be part of any systematic study, for a systematic study can only progress: whatever dithers or vacillates or reacts is merely leisure-class gossip. (18)

Eliot is thus doubly cursed, both as a poet who by nature is unable to invest himself dispassionately in criticism and as one of those of the leisure class who, by casual evaluation, is exempted from the true scientistic, systematizing labor behind the critical process. Significantly, Frye condemns Eliot for not taking on the essentially evolutionary view of the scientistic progress inherent in a systematics of criticism. And Eliot, finally, represents just one more rendition in the "history of taste" that has nothing to do with the *structure* of criticism.

The scientistic authority of this structure is driven home by Frye through renditions of the classic Frazerian bifurcation of fact versus theory. In Frye's case the "facts" garnered by the truly systematic critic are set against the soft interpretation of the other, more impressionable types of critics. "In the history of taste, where there are no facts," Frye claims, "we perhaps do feel that the study of literature is too relative and subjective ever to make any consistent sense" (AC 18). Frye's Frazerlike insistence upon the security of "facts" is further illustrated in an essay entitled "Criticism, Visible and Invisible," where Frye, objecting to the "'X is a failure because' formula," asserts that "the fact is a fact about literature, and . . . nothing can follow 'because' except some kind of pseudo-critical moral anxiety" (SS 78).

The faulty critic is portrayed by Frye as having taken a bad turn off the path of induction, of having, like Frazer's erring anthropologist, ignored the prime responsibilities of fact collection and classification that lead to the best possible theories: "The substitution of subordination and value-judgement for coordination and description, the substitution of 'all poets should' for 'some poets do,' is only a sign that all the relevant facts have not yet been considered" (AC 26). Frye's dichotomization of subjective evaluation versus objective criticism is deliberately illustrated through the simplest of examples: "Shakespeare, we say, was one of a group of English dramatists working around 1600, and also one of the great poets of the world. The first part of this is a statement of fact, the second a value-judgement so generally accepted as to pass for a statement of fact. But it is not a statement of fact. It remains a value-judgement, and not a shred of systematic criticism can ever be attached to it" (20).

As with Eliot, for Frye the "fact" amid the welter of interpretive process functions as an ideal pointed to, an authority invoked, a construct whose importance as something other than construct impels a willing suspension of disbelief. Certainly this simulacrum of certainty, once adopted by different authors, serves divergent ends. For example, Frye's comment that the systematic critic "sees what is there, as distinct from seeing a Narcissus mirror of our own experience" (SS 68) implements that notion of fact and turns it against Eliot, whose insistence upon evaluation is viewed in this light as profoundly unempirical, disastrously unscientific. And yet Eliot also wielded the authority of scientistic "fact" in his own campaign to make criticism a legitimate professional pursuit apart from the "leisure-class gossip" of amateurs. Their different uses testify to the fact that each age demanded that for criticism to become autonomous and authorizing, different routes were necessary.

Frye claims to unveil the ideologies underlying evaluative criticism in order to erect the possibility of the opposite: a "value-free" criticism that is shorn of ideology.[11] But, ironically, Frye's remark that "every deliberately constructed hierarchy of values in literature known to me is based on a concealed social, moral, or intellectual analogy" (AC 23) applies inevitably, and quite fittingly, to Frye himself. Frye rightfully points to the mystification of ideology behind criticism; his error is in assuming that his own system, mainly because of its sheer capacity to systematize on a grand scale, is able to transcend ideology. His comment that "a selective approach," as opposed to his all-inclusive method, "invariably has some ultra-critical joker concealed in it" (23) underlines the assumption that floating free of cramping ideology is simply a matter of drawing larger circles around one's subjects.[12]

It is significant that, immediately after Frye denigrates Eliot as a leisure-class "man of taste," he heralds Eliot's conception of a literary order as critical to his own enterprise. Frye, citing Eliot's notion that "the existing monuments of literature form an ideal order among themselves, and are not simply collections of the writings of individuals," asserts that "this is criticism, and very fundamental criticism. Much of this book attempts to annotate it" (AC 18). Here Frye aligns himself with Eliot's critical program by a valorization of order over the mere sequence of texts. Frye resolutely promotes the classifying and theorizing capacities of the comparativist as a way of defeating the seemingly chaotic diachrony of agglomeration. Unlike Frazer, Frye is not content, at least explicitly, to celebrate collection as an end in itself, and so trots out, not the Eliot who proliferates the lump aggregates of "facts," but the Eliot who sculpts that mass of cultural material into a symmetrical and hence satisfying shape.

Frye's fear of the unrecognizable mess of texts spread through time is well illustrated in *Anatomy*'s second essay, where he holds that "unless there is . . . a center [to literature as a body], there is nothing to prevent the analogies supplied by convention and genre from being an endless series of free associations, perhaps suggestive, perhaps tantalizing, but never creating a real structure" (118). Frye's aversion to indeterminacy involves, significantly, a shift in dimension. "We begin to wonder," Frye avers in his Polemical Introduction, "if we cannot see literature, not only as complicating itself in time, but as spread out in conceptual space from some kind of center that criticism could locate" (17). That Frye's system becomes spatialized in form and hence highly resistant to diachronic processes is hardly a new observation. Harold Bloom firmly links the "simultaneity" of Frye's "order" to Eliot's myth of "Tradition and the Individual Talent," holding it as a "fiction that Frye, like Eliot, passes upon himself." "This fiction is a noble idealization," Bloom asserts, "and as a lie against time will go the way of every idealization."[13]

While Frye himself interprets his project as an extension beyond diachronic interpretation, not the replacement of diachronic for synchronic readings, the fact remains that his tendency is to view literary texts in successions or evolutions that promote not the particularity of their placement in time, but the generality of their time as revealed by the ways in which those texts combine, according to Frye's own unifying principles, with other texts from other times. Frye's drive toward generalities of modes, symbols, myths, and genres inevitably quashes temporal as well as cultural particularity. Poirier asserts that Frye's notion of scientistic "progress" in criticism amounts to "a progress that distances us from the play, that takes on a spatial excursion from 'the individual plays to the class of things called plays,' and then on to the meaning of the drama as a whole" (*Performing Self* 78).

Frye freezes temporal flow by placing a flurry of time zones next to each other in such a way that their conceptual similarities are suggested. The analogy to the Frazerian comparative method is obvious, as is the relation to Eliot's concept of "mythical method." Rahv observes that the myth criticism of the 1950s replicates Joseph Frank's notion of the spatial form of high Modernist literature, which is defined by Frank as "a continuum in which distinctions of past and present are obliterated . . . past and present are seen spatially, locked in a timeless unity" (quoted in "Myth and Powerhouse" 115). Frye, like other myth critics, found quite useful the side of Eliot that suggests the comparativist's carefully orchestrated suspension of dazzlingly various cultures, periods, and texts.

Frye justifies his essentially antihistorical frame by representing his subject, art, as oppositionally related to history. "The imaginative element in works of art," Frye claims in his Tentative Conclusion, "lifts them clear of the bondage of history" (347). It is rare, Frye claims in the more recent *Critical Path,* that "literature is itself an active part of the historical process."[14] This separation, like the divorce between criticism and literature, enables Frye to carve out an autonomy for literature that separates it from history while enabling it to partake of time's materials. Literature, Frye states in *The Critical Path,* is "a coherent structure, historically conditioned but shaping its own history, responding to but not determined in its form by an external historical process" (24).[15]

Frye's dichotomization of literature from history is in one sense simply a separation of the supremely general or identical from the merely particular or different. In *The Educated Imagination* Frye states that the poet's job is "not to tell you what happened, but what happens. . . . He gives you the typical, recurring, or what Aristotle calls universal event." Eagleton in this respect holds that Frye's "modes" and "myths," what constitute his "substitute history," are themselves "transhistorical, collapsing history to sameness" (*Literary Theory* 92). And Fredric Jameson's assertion that "the driving force of Frye's system is the idea of historical *identity*" suggests the comparativist nature of Frye's surrogate history, in which we are led on a grandly multidimensional, diachronic search for monochromatic identity.[16]

Frye's bifurcation of history from literature takes on special purport in his treatment of the Bible. In this respect Frazer's rendition of the Bible as not "science and history" but rather "noble literature" (*Passages* viii) looks forward to Frye's denigration of the historical or factual interpretations of the Bible and his promotion of its literary and mythical aspects. In the "Theory of Genres" section of *Anatomy,* Frye holds that "the priority of myth to fact is religious as well as literary; in both contexts the significance of the flood story is in its imaginative status as an archetype, a status which no layer of mud on top of Sumeria will ever account for" (325). And in *The Critical Path* Frye, claiming that the Bible endures not "because it is historically accurate," asserts that the Book of Job is "avowedly an imaginative drama" that is "more significant" than the " 'begats' " which "may contain historical records" (112–13).

In *The Great Code: The Bible and Literature* (1982), Frye, assuming that "the Biblical myths are closer to being poetic than to being history," suggests that "perhaps the myths of the Bible should be read poetically, just as we read Homer and the Gilgamesh epic poetically."[17] Frye's thesis doubles Frazer's intent, in his own book on the Bible, of disengaging the aesthetic gems of the Bible from their setting in history so that they can be appreciated for the literature that they constitute. Now Frye does not simply maintain that the Bible is pure poetry. Indeed, he states that "trying to reduce the Bible entirely to the hypothetical basis of poetry clearly will not do" (TGC 47). However, Frye does not base his qualification on the premise that what is nonliterary about the Bible is thus historic. Rather, he explains that there are "two aspects of myth: one is its story-structure, which attaches it to literature, the other is its social function as concerned knowledge, what it is important for a society to know" (47). In this latter, important sense, the Bible functions as "a program of action for a specific society" (49). And, significantly, what the social function of a myth has in common with the story-structure is its dichotomizing relation to history: "a program of action," Frye states, "while it cannot ignore history, often sets itself in opposition to history" (49).

Frye's point on the social function of myth's opposition to history leads him to the conclusion that time-bound particulars—places, peoples, cultures, dates—appear in the Bible not because they are historically true but because they serve important social purposes. Hence the significance of ancient Egypt in the Bible is not tied to historical accuracy but to the values expressed through it: "the symbolic Egypt," the vessel for the exportation of those values, "is not in history: it extends over past, present, and future" (TGC 49).

Frye uses similar rhetoric in his discussion of the value of Frazer's *Golden Bough*. In a 1959 radio broadcast in which he discusses Frazer's significance for our century, Frye claims that *The Golden Bough* is "more a book for literary critics than for anthropologists" in that it "isn't really about what people did in a remote and savage past; it is about what the human imagination does when it tries to express itself about the greatest mysteries" (NFCL 88, 89). *The Golden Bough*'s significance as a prime symbolic vessel of cultural import (revealing fundamental truths about the imagination) is complemented by its value as a literary product—the "poetic" element of myth that is "re-created in literature" (TGC 49). According to Frye, Frazer went wrong when trying to prove broader, timebound evolutionary theories but succeeded as a writer whose poetic figurations were re-created in modern literature. Frye describes Frazer as "a devotee of what he thought was a rigorous scientific method who profoundly affected the imagery of modern poetry" (NFCL 94). One of the reasons why Frazer affected poets and antagonized others, Frye states, is quite simply that he wrote well:

> In Oxford, Frazer used to be referred to as "the Cambridge fellow who can write," and it is certainly true that he can write. He can take a great mass of evidence and with a few selective touches make it into a lively narrative that keeps you turning the pages into the small hours. Of course, people who cannot write are not only apt to be jealous of people who can, but often believe quite sincerely that anybody who is readable must be superficial. That is why you get so many sniffy remarks about Frazer's "highly imaginative" or "picturesque" style in books that are a lot harder to get through than his are. But no matter what happens to the subjects he deals with, Frazer will always be read, because he can be. (90–91)

Frye's valorization of the symbolic and literary over the merely historic-empirical is even more clearly seen in his discussions of three writerly historians: Gibbon, Oswald Spengler, and Arnold Toynbee. In an early review

Frye holds that Toynbee is "not writing a philosophy of history so much as unrolling a vast historical panorama. His material doesn't really 'prove' anything: it provides the detail of his vision, and he leads us toward an imaginative total apprehension which can skip over the logical, and even factual, stage" (NFCL 76). And in another review Frye notes that "for sheer power to organize material [Frazer] ranks in the first class, with Gibbon or Macaulay, and a more recent encyclopedic writer, Toynbee, has learned a lot from him" (91). Frye's praise of Toynbee's vision that leaps over the actual facts recalls his claim that *The Golden Bough* tells us more about the human imagination than about what primitive tribes actually did. And it also brings to mind Hyman's rationalization that Frazer knew that "primitive tribes did not evolve from one to the other": *The Golden Bough* is no history to be judged by empirical standards but, rather, is an "epic" of "idealized ascent" (TTB 247).[18] Frye's justifications of Frazer and the three historians resoundingly replicate the rhetoric in which Frazer defended himself against the collapse of his ideas by suggesting the imaginative capacity of his corpus. Essentially Frye is claiming that Frazer and these historians "possess" what Frazer, in a thinly veiled celebration of his own literariness, claimed that his fieldworker sources lacked: "that magic charm of style which . . . can alone confer what we fondly call immortality upon a work of literature" (quoted in Leach, " 'Founding Fathers' " 561).

What is perhaps most significant about Frye's use of the Frazerian rhetoric of literary over empirical, style over substance, is that it encourages readers to enroll Frye's own corpus in that much-honored order of words wherein graceful encyclopedic works outstrip their usefulness as factual chronicles and become "literature." Frye's celebrations of social-scientific texts revealed as literature become, then, press releases on the efficacy of his own creations. Thus, in line with Frazerian rhetoric, the status of Frye's work as literature can be used to defuse his theoretical failings; if it is "wrong" or short-sided in content, then at least it is impressive in its comprehensive and intricate patternings. It is in this sense that George Woodcock refers to *Anatomy* as a "great and intricate edifice," one of those works which "impress and move by their skill and grandeur long after their subjects have ceased to interest us" (quoted in Denham, NFCM 224).

Frye's insistence upon the autonomous nature of literary criticism reflects not only the belief that the critic ought to be elevated to the status of artist, but that the critic, like Frazer the anthropologist, actually can assume the artist's position.[19] It is not fortuitous that Frye states in *The Critical Path* that "students of mythology often acquire the primitive qualities of mythopoeic poets" and gives as "the greatest" of such students Frazer and Freud (98).

The relation between the aesthetic qualities of Frye's work and Frazer's comparativist artistry has not escaped critics. George Woodcock, who views Frazer as Frye's chief "master," observes that Frye's work, like *The Golden Bough,* is "imaginative in its own right," and he cites the resemblance between the two writers "as disguised creative artists." Graham Hough baldly states that "Frye has written his own compendious *The Golden Bough,* using literary rather than anthropological material. It is a highly personal *Golden Bough,* suffused with the quality of his own imagination."[20] Yet it is not necessary to demonstrate Frye's intention to create a work of literature. Intention is hard to prove. More important, *Anatomy of Criticism,* like *The Golden Bough,* functions as a powerful rhetorical tool because it is not simply and easily categorized as art, or science, or anatomy, for that matter. In duplicating the rhetoric of *The Golden Bough, Anatomy* proliferates itself, suggesting several selves that are themselves made possible by bifurcations inherited, in part, from Frazer and reinscribed for the benefit of the all-inclusive text. What unites these multiple versions of genre or type is not only the signature of the acclaimed author, but also the system of theories, often assumed and mystified, that narrow plurality of genre, voice, and source to the oneness of a containing ideology.

Myth, Ritual, and the Metaphysics of Evolutionism

A century ago, many scholars, influenced partly by a naive identifying of evolution with progress, assumed that mythological thinking was an early form of conceptual thinking. This of course led immediately to the discovery that it was very bad conceptual thinking. Thus Frazer, again, in another fit of rational *tic doloreux*: "By myths I understand mistaken explanations of phenomena, whether of human life or of external nature." This was obviously part of an ideology designed to rationalize the European treatment of "natives" on darker continents, and the less attention given it now the better. (TGC 38)

Frye's departure from Frazer on the nature of mythological thinking is crucial to our understanding of both Frazer's work and most myth criticism of the mid-century. The Frazer who exposed the world to cyclical and king-killing rituals was essential to those who looked to myth and ritual as the structural, and often originary, principles of all of literature. However, the

Frazer who branded mythical thinking as "bad reasoning" on its way to becoming better was found to be of little use to those who desired to ground criticism in the valorization of an original mystical mentality: the "social science" of Jung and Lévy-Bruhl was more appropriate toward that end.

Frye, like Hyman, Campbell, and a host of other myth critics, found it necessary to preserve the realm of myth from the infringement of science and give to the former a separate and, at the least, equal status. In *The Stubborn Structure* he inscribes that separation by the claim that "science is its own world-view, and should be distinguished from the mythical one"; indeed, he goes so far as to say that "the physical sciences have never contributed anything to the mythopoeic world-picture except through misunderstanding and misapplication" (18). Frye's insistence upon this division may at first seem contradictory to his own application of science to mythic structures in literature. But his rhetoric resolves the seeming inconsistency by insisting that the "science" he imports is the pure method that enables structural analysis of mythic patterns: it does not penetrate or change the actual mythic structures.

Thus Frye's system reveals but does not alter the myths that tell a culture "what it is and how it came to be, in their own mythical terms." Reading myth aright, then, means, on a basic level, reading culture, a process that is essentially the same from culture to culture, though in "highly developed cultures" myths form more complex systems called "mythologies."[21] The developmental schema of Frye's mythical system, in which simpler cultures produce simpler myths, and so forth, recalls Frazerian evolutionism. This comparativist legacy is especially noticeable, and significant, in Frye's figuring of the uniform progression of "primitive" mythologies into civilized literatures. In *The Stubborn Structure,* for example, Frye holds that the plots of folktales show "a clear line of descent from the myths of early mythologies, and illustrate [literature] as a cultural descendent of mythology" (64). And in *The Educated Imagination* he asserts as his "general principle" that "in the history of civilization literature follows after a mythology" (110).

While Frye does not agree with Frazer on the nature of myth, on the most elementary level he doubles Frazer's rhetorical habit of laying a simplified evolutionary grid (the myth-to-literature paradigm) over the plethora of world cultures. But such schemas, as Frye himself was well aware, were out of sync with the anthropological present and recognized, even by those outside social science, as potentially racist. So we see Frye jettisoning the most blatant evolutionism of Frazer's text while obscuring his use of

the fundamental developmental framework that fulfills the desire for Frazerian cultural patterning. This crucial mystification is clearly seen in Frye's
reading of *The Golden Bough*:

> Frazer's *The Golden Bough* is, as literary criticism, an essay on the ritual
> content of naive drama: that is, it reconstructs an archetypal ritual
> from which the structural and generic principles of drama may be log-
> ically derived. It does not matter two pins to the critic whether this
> ritual ever had any *historical* existence or not. Frazer's hypothetical rit-
> ual would inevitably have many and striking analogies to actual rituals,
> and such analogies are part of his argument. But the relation of ritual
> to drama is a relation of content to form, not of source to derivation.
> (NFCL 125)[22]

Here Frye replicates the ritualist assumption, first brought to light by
Frazer and then propounded by the Cambridge Hellenists, that the ritual
represents the primal "thing done," the originary imitation of the physical
universe. In fact, in *Anatomy* Frye characterizes ritual as the "pre-logical,
pre-verbal" imitation of the yearly round: "Its attachment to the calendar
seems to link human life to the biological dependence on the natural cycle"
(106). The evolutionary nature of Frye's schema comes clear when this
most primal of human imitative actions is prominently perceived in the
most "primitive" of dramatic forms; and, importantly, Frazer's work is
celebrated as the classic work that, in archaeological fashion, "reconstructs"
the primal imitation, burrowing back to the originary site of ritual.

But, significantly, Frye mystifies the essential evolutionism of his use of
Frazer by denying the source searching that is at work in Frazer's text.
Perhaps more accurately, Frye bifurcates Frazer's text according to two
readings, as social science and as literary criticism, and relegates to the
former the onerous task of tracing derivation: "the critic need not take sides
in the quite separate historical controversy over the ritual *origin* of Greek
drama," Frye adds to his discussion in *Anatomy* (109). Frye disavows the
need to demonstrate the equation that led to the result: the critic, Frye notes
in *Anatomy*, "is concerned only with the ritual or dream patterns which are
actually in what he is studying, however they got there" (109).

Frye wrenches the essentially developmental aspect of ritual from the
ritual itself when insisting upon reading it as the "content" of drama rather
than the source. Essentially, he does this by temporarily removing the diachronic dimension from ritual: we are to forget his own evocation of the
complication of ritual in the development of culture. Frye's scientific
method is brought out to deny the temporal dimension and, pure method

that it is, to spatialize the relation of ritual to drama as a schema in which the "content" fills the form, and has always already been there, filling that form. Any attempt to follow ritual to its source gets one bogged down in the quagmire of historical speculation and hence threatens the precious autonomy of the critics by making them resort to extradisciplinary explanations. Hence Frye refers to the mistaken attitude of some "archetypal critics" that "all such ritual elements ought to be traced directly, like the lineage of royalty, as far back as a willing suspension of disbelief will allow. The vast chronological gaps resulting are usually bridged by some theory of race memory, or by some conspiratorial conception of history involving secrets jealously guarded for centuries by esoteric cults or traditions" (AC 109).

In his effort to mystify the nature of *Anatomy* as an ultimate exercise in literary reconstruction, as the rendering of literature down to its ur-forms,[23] Frye renders the ritual itself as the ultimate "fact" of the mythic process. He is careful to avoid a term suggesting origination: in *Spiritus Mundi* he calls it "the epiphany or manifestation of myth" (136). It functions rhetorically as did Frazer's "fact" and Eliot's "rite": as the irreducible site for contemplation, wholly open to but autonomous from interpretation, manifested in history but not dependent upon it. The archetypal critic, in analyzing a plot, reveals the pattern of "the generic, recurring, or conventional actions which show analogies to ritual" (AC 105). Ritual is the very basis or bedrock for such a pursuit, to which Frank Kermode, in his 1959 review of *Anatomy*, attests when he notes that "everything in this book points downward to preconscious ritual, which is the necessary base of the structure."[24] But like Frazer, Frye cannot permit that irreducible unit to be put into question, so he avoids the historical route by which the concept can be made vulnerable. We simply recognize and trace its inexplicable yet undeniable presence.

Frye's denial of "archetypal critics" who depend upon suspect extra-disciplinary beliefs promotes the portrait of the correct archetypal critic who scientifically records and traces the pattern of the highly communicable and suggestive "ritual." Frye explicitly denies any overt attachment to mystical values, such as the "theory of a collective consciousness," which he terms "an unnecessary hypothesis in literary criticism" (AC 112). However, his rhetoric certainly benefits from the aura projected from the alluringly "pre-logical, pre-verbal" rituals that somehow map out our literatures. W. K. Wimsatt points out that Frye "may well disclaim Frazer and Jung; they may be an embarrassment; they are not strictly needed.

What *is* needed, however, is some constant implication or intimation of the primordial."[25]

Though Frye may deny concern over the ultimate origin of rituals, and deemphasize evolutionary movement in the workings of ritual in literature, still a finger points powerfully back to originary forces when ritual emerges, however it got there; indeed, that we do not know how it got there provides a good part of that mysterious pull. Frye notes that "the instant drama becomes primitive and popular," as it does "even in the nineteenth century" with *The Mikado,* for example, then "back comes all Frazer's apparatus, the king's son, the mock sacrifice, the analogy with the festival at Sacaea, and many other things that Gilbert and Sullivan knew and cared nothing about" (AC 109). Frye denies the centrality of a collective consciousness in this phenomenon; indeed, he expressly states that "it comes back because it is still the best way of holding an audience's attention" (109), but that answer returns us even more persistently to the inexplicably enduring pull of elemental ritual.

Frye, like Eliot, while hardly promoting the poet's return to the "savage" state, nonetheless recognizes the appeal of the return to primitivistic coherence. When commenting on "the quality of primitive simplicity . . . that keeps eluding the poets of a more complex society," Frye notes: "One might start drawing morals here about what kind of society we should reconstruct or return to in order to achieve such simplicity, but most of them would be pretty silly. I merely stress the possibility, importance, and genuineness of a response to the arts in which we can no longer separate that response from our social context and personal commitments" (SM 121).

Like Eliot, Frye attempts to empower modern art through appeal to a myth of originary social purpose. In this respect he echoes Eliot's claim that the arts began as practical activities that in time splintered into nonfunctional, ornamental activities. In *Anatomy* Frye notes that "nearly every work of art had a social function in its own time, a function which was often not primarily an aesthetic function at all" (344). When we see in primitive art "an aesthetic impulse at work," what is happening is that we are making "a sophisticated abstraction which may well have been outside the mental habits of the people who produced them" (345). Here Frye recalls Eliot's primitive ritual; for Frye it is almost inevitable that critical approaches to literary works insert their own functions and hence the artifact "loses much of its original function" (345). Frye, like Eliot, adopts the reconstructionist mission of the evolutionary comparativist when he announces that "we can hardly be satisfied with an approach to works of art that strips from them their original function. One of the tasks of criticism is that of the recovery of function, not of course the restoration of an original function, which is out of the question, but the recreation of function in a new context" (345).[26]

The myth of wholly functional, socially integral and hence powerful primitive art is really part of the larger master narrative of the fall from a hypothetical state of primitive unity and simplicity. Frye's narrative tells the tale of "a state of identity, a feeling that everything around us was part of us," and the consequent "split" or separation of that unity which marks, among other things, "where science and art began" (EI 28). But societal differentiation really only repeats what Frye sees as a fundamental shift in consciousness, in which the very vessel of conceptualization is now broken into distinct mental categories. In a review published several years before *Anatomy,* Frye points to Cassirer's use of "the Polynesian *mana*" and "the Iroquois *orenda*" as "fluid primitive conceptions" that function grammatically as "participial or gerundive conceptions." Frye elaborates on this conceptual-linguistic prelapsarian state when he states that these primitive forms "belong in a world where energy and matter have not been clearly separated, either in thought or into the verbs and nouns of our own less flexible language structures" (NFCL 70). He attempts a contemporary legitimacy for his primal-logocentric yearning when he states that "as energy and matter are not clearly separated in physics either, we might do well to return to such 'primitive' words ourselves" (70).

In *Anatomy* Frye finds the ultimate ur-unity of those primitive words in the metaphor that distinguishes poetry. There he defines metaphor "in its radical form" as "a statement of the identity of the 'A is B' type" (123). Recalling Lévy-Bruhl and Eliot's use of him, Frye posits this process as mystical and prelogical: "In the metaphor two things are identified while each retains its own form. Thus if we say 'the hero was a lion' we identify the hero *with* the lion, while at the same time both the hero and the lion are identified *as* themselves" (123). Eliot, discussing Lévy-Bruhl's example of the Bororo tribe who have a mystical identification with the parrot, makes the following observation: "In practical life, the Bororo never confuses himself with a parrot, nor is he so sophisticated as to think black is white. But he is capable of a state of mind in which we cannot put ourselves, in which he *is* a parrot, while at the same time a man."[27]

Frye then provides Pound's version of Fenellosa's ideogram as an example of radical metaphoricization, in which metaphor is manifested in "simple juxtaposition" and civilized "predication" is removed. According to Frye, "in Pound's famous blackboard example of such a metaphor, the two-line poem 'In a Station of the Metro,' the images of the faces in the crowd and the petals on the black bough are juxtaposed with no predicate of any kind connecting them. Predication belongs to assertion and descriptive meaning, not to the literal structure of poetry" (AC 123). But Pound's poem functions as merely a scattered Modernist recreation of fusion of identity. Frye's real interest lies in bringing into existence an all-encompassing form of primal identificatory metaphor, which he calls the "anagogic phase of meaning" (AC 124). There, according to Frye, "we are dealing with poetry in its totality, in which the formula 'A is B' may be hypothetically applied to anything. . . . The literary universe, therefore, is a universe in which everything is identical with everything else" (124). Frye's evocation of this radical metaphorical state, like his appeal to ultimate, pure ritual, is significantly hypothetical, constructed out of a barely mystified urge toward the ultimate predissociative fluidity of mana, in which distinctions between subject and object, matter and energy, and noun and verb cease to matter.

Like Frazer and the Cambridge Hellenists, Frye charts a development by which what begins in the figure of nondifferentiated fusion—or, more accurately, through the simulacrum of primal identity that obscures essential difference—is charted as a progressive attribution of anthropomorphic qualities to nature.[28] That this anthropomorphic progression is tied to Frazerian and Cambridge-Hellenist conceptions of the development of totemistic gods is openly verified by Frye in several places. In *Anatomy* Frye states that the "identifications of gods with animals or plants and . . . human society form the basis of totemic symbolism" (144). And in *The Educated Imagination,* Frye constructs a classic "If I were a horse" rendition of the development of the primitive imagination:

> But suppose you were enough of a primitive to develop a genuinely imaginative life of your own. You'd start by identifying the human and the non-human worlds in all sorts of ways. The commonest, and the most important for literature, is the god, the being who is human in general form and character, but seems to have some particular connection with the outer world, a storm-god or sun-god or tree-god. Some people identify themselves with certain animals or plants, called totems. . . . You may say that these things belong to comparative religion or anthropology, not to literary criticism. I'm saying that they're all products of an impulse to identify human and natural worlds. (38–39)

This conception of primitive god is of course integrally tied to the metaphoric process. In *The Educated Imagination* Frye states that these god-nature weldings, born out of the "impulse to identify," are "really meta-phors" (39). And in *The Great Code* he holds that "the central expression of metaphor is the 'god,' the being who, as sun-god, war-god, sea-god, or whatever, identifies a form of personality with an aspect of nature" (7). Finally, in *Anatomy* Frye poses Christ himself as the ultimate metaphor, as he "unites all these categories [of 'divine,' 'human,' 'animal,' 'vegetable,' and 'mineral'] in identity: Christ *is* both the one God and the one Man, the Lamb of God, the tree of life, or vine of which we are the branches, the stone which the builders rejected, and the rebuilt temple which is identical with his risen body" (141–42).

While Christ is identical to all elements, Frye nonetheless poses a hier-archic arrangement that charts, in backward order, the evolution from min-eral to man to god. His progression brings to mind the drive toward the godhead in *The Waste Land* but recalls even more strikingly the gradual but resolute separation of the god from the lower elements envisioned by Frazer and the Cambridge Hellenists. Frye's replication of this developmental schema perhaps takes its most significant and overt form in *Anatomy,* where he speaks of "undisplaced myth" as "total metaphoric identification" and underscores the tendency of romance, as a less extreme form, "to displace myth in a human direction" (136–37). Actually, Frye places romance be-tween the extremes of myth and realism: whereas in myth a word such as *sun-god* functions as an example of "pure ideogram," indissolubly fusing the god to the element in the act of "implicit metaphorical identity," realism at the other extreme functions as the more developed and yet less powerful "art of extended or implied simile," in which "what is written is *like* what is known" (136).

Frye is careful not to pronounce romance a genre that is evaluatively weaker than or developmentally subsequent to myth. Still, we sense in Frye's rhetoric the barely concealed attempt to enshrine mythic metaphor-ical identity and denigrate, in dissociative fashion, the falling-off from "un-displaced" originary form that is exemplified by romance: metaphor is mystical fusion, after all, and romance mere comparison. This becomes clear in *Anatomy* when Frye declares: "The central principle of displacement is that what can be metaphorically identified in a myth can only be linked in romance by some form of simile: analogy, significant association, inci-dental accompanying imagery, and the like. In a myth we can have a sun-god or a tree-god; in a romance we may have a person who is significantly associated with the sun or trees" (137). Frye's reference to "romance, where the hero is still half a god" suggests that romance is positioned midway on the Great Chain, between realism dangling at bottom and myth poised at top.[29]

The affiliations of Frye's metaphoric schema to anthropological theories of totemism are strong. Indeed, Frye reads the metaphoric process as a linguistic version of the totemic march articulated by Frazer, in which spirits residing in the natural elements evolve into gods merely "associated" with those same elements. In *The Great Code* he refers to the "social development in which subordinate gods move from local deities of woods and rivers and fields into an analogy of a human aristocracy like the Olympian gods of Greece" (70). Like both Frazer and Harrison, he emphasizes the social inequality inherent in the later Olympian model: "The Olympians treat humanity as aristocrats do their inferiors. . . . Their habitation on the top of a mountain is symbolically 'over' mankind" (70). And he stresses, like Frazer and Harrison, how mythologies of the more civilized nations have become progressively more effete and polite in their accounts of their gods. Narrating a fall from primitive originary directness that could have been torn from a page of *Themis,* Frye in *Anatomy* calls this phenomenon "displacement in the direction of the moral," acknowledging the comparativist base from which he has drawn: "The student of comparative mythology occasionally turns up, in a primitive or ancient cult, a bit of uninhibited mythopoeia that makes him realize how completely all the higher religions have limited their apocalyptic visions to morally acceptable ones. A good deal of expurgation clearly lies behind the development of Jewish, Greek, and other mythologies; or, as Victorian students of myth used to say, a repulsive and grotesque barbarism has been purified by a growing ethical refinement" (156).

Also like Frazer and Harrison, Frye sees this progression as concomitant with the evolution from polytheism to monotheism. In *The Great Code* Frye speaks of "the polytheistic gods" as "metaphors begotten of man's close association with nature and his sense that nature has a life and energy identifiable with his own" (67). He also holds that "the mythology of paganism . . . begins with local epiphanic gods and moves on to departmental gods with established functions"; from there we move to "an imperial monotheism," politically motivated by earthly rulers, in which "local cults" are regarded "as manifestations of a single god" (TGC 93). Like Frazer, Frye works this progression both ways: appealing to the fluid primitivist aura that begins it but pointing as well to the comprehensive historical inexorableness by which the many are ultimately and always reduced to the one.

In *The Great Code* Frye borrows from Roman Jakobson when he recasts his figure of the fall from identity as a shift "from the metaphorical, with its sense of identity of life or power or energy between man and nature ('this is that'), to a relationship that is rather metonymic ('this is put for that')" (7). Significantly, Frye inscribes this shift as a transition from the polytheistic to the monotheistic: "In metaphorical language the central conception which unifies human thought and imagination is the conception of a plurality of gods, or embodiments of the identity of personality and nature. In metonymic language this unifying conception becomes a monotheistic 'God,' a transcendent reality or perfect being that all verbal analogy points to" (9). Again hearkening back to Frazer and Harrison, Frye figures the monotheistic God as the ultimate civilizing site of analogy, toward which all things bear homage (from below) but do not identify with. Frye adds to this by noting that "the word 'God,' however great its number of referents, is practically a linguistic requisite for metonymic thinking. There is no point in making analogic constructs out of words unless we have something to relate the analogy to" (10).[30]

Frye defines the metonymic as "a mode of analogical thinking and writing in which the verbal expression is 'put for' something that by definition transcends adequate verbal expression" (TGC 15). The conception of "the language of transcendence, which is founded on metonymy" is what Frye opposes to "the language of immanence, which is founded on metaphor" (15). This dichotomy of immanence and transcendence, in which the "personal nature-spirit" virtually evolves into "the conception of a transcendent 'God,'" strikingly recalls Frazer's figuring of the progress from unmediated animistic presences to the overtly representing or symbolizing god, in which, in Frazer's words, the "tree-spirit," "incorporate or immanent in the tree," becomes "detached from the tree and clothed in human form" (*Magic Art* 71). That detachment in Frazer as well corresponds to a social separation from humanity, in which the god is unavailably above its subjects.

Through his developmental schema of metaphor Frye, like Eliot, poses a reversion to primitive figuration. In *The Great Code* he asserts that "it is the primary function of literature, more particularly of poetry, to keep recreating the first or metaphorical phase of language during the domination of the later phases, to keep presenting it to us as a mode of language that we must never be allowed to underestimate, much less lose sight of" (23). But as in Eliot's work, Frye's power comes not simply from the presentation of the recovered primal but from a simulacrum of the bountiful primal wrought out of a highly skewed representation of a lean and ragged contemporaneity. The poet, as Frye articulates it, *does* the recreating, more or less instinctively, but the critic-comparativist has the breadth of vision to recognize its necessity.

In *The Great Code* Frye argues strongly against the notion that "poetry, however ancient, is still a later development out of an original demotic speech" and presses instead the argument that "poetry is genuinely primitive, and not an artificial way of decorating and distorting ordinary 'prose'" (23). In this respect Frye appears to condemn the Frazerian notion of the figure as ornament. And in this sense he agrees with Lévi-Strauss that metaphor is not a "later embellishment of language but one of its fundamental modes" (Lévi-Strauss, *Totemism* 102). Indeed, in language that appears to anticipate deconstructionist assumptions, Frye in *The Critical Path* goes so far as to question "the degree to which anything in words can tell the truth at all" (119). Of course Frye is not so much saying that language lies but, rather, that as an autonomous system it cannot serve as a transparent representation of "reality." This is made clear when he asserts, again in apparently post-structuralist fashion, that "even the subject-predicate-object relation is a verbal fiction, and arises from the condition of grammar" (CP 119).

Frye's denial of a "truth" emerging from language resembles Eliot's imperative on the avoidance of meaning in poetry. Indeed, in *The Critical Path* Frye states that "there can be no definitive rendering of the real poetic meaning" (70); and in *Anatomy* he, in the structuralist vein, holds that "it is better to think . . . not simply of a sequence of meanings, but of a sequence of contexts or relationships in which the whole work of literary art can be placed" (73). Rejecting the goal of "meaning" in this respect means jettisoning the assumption of a windowlike transparency to reality. Modernist art, according to Frye, has anticipated this critical imperative, having "shifted the center of interest back to the linguistic structure itself, after having destroyed much of our naive confidence that words have an unlimited ability to represent things outside ourselves" (ss 46). It is in this respect that Frye in *The Great Code* welcomes the recent orientation toward language in contemporary criticism: he finds it "rather reassuring that there should be so heavy an emphasis on language and linguistic models in contemporary thought, apart from whatever embodies the emphasis" (15).

And yet while Frye applauds the renewed focus upon the primacy of the linguistic structure, in an even more essential sense he shares Frazer's semiotics of transparency. For what Frye insists on as the "*radically* metaphorical" (TGC 24) in language boils down to a backward rush toward identity, an urge toward a prelogical, predissociative fusion in which difference is obliterated. Frye is indeed worlds away from a post-structuralist mode of thinking of metaphor as at bottom a matter of slippages, ruptures, and discontinuities. In the appropriately entitled *Stubborn Structure,* he appears to contradict his other statements on the irreducibility of "meaning" in literature when he states that "I do not see how literature can ever lose its kernel of externalizable meaning" (46). In fact, Frye laments that this transparency is not greater, for the opaqueness of literature limits "the capacity of words for informing other disciplines. . . . Compared with mathematics at least, words are incurably associative: multiple meanings lurk in them and the structures of grammar twist them into non-representational forms" (46).

Clearly Frye fears the indeterminacy of words, their resistance to being comfortably pegged and thus appropriated for institutional and personal ends. This is strikingly illustrated in *The Stubborn Structure* when, after mourning the associative tendency of language, Frye states: "When I read or try to read Heidegger I get the same feeling that I get when trying to read *Finnegans Wake,* of language dissolving into a mass of associative puns, and language of this kind is surely heading in the direction indicated by the squeals and groans of electronic music" (47). The need for the secure destination of the word explains Frye's gravitation toward Blake just as it clarifies his unease with Joyce (and rock music), for Frye in his concluding paragraph of *Fearful Symmetry* proclaims that "to Blake there are no puns for ambiguities or accidents in the range of the meaning of 'word,' but a single and comprehensible form" (428).[31]

Blake's system is celebrated by Frye because, along with the Bible, it represents an ultimate attempt to make the universe into man's image. In this turn of his rhetoric Frye clearly asserts that the return to a state of identificatory mana, though desirable, is not possible: instead we use verbal fictions, within the limits of "the conditions of grammar" (CP 119), to create full-bodied, systematic approximations of higher realities. In holy works, according to Frye, "God speaks, by hypothesis, in *accommodated* language, putting his thoughts and commandments into a humanly comprehensible form" (120). In fact, Frye states elsewhere, "where a divine personality is presented, the only possible literary form would be that of a discontinuous sequence of epiphanies."[32] These epiphanic fragments as found in the Bible bring to mind the shreds or bits of culture that jaggedly surface in *The Waste Land,* mere anthropomorphic approximations that serve primarily to point to what is not figurable at all.

While Frye openly accedes to the limits of the linguistic system, the ever-present veil between god and word, he, like Eliot, gains great authority by pointing toward the semantic open space where truth is not conditional or screened by his own anthropomorphic figurings. In *The Stubborn Structure* Frye proclaims that "all poet or critic can do is to hope that somehow, somewhere, and for someone, the struggle to unify and to relate . . . may be touched with a radiance not its own" (89). The curtain drawn between god and human approximation in the word is underscored at the conclusion to *The Secular Scripture,* where Frye holds that "the real silence is the end of speech, not the stopping of it" (188). And here we are reminded of the semiotics of *The Waste Land,* in which ultimate value is given over to what is not us at all. Like Eliot and Frazer, Frye gains in authority through the revelation of limitation: his corpus, like *The Waste Land,* derives its power from invoking what cannot be imagined: the perfect, ultimate originary unity of things.

READING THE ARCHETYPES OF CULTURE

At first it may seem curious that Frye, with his vision of a hermetically sealed literary universe, would emerge as a fairly prominent social critic in his own right. And yet a parallel to Eliot might be illuminating: both pushed for the tough, unimpressionistic, and even technical autonomy of literary criticism, yet once they were established as literary critics, both moved with aplomb from literary to social criticism. Like Eliot, Frye made that move by dividing the social and literary realms in order to become the agent who welded them. In *The Critical Path: An Essay on the Social Context of Literature* (1971) Frye notes that the critic works with two poles, the literary and the social, and that correct criticism is a mediation between the two extremes: "Criticism will always have two aspects, one turned toward the structure of literature and one turned toward the other cultural phenomena that form the social environment of literature. Together, they balance each other: when one is worked on to the exclusion of the other, the critical perspective goes out of focus. If criticism is in proper balance, the tendency of critics to move from critical to larger social issues becomes more intelligible" (25).

Yet in another sense that shift is effected, Frye argues, by the *extension* of mythic-literary modes of analysis to the social sphere. Reading cultural-wide myths is a process "very similar to criticism in literature, and it is clear that the different forms of critical interpretation cannot be sharply separated, whether they are applied to the plays of Shakespeare, the manuscripts of the Bible, the American Constitution, or the oral traditions of an aboriginal tribe" (CP 123). In this respect Geoffrey Hartman makes the point that "though Frye's theory is unified only for literature, it has larger

implicit ambitions and is concerned with the 'fables of identity' latent in
all cultural or symbolic forms."[33]

Contained within Frye's system is the all-important assumption that literature functions as a microcosm of culture, so that the abilities involved
in the right reading of literature qualify one to interpret culture. What one
ends up finding in Frye's social criticism is society rendered in terms of
his conception of the literary universe, informed as the latter is by the predominant influences of the Bible, Blake, Frazer, and others. So what might
sound like the harbinger of the fall of literary studies and a prophetic call
for popular or cultural studies—tribes and legal documents ought to be
read like, and alongside, literary texts—is actually Frye's own distinct literary criticism writ large: savages and the Constitution end up being read
as versions of Frye's versions of Blake and the Bible.

While the horizons of Frye's interpretive focus have expanded, the rhetoric, methods, and assumptions have fundamentally remained the same.
This becomes clear in Frye's primary reading of culture, in which all societies' myths are bifurcated into two encompassing categories, myths of
concern and myths of freedom. The system of myths referred to as the
"mythology of concern," Frye explains, "comprises everything that it [that
mythology] most concerns its society to know" (CP 36). The mythology
of concern is intensively traditional, becoming "the way of the elders" (37)
and giving to culture a "limited orbit" of possibilities. Not surprisingly,
Frye articulates the myth of concern in evolutionary terms: it begins and
thrives in the "oral" phase of a culture (38); that phase is "largely undif-
ferentiated," but then in time it "develops different social, political, legal,
and literary branches" (36).

Frye posits against this the mythology of freedom, which stresses the
"non-mythical elements of culture" that are "studied rather than created"
(CP 44). He relates this impulse to the "liberal" and to liberal issues such
as "tolerance of opinion" (45, 44) and again, attaches developmental assumptions: myths of freedom, for instance, are integrally related to the
phase of writing in cultures. Frye applies patently Arnoldian assumptions
here: Greek writing culture has given us roots in myths of freedom, He-
braic culture ("the Old Testament maintains a much closer link with the
oral tradition") promotes concern (46).

Just as right criticism constitutes a mediation between a closed linguistic
system and a tie to social context, so right culture functions when the conservative myth of concern and the liberal myth of freedom negotiate a
proper centrism. Perhaps Eagleton is too harsh in characterizing Frye's delicate balance as "a position somewhere between liberal Republican and

conservative Democrat" (*Literary Theory* 94), but that depiction does emphasize both the posed importance of centrism and Frye's own narrowly culture-bound notion of social change. There is little room in Frye's system, as in his literary criticism, for the legitimizing of fringe or radical cultural elements: as Eagleton tellingly puts it, "the only mistake" in Frye's system "is that of the revolutionary, who naively misinterprets myths of freedom as historically realizable goals" (94). To be legitimated, any cultural extremity must display the impulse toward a center of Frye's own positioning.

Frye does not view the meeting of concern and freedom as simply harmonious: indeed, he insists upon "the recognition of the tension between concern and freedom" (CP 108). Nonetheless, he characterizes recognition as the liberal tolerance that constitutes "the condition in which a plurality of concerns can co-exist" (108). In other words, Frye points to a utopian state in which one can choose, in comparative fashion, between a wide stratum of constricting articles of faith, much as his literary criticism offers the multiple possibilities of reductive mythic patternings. What does not seem possible is the emergence of a genuinely new cultural pattern, a limitation seen in literary critical terms as the inability to recognize new or "fringe" literary properties that could conceivably develop into a new genre.[34]

While "literature is not itself a myth of concern," it nonetheless contains all cultural possibilities, for "it displays the imaginative possibilities of concern, the total range of verbal fictions . . . out of which all myths of concern are constructed" (CP 98). The dilemma is that "the critic wants to get into the concern game himself, choosing a canon out of literature and so making literature a single gigantic allegory of his own anxieties" (127). Extending his application beyond literary criticism, Frye holds that Freud and Marx failed to divest themselves of belief and thus produced "an encyclopedic programme that they called scientific" but, Frye adds, "nine-tenths of the science of both turns out to be applied mythology" (SS 54). In Frye's mind these encyclopedists have drifted unknowingly into "mythological expressions of concern, in which man expresses his own attitude to the culture he has built"; this leaves them prey to "a disease of thinking which is best called anxiety" (SS 54). But of course Frye's formula for reading Freud and Marx can with some striking parallels be turned on him, for Frye has also constructed encyclopedic, comprehensive writings that mystify a set of mythological concerns held dear by the author. And, like Marx and Freud, he has given to this mass of selective concerns the rubric of scientism.

Perhaps his own "anxiety" is nowhere more significantly veiled than in his treatment of Christian religion, particularly his rendering of Protestant versus Catholic traditions. Typically, Frye denies partisanship on the issue of belief, while in fact his work rests on certain implicit theological and religio-cultural assumptions. Although Frye denies that commitment to a particular belief colors *The Great Code,* for example, the book is, as George Woodcock notes, "indissolubly linked with Frye's religious background. It is the kind of book one cannot imagine a Jew or a Catholic, or even an Anglican, writing about the Bible. It comes out of the heart of the English dissenting tradition which, dispensing with liturgy, gave the Bible a centrality rivalled only in other puritan and book-obsessed traditions."[35]

Frye's barely veiled judgments on Catholicism emerge, for example, in his discussion of the Bible as supreme interpretive text. Heralding it as "a structure of universalized poetic meaning that can sustain a number of discursive theological interpretations," Frye then states that "when the Catholic Church achieved temporal power, it was able to confine acceptable discursive renderings of the Bible's meaning to a very narrow orbit, but after the Reformation it became obvious that secondary or discursive meanings of the Bible could take on many different but internally consistent forms" (TGC 65). The point here is not to disprove Frye's assertion but to show that his insistence upon the Bible as well-wrought urn is framed within the Protestant insistence on free reading.

Characteristically, Frye in *Fables of Identity* asserts the preeminence of the "Protestant, radical, and Romantic qualities" in the British literary tradition and yet notes that he has "no thought of trying to prefer one kind of English culture to another"; indeed, he insists, "I regard all value-judgements that inhibit one's sympathies with anything outside a given tradition as dismally uncritical."[36] But he then delivers a biting diatribe on what he perceives as Eliot's "reaction" against these elements:

> During the twenties of the present century, after the shock of the First World War, this intellectual reaction gathered strength. Its most articulate supporters were cultural evangelists who came from places like Missouri and Idaho, and who had a clear sense of the shape of the true English tradition, from its beginnings in Provence and mediaeval Italy to its later developments in France. Mr. Eliot's version of this tradition was finally announced as Classical, royalist, and Anglo-Catholic, implying that whatever was Protestant, radical, and Romantic would have to go into the intellectual doghouse. (149)

Now Eliot and Pound did not stress the French and Italian elements of British literary tradition so much as they did the influences of those elements upon emergent Modernist art (their own included). But the point here is not that Eliot is correct and Frye wrong, or even that Eliot is taken out of context. Rather, it is that, disclaimers to the contrary, Frye's charge amounts to a tit-for-tat rendering of literary tradition.

Again, the similarities between Eliot and Frye may be more revealing than their differences. It is important to note that Eliot's alternative reading of the canon is hardly a freewheeling dismantling of the notion of time-honored canon but rather a reinscription that merely emphasizes a different set of authors. Harold Bloom succinctly articulates this continuity when he states that Frye's notion of the myth of concern as it applies to literary interpretation "turns out to be a Low Church version of T. S. Eliot's Anglo-Catholic myth of Tradition and the Individual Talent. . . . Freedom for Frye, as for Eliot, is the change, however slight, that any genuine single consciousness brings about in the order of literature simply by joining the simultaneity of such order" (*Map of Misreading* 30).

Bloom goes on to label Frye's notion of simultaneous order as a "noble idealization" and asserts that "such positive thinking served many purposes during the sixties, when continuities, of any kind, badly needed to be summoned, even if they did not come to our call" (*Map of Misreading* 30). Bloom's words could well be describing Frye's own rhetoric on the youth culture in the 1960s. Indeed, Frye handles sixties counterculture exactly as he does literary works on the periphery of the great tradition: he charts their position within a continuous order, defining them in relation to the centering traditional or archetypal elements of culture and thus disarming them of actual social impact. In *The Critical Path* Frye effectively contains the sixties movement through his own comparative method, similar to Eliot's mythical method, in which he brings to light "parallels between the present and the nineteenth-century American scene, between contemporary turn-on sessions and nineteenth-century ecstatic revivals, between beatnik and hippie communes and some of the nineteenth-century Utopian projects; . . . the populist movements at the turn of the century showed the same revolutionary ambivalence, tending equally to the left or to the right, that one sees today" (140).

Throughout *The Critical Path* Frye trots out contemporary slang of the counterculture ("turn-on sessions") in order both to authenticate his own familiarity with that culture and to render the novelty or urgency of the terms on the level of contained history: the effect is to deaden any sense of freshness in the current form by bracketing it within a continuous tradition. Extremist movements, typified above in the parallel of populist movements with the counterculture uprising, are characterized structurally according to their off-centeredness.

Even when Frye recognizes the novelty of the counterculture within its own specific cultural context—he concedes that "the situation is so new that not all its social implications are clear yet" (CP 145)—he is still quick to place the novelty within the containing parameters of his own discursive system. What he views as the current "absorption of the poetic habit of mind into ordinary experience" (which is the opposite of making life into great art, he notes) manifests itself in, among other things, the return of the primitivist oral stage of literature. So, though the particular shape of radical social change is not yet realized, Frye has already anticipated its filiations and thus framed its contours: "Both oral poetry and the life it reflects rely on a spontaneity which has a thoroughly predictable general convention underlying it" (145–46). Countercultural social activity, then, is figured as a collective attempt at retrogression, "a concerted effort to break down the barrier between art and life, between stage and audience, drama and event or 'happening'" (146). Frye labels these performances "improvised symbolic dramas" and provides, like a good folklorist, the item, classifying type, and interpretation:

> An example that I witnessed recently was the extraordinary sleep-walking ritual of the "people's park" crisis in Berkeley in the summer of 1969. Here a vacant lot with a fence around it became assimilated to the archetype of the expulsion from Eden, dramatizing the conflict of the democratic community and the oligarchic conspiracy in a pastoral mode related to some common conventions of the Western story. A student editorial informed us that the lot was "covered with blood" because, like all the rest of the land in North America, it had been stolen from the Indians (murder of Abel archetype). The expelling of angels in this symbolism were (as in Blake's version of it) demonic, and the police, with their helmets and bayonets and gas masks, were endeavoring, with considerable success, to represent the demonic in its popular science fiction form, of robots or bug-eyed monsters in outer space. (146)

Crucial to Frye's rhetoric is the vertical relation between the author as folklorist-mythologist and the participants as subjects. The sleepwalkers are represented as primitive tribespeople, spontaneously, ritualistically acting out the archetypal elements that the social scientist has brought to light. The participant's explanation of the ritual ("'covered in blood' because . . .") serves not as an opening through which the subject can speak so much as proof of the appropriateness of the folklorist's classification of type ("murder of Abel archetype"). In classic Frazerian manner, Frye's rendition of the scene illumines not the particular urgency of the situation but the adeptness and brilliance with which the comparativist has welded these unlikely events to a recognizable pattern. Meanwhile, Frye's fitting of the new to the old itself acts as a panacea, a staving-off of the panic engendered by the recognition of discontinuities. This pacification of the fear of chaos is underscored by the fence that surrounds the happening, that encloses and hence makes controllable, containable, the conflict ensuing inside.

Frye's clear delight in his own figuring of the police as Blakean demons demonstrates a certain sympathy on his part for the protesters; indeed, it must be said that Frye in *The Critical Path* indicates his understanding of the frustrations motivating the protesters, especially in regard to the Vietnam war (138). The point here is not whether Frye was politically correct but that he found it necessary to place the counterculture of the sixties into his own controlling comparativist framework. What he finds objectionable in counterculture protesters is not usually their stand on the issues themselves, but rather their feeling that they were embarking on something new: he really cannot stand the enthusiasm that arises from the feeling that there is something new under the sun, uncontainable within his own code. He needs to remove any sense of radical cultural break and refigure the novelty as a progressively continuous realization of essence: "all genuine effort at social change aims, not at creating 'another society,'" Frye notes, "but at releasing the real form of the society it is in" (156).

So Frye in his essay "The University and the Personal Life" laments the New Left's lack of recognition of the "traditions or context of anarchism" (SM 27). And in the same essay, although he praises the radical protests against the Vietnam war, he is harshly critical of "the general panic, even hysteria, that the loss of reference to temporal context has left us with" (34). Indeed, he goes so far as to suggest that this panic, originating from that lost connection to tradition, constitutes college campus protests. Frye thus attempts to separate the general movement from the specific cause (Vietnam war) and relegate the former to the status of simple maladjustment. "Student unrest is not a genuine social movement," Frye claims, "it has no roots in a specific social injustice, as Negro unrest has" (47). The all-embracing collectivity of the Great Tradition, which was used to contain not only the student movement but the whole counterculture, now shuttles them to the periphery of social significance: "Like the beatniks, who have gone, the hippies, who are on the skids, and the LSD cults, which are breaking up, student unrest is not so much social as an aggregate of individual bewilderments, frustrations, disillusionments, and egotisms" (47).

Frye extends his criticisms to counterculture literary artists, who "with their mystiques of orgasm, drugs, and quasi-Buddhist moments of enlightenment" fall predictably and with pedestrian effect into the pattern of striving toward "ideal experience" (CP 30), and to drugs and rock music, which he groups together as "more strenuous forms of resistance" to "mass communication," more vigorous that is than simple "apathy." Drugs, on the one hand, "may promise genuinely new sensory experiences, of a kind that mass media cheat us out of and that the socially approved narcotics fail to provide"; rock music, on the other hand, "wraps up the listener in an impermeable cloak of noise" (149): both are characterized as aberrations, mutual signifiers of a sick and misguided society.

The aspect of the counterculture that hits Frye closest to home, dissent within the walls of the university, is treated to a combination of the strategies of containment, belittlement, and marginalization. Frye presents campus protesters as a simple lot who believe that since "complete objectivity is impossible," then "differences in degree are not significant" (CP 109). They do not realize, as do academics, that "concern" and "freedom" "interpenetrate"; indeed, Frye notes, "it is clearly one of the unavoidable responsibilities of educated people to show by example that beliefs may be held and examined at the same time" (109). Indeed, Frye goes so far as to liken the protesters, in their incapacity for reflection that is tied to their ideological insistence upon the "relevant," to fascists: "A certain amount of contemporary agitation seems to be beating the track of the 'think with your blood' exhortations of the Nazis a generation ago, for whom also 'relevance' . . . was a constant watchword" (155).

In *Spiritus Mundi* Frye again refers to the "neo-Nazi slogan of 'relevance'" and ties it to a "feeling" among the undergraduate population "that departments of English in universities were under a moral obligation to be as contemporary as possible" (5). In *The Critical Path* he claims that "only the student himself establishes the relevance of what he studies" (156); the university has done its job by providing the wide wealth of the Great Tradition which, like *The Golden Bough,* represents an almost limitless storehouse of treasures that can be variously interpreted. For Frye, the university functions as "an engine-room" of ideas, the "power" of which "can last only so long as the university keeps operating" (SM 43). He mystifies the ideological filiations and political and economic contingencies of the university when he asserts that it figures as "the source of free authority in society, not as an institution, but as the place where the appeal to reason, experiment, evidence, and imagination is continuously going on" (43).

Bell-Villada notes Frye's relation to a typical attitude of midcentury
centrist liberalism, in which the university is considered a "universalist
institution . . . with its ideal of standing above all conflicts and prefer-
ences and studying all phenomena with equally disinterested objectivity"
("Northrop Frye" 280). The tie of this view to Frye's notion of a scientistic,
value-free criticism is significant: in the broadest sense, the university
serves as the ideal site at which the scientist-critic can practice his trade, for
it is a locus shorn of all judgmental bias. In "On Value-Judgements" Frye
extends the value of the conception of value-free not only to the criticism
written within the university but to the classroom as well:

> The more consistently one conceives of criticism as the pursuit of val-
> ues, the more firmly one becomes attached to that great sect of anti-
> intellectualism. At present it seems fashionable to take an aggressive
> stand in the undergraduate classroom, and demand to know what,
> after all, we are really trying to teach. It appears that we are concerned,
> as teachers, with the uniqueness of human beings, or with the fullness
> of humanity . . . or in fact with anything at all, so long as it sounds
> vaguely impressive and is not reducible to treating literature as some-
> thing to be taught and studied like anything else. (ss 73)

Frye's disdain for value-related conceptions of pedagogy is integrally tied
to his insistence that literature or English is a subject, like chemistry or
biology, that is made up of the genuine building blocks of knowledge. Frye,
bringing to mind recent rhetoric on "cultural literacy," indicatively notes
the fallacy leading people "to doubt that genuine knowledge of literature is
possible" (ss 72). His assumption of literature's empirical primacy, as an
order of irreducible cultural fact, leads inexorably to the notion that a teacher
ought to perform not as an "opaque substitute for his subject" but as a
"transparent medium of it" (73). Teachers function as clear windows
through which the radiance of cultural nuggets shine; later, of course, the
students can go their own ways and disseminate multiple interpretations
of the revelation. Freedom, as structured by Frye, is the room in which the
student's subsequent interpretive efforts move.

In spite of the fact that Frye figures the university as a free forum, the
actual learning process is decidedly antidemocratic. The student demand
for relevance in subject matter is scornfully refused, and faculty participation in the push for curricular change is called collusion "with the student's innate resistance to the learning project" (ss 73). More broadly,
"dialogue" in pedagogy is posed as fallacy, "a literary convention taken to
be a fact of life" (sm 46). Frye's reading of Plato, for example, repeats Fra-

zer's strategy of narrowing the conception of dialogue into an orchestrated version of the multivocal: "Nothing happens in Plato until one person, generally Socrates, assumes control of the argument and the contributions of the others are largely reduced to punctuation" (46). *Control* for Frye predictably means form or structure, the prerequisite for learning that, in Eliotic terms, necessarily removes the originality of the individual: "Everything connected with the university, with education, and with knowledge, must be structured and continuous. Until this is grasped, there can be no question of 'learning to think for oneself.' In education one cannot think at random. . . . We do not start to think about a subject: we enter into a body of thought and try to add to it" (47).

Frye's discussion of the structure (rather than the dynamics) of the learning process duplicates his rhetoric on the structure of social change, which in turn is a doubling of his rhetoric of literary and ultimately semiotic processes. All function by drawing large circles around their subjects. At bottom is an insistence on structured continuity and a fear of the haphazardly or spontaneously discontinuous. The essentialist nature of the order of words, social formations, and knowledge is necessary in order that the historically contingent and ideologically fueled aspects of that order be mystified. The comparativist critic steps in as the mediator of the comprehensive universal, which he has himself garnered and arranged. To others are left the sundry onerous tasks of adding bricks to the order, but the comparativist himself, through the genius of his arrangement, has made its terms (whether literary, mythic, social, or professional) his own.

4

Joseph Campbell:
Authority's Thousand Faces

READING MODERNISM, READING MYTH

Like Frazer, Joseph Campbell has achieved great popularity as a reader of comparative cultures. Campbell's corpus, like Frazer's *Golden Bough,* has made the difficult transition from a modest scholarly readership to a massive popular audience. By July 1989, the posthumously published version of *The Power of Myth,* the book fashioned from Bill Moyers's interviews with Campbell airing on Public Broadcasting, had remained on the *New York Times* paperback bestseller list for fifty-seven weeks. The forty-year-old *Hero with a Thousand Faces* also made the list that year. The famous account of the policeman reporting to Jane Harrison that *The Golden Bough* "changed my life" finds strong parallels in the popular reception of Campbell today. In Campbell's case, the broad appeal has much to do with the message he sends to readers: myth *can* change your life. The titles of a number of his many books—*The Power of Myth, Myths to Live By*—underline the *use* that individuals can make of myth. In precisely this respect Mary Lefkowitz refers to Campbell as "a priest of a new and appealing hero-cult—the religion of self-development."[1]

But of course the therapeutic uses ascribed to myth by Campbell could not be further from Frazer's conception of the essentially and pejoratively "primitive" nature of myth as an early and fumbling form of science. As Robert Segal points out, whereas Frazer types myth as "superfluous" and "impossible for moderns, who by definition have science," Campbell views myth as "indispensable" to all humanity and especially necessary in the modern age.[2] Like Frye, Campbell finds it necessary to jettison Frazer's notion of mythical thinking as "bad reasoning" becoming better (becoming, ultimately, science) in order to preserve myth's autonomy from science.

And yet this important distinction between Frazer and Campbell should not blur the even more crucial bond between the two as immensely influential readers of comparative culture. Indeed, a key contention of this chapter is that grasping Campbell's popularity involves understanding the

151

comparativist rhetorical authority, in the genealogy traced from Frazer, that organizes the myriad voices of comparative cultures into the one authorial chord. Here the parallels to Frazer can help in understanding Campbell's rhetorical authority. For example, Campbell like Frazer had a mentor whose own writings and personal magnetism had a direct impact on his development as comparativist. But the writings of Heinrich Zimmer and William Robertson Smith never grasped the public imagination like those of their pupils. In each case the bolder, extended comparative method of the pupil was welded to a conspicuously "literary" style. And in each case the pupil took great rhetorical advantage of "literary" influences, properties, and tendencies, all of which are made to augment and defend the author's agenda.

Campbell's appropriation of the literary, like Eliot's and Frye's, also involved interpreting literary texts and, more specifically, rewriting literary Modernism. Few people who pick up his monumental volumes on world myth realize that Campbell began his career by coauthoring the first important analysis of a central Modernist text. *A Skeleton Key to* Finnegans Wake, published in 1944 under the joint authorship of Campbell and Henry Morton Robinson, was the first major full-length attempt to interpret Joyce's last and most enigmatic work.[3] Like Eliot's reading of Joyce and Frye's reading of Eliot, Campbell's reading of Joyce would serve as a press release for his own authorial ends. Indeed, Campbell's reading of Joyce is significant not only because it sites the mythographer's place within the contentious arena of Modernism and Modernist interpretation, but also because it provides a blueprint for the aesthetics, semiotics, and rhetorical strategies of his later work on myth.

The purpose of *A Skeleton Key to* Finnegans Wake is precisely to function as a key toward understanding Joyce's puzzling text. Such understanding is obtained, Campbell maintains, through the study's "thin line-tracing of the skeletal structure of *Finnegans Wake*. Here for the first time the complex and amazing narrative of Joyce's dream-saga is laid bare" (x). As he explicitly lays out in the introduction, Campbell aspires "to indicate the fundamental narrative itself" through the reduction of Joyce's text to its essentials:

> From sentence to sentence we had to select and again select (among the crowding, curiously melting nuances of implication) precisely the one or two lines to be fixed and rendered. Wherever possible we have clung to Joyce's own language, but in order to stress the narrative we have freely condensed, simplified, and paraphrased the heavily

freighted text. No one can be more conscious than ourselves of our numberless inept decisions. Nevertheless, even through our failures the great skeleton emerges, and clearly enough to disclose the majestic logic of *Finnegans Wake*. (x)

Campbell's account of the book's methodology stresses the reduction of distracting difference to sameness, the deletion of the difficult and shifting to the simple and stable. In this condensed version, the dense, even dizzying metaphors of Joyce's text are seen as obstacles to overcome, unfortunate accidents around which one must detour. Though the multiple possibilities within Joyce's text are signs of its greatness, they are only valuable if they can be pared to their essential meanings in the neverending "struggle for the unimaginable prize of complete understanding" (SK ix). Campbell admits to failures in deleting and interpreting, but those editorial shortcomings are absolved by the ultimate success of reducing *Finnegans Wake* to its primary structure: nowhere does Campbell question the motivation to cut the text down to its underlying "logic." In fact, the desire to make "sense" of the text leads inexorably to the claim that there is nothing in Joyce's text that cannot be traced to a logical equivalent: "Amidst a sea of uncertainties, of one thing we can be sure: *there are no nonsense syllables in Joyce!*" (360).

Deconstructionist interpretations of Joyce's work, and especially of *Finnegans Wake,* for example, strongly emphasize the impossibility of rendering Joyce's highly suggestive texts into the "sensible." Indeed, Derridean interpretation valorizes the *Wake* precisely because of its metaphoric elusiveness, what Shari Benstock terms "the compacted linguistic structure of Joyce's text, a stream that cannot contain the multiplicity of its own meanings, whose borders are overrun by excess of language."[4] From this perspective Campbell's attempt to fix the text's meaning not only is a naive effort at signification but also manages to cut against the grain of what makes the *Wake* so interesting. Benstock's description of the fate of a traditional literary approach to *Finnegans Wake* appears tailormade to Campbell's efforts: "hard as the reader peers through the concentric rings of language that envelop the story in search of its center, its locus, the meaning that will illuminate the internal void, the more the essence of the story eludes him" ("Letter of the Law" 165).

But we hardly need to theorize what post-structural Joycean criticism would say about Campbell's approach to the *Wake*. Margot C. Norris provides a history of *Wake* criticism that isolates two strands, a "radical" and a "conservative." The radical approach, initiated by Samuel Beckett, celebrates the text's resistance to signification and claims that it "subverts . . .

the most cherished intellectual preconceptions of Western culture as well."
The conservative approach, on the other hand,

> is characterized chiefly by a belief that the work contains fixed points
> of reference in the manner of the traditional novel. *A Skeleton Key to
> Finnegans Wake,* whose publication essentially initiated this critical
> trend, first outlined the completely naturalistic narrative level toward
> which the mythic elements in the novel purportedly refer. By assigning
> this literal level as the point of reference in the work, the mythic events
> . . . are relegated to the subordinate function of illustrating, univer-
> salizing and inflating the naturalistic events.[5]

Norris's discussion of the *Skeleton Key*'s preeminent place in the conservative camp is well taken, though perhaps the more telling term is mythic
equation, rather than *subordination,* to the naturalistic: what in *A Skeleton
Key* contrasts most dramatically to a deconstructionist reading of Joyce is
the ease with which the multiple signifiers can be traced to their few mythic
messages or signifieds. The windowlike nature of Joyce's language is assumed, a notion that critics such as Perry Meisel roundly reject: "For Joyce,
language is not a transparent instrument designed to signify alinguistic
truths . . . but a palace of reverberations" (*Myth of the Modern* 127).

In the foreword to *Skeleton Key,* the authors write of how they were "pro-
voked by the sheer magnitude of the work" (ix). As with Hyman's reading
of *The Golden Bough,* the utter mass of the text attracts the critic. And yet,
as is also the case with Hyman, for Campbell the gargantuan text must be
contained, mapped into a recognizable and hence controllable grid. The
text's size and complexity are not obstacles to understanding: indeed, "the
unimaginable prize of understanding" is treasured precisely in proportion
to the text's massiveness and seeming uncontrollability. Size and complexity are insisted upon in order to demonstrate the authority of the author-
reader who can break them down into manageable units. Just as Frazer, and
by extension Hyman, gain authority by figuring the mighty web of culture
and then isolating and signifying its threads, so Campbell inscribes a
Joycean tapestry whose pattern, he claims, is ultimately readable:

> This complex fabric of semantics, associative overtones, and stem
> rhythms is merely the *materia prima* of Joyce's communication. To this,
> add an enormous freight of mythological, historical, and psychologic
> reference. It would be well-nigh hopeless to attempt to trace the design
> of any page were it not that a thread of logic runs through every par-
> agraph. True, the thread always frays out into lateral associations

which in turn disappear into almost inaccessible tenuities of meaning. Yet the main lines can all be followed. (SK 359)

Just as Hyman reads Frazer's "common image for culture" as both "a great fabric" and "an orderly tangled bank," a jungle barely capable of being tidily organized, so Campbell similarly reads Joyce's text as a wilderness that, with the expertise and doggedness of the right critics, can be plotted:

> The vast scope and intricate structure of *Finnegans Wake* give the book a forbidding aspect of impenetrability. It appears to be a dense and baffling jungle, trackless and overgrown with wanton perversities of form and language. Clearly, such a book is not meant to be idly fingered. It tasks the imagination, exacts discipline and tenacity from those who would march with it. Yet some of the difficulties disappear as soon as the well-disposed reader picks up a few compass clues and gets his bearings. Then the enormous map of *Finnegans Wake* begins slowly to unfold, characters and motifs emerge, themes become recognizable, and Joyce's vocabulary falls more and more familiarly on the accustomed ear. (SK 3–4)

The appeal of Campbell's approach has much to do with a calculated egalitarian message, later to be used, in self-help fashion, in the books on myth: you too can perform this difficult task, with a little help from friends. The authors become advance guards, scouts who first break the trail in order to make the journey as effortless as possible. In some respects the authors play the role of Anne Tyler's Accidental Tourist: they take the journey first and map out the territory so that future travelers through the novel encumber the fewest difficulties and feel as close to home as possible in the strangest and most difficult of places.

Clearly Campbell's approach entails more than the interpretation of a single work by a single Modernist. Indeed, the philosophy of language articulated here and explored in later works by Campbell represents a fundamental position not only on literary Modernism but on literature itself. In opposition to post-structural approaches, Campbell's reading of Joyce holds that Modernist literary language at its best (that is, at its most comprehensive and universal) functions as a conduit through which flows mythic content. For a critic such as Meisel, Joyce's language works on the "notion of the relational buoyancy of language rather than the fixed or transparent signification of alinguistic states or objects that Arnold and Eliot, by contrast, hold language to be" (*Myth of the Modern* 135–36). Meisel points to Eliot in particular as the culprit in the conservative effort to tie Modernist language to signification, viewing Eliot's famous review of *Ulysses* (which isolates the "mythical method" as the operating principle in Joyce's novel) as an attempt to "normalize" Joyce's literary production: "It is Eliot we may thank for promoting a reading of *Ulysses* based on taking, without apparent irony, its wryly announced correspondences to *The Odyssey* as a way not simply of beginning to contextualize the novel, but as a way of decoding it" (142).

Although Eliot's semiotics clearly do more than attempt to make language transparent, still the relation between Eliot's reading of *Ulysses* and Campbell's interpretation of the *Wake* is significant. Each represents an early and highly influential reading of a Joyce masterwork. Each announces the pattern, "key," or "method" that makes "sense" of (and makes significant) Joyce's essentially disruptive text. Each activates what Meisel calls a "mythic replication" at work in the novel that tends to freeze temporal flow (in Eliot's case, by the paralleling of epochs) and in general to minimize historical and cultural particularity. And finally, and perhaps most important, each takes the occasion of a Joyce text to promote a method that the author himself was using (in Eliot's case, in *The Waste Land*; in Campbell's, in the study of the *Wake* itself).

Meisel's belief that Eliot in *The Waste Land* attempts "an isomorphic symbolism that yokes all myths, religions, all literatures in a serene and pacifying conclusion" (*Myth of the Modern* 87) represents precisely what Campbell views as the triumphant principle activating *Finnegans Wake*. For Campbell, Joyce's preeminence as a mythic author, his mythographic authority in effect, lies in his ability to present particular cultural phenomena as universal: "Under the seeming aspect of diversity—in the individual, the family, the state, the atom, or the cosmos—these constants remain unchanged" (SK 14). As was the case for myth critics such as Hyman, mythic universalization amounts to a temporal stasis that is justified in the name of the "eternal" or "timeless." "Amid trivia and tumult," amid the messy particulars of history, Joyce, Campbell claims, clarifies the "eternal dynamic implicit in birth, conflict, death, and resurrection" (14).

Campbell does not deny that *Finnegans Wake* contains internal warring elements that produce a seeming fragmentation (after all, he refers to the book as "all compact of *mutually supplementary antagonisms*" [14]);[6] his Joyce, however, like Meisel's pejoratively cast Eliot, contains conflict within a mythic form that promotes the comforting illusion of representational impermeability and completeness. Campbell would agree with Benstock that Joyce's text represents a "compacted linguistic structure"; however, the "borders" of Campbell's version of that structure are anything but "overrun by the excess of language," as Benstock claims. Indeed, the book becomes for Campbell what Meisel and others claim *The Waste Land* has mistakenly come to signify: a hermetically sealed rendering of an epoch. Campbell's figuring of *Finnegans Wake* as "a huge time-capsule, a complete and permanent record of our age" is quite telling in this respect. This is a freeze-dried version of world culture that, through myth-induced strategies of containment, encourages readers to breathe easy, knowing that the sprawling, terrifyingly vital mess is representable and hence controllable.

Campbell's assuring mythic replication of culture, extending well beyond *A Skeleton Key,* often takes the form of Clifford's figure of the ethnography of salvage, which justifies other-cultural representation through the claim that a "last chance rescue operation" is underway (WC 112–13). Campbell in this respect is part of a larger legacy of authors, including Eliot, who claim cultural ruin as a pretext for authorial emergence and control. In the foreword to *A Skeleton Key,* Campbell holds out the comforting notion that whatever apocalyptic fears we might harbor about the future, Joyce has so well staked out the outlines of our culture that we will be eminently representable: "If our society should go smash tomorrow (which, as Joyce implies, it may) one could find all the pieces, together with the forces that broke them, in *Finnegans Wake.* The book is a kind of terminal moraine in which lie buried all the myths, programs, slogans, hopes, prayers, tools, educational theories, and theological bric-a-brac of the past millennium" (x).

Campbell's version of *Finnegans Wake* rehearses what Clifford describes as the trope of "the persistent and repetitious 'disappearance' of social forms at the moment of their ethnographic representation" (WC 112). According to Campbell, Joyce's text is sited at the point of extinction, where the glacial flow of culture has now ceased; like many a modern ethnographer, Joyce is figured as the rescuer of a civilization already disappearing from the horizons of history.

Like *The Waste Land,* Campbell's *Wake* figures the various aspects of human culture as debris that is brilliantly configured into value by the author–culture reader. The image of the "terminal moraine" fortifies the notion that the pieces of culture are scattered remains when separated from the pattern the author makes of them, just as the parts of culture represented in *The Waste Land* are figured as "fragments," debris to be "shored against" the personal "ruins" of the author. Meisel's claim that Eliot's fragmentation of the world operates as self-serving figure, as "a state that really inheres largely in the history of imagination alone" (*Myth of the Modern* 89), proves relevant here. And yet, if we accept the "radical" reading of *Finnegans Wake,* it is not Joyce who gains authority through the tidy configuration of debris. Rather, Campbell, like Eliot, reads that authority into Joyce so that it is projected back upon the critic. Even if we grant that *Finnegans Wake* constitutes the terminal moraine of culture, it is the critic who excavates that moraine, maps it out, takes samples, and provides an analysis of its content and structure. Campbell's representation of Joyce's text as excavation site creates the need for an archaeologist-geologist, a role that the critic Campbell is only too happy to fill and, later, extend from the study of literature to mythic structures themselves.

Throughout *A Skeleton Key* Campbell projects his own methodological and ideological program onto Joyce, and in the process creates a gap that only he can fill. Perhaps nowhere is that tactic so conspicuous as in the book's concluding pages: "Joyce early understood that unless we transcend every limitation of individual, national, racial, and hemispherical prejudice, our minds and hearts will not be opened to the full stature of Man Everlasting. Hence his zeal to shatter and amalgamate the many gods. Through the lineaments of local tradition he sends an X-ray, and on the fluorescent screen of *Finnegans Wake* projects the permanent architecture of all vision and life" (362).

The figure Campbell provides for Joyce's activity actually describes his own: the radiologist is not so much Joyce, making transparent the outer differentiated trappings of local cultures, as Campbell, piercing the thick layers of Joyce's language to get to the very skeleton of the corpus. As such, the X-ray, shot through the myriad local signifiers, is sent not by Joyce but by Campbell, and projects onto the novel Campbell's version of a permanent architecture, his own map of ultimate, universal meaning. What Campbell claims through the analogy of the X-ray is nothing less than the capability to make the opaque medium of signification transparent, and in the process to enable the leap from local to universal, from common many to transcendent One.

Campbell's books after *A Skeleton Key* fan out from the study of literature to world myth, as Campbell himself moves into progressively more powerful positions, from literary critic to mythologist to self-styled guru.[7] Still, the methodology inscribed in the figure of the X-ray and the conception of semiotics at the base of his rhetoric remain constant. In *The Hero with a Thousand Faces,* Campbell's second and most influential book, the analogy of the X-ray is again applied but this time the ostensible subject is not a single novel, but the hero as he is revealed in world myth:

Mythology . . . is psychology misread as biography, history, and cosmology. The modern psychologist can translate it back to its proper denotations and thus rescue for the contemporary world a rich and eloquent document of the profoundest depths of human character. Exhibited here, as in a fluoroscope, stand revealed the hidden processes of the enigma *Homo sapiens*—Occidental and Oriental, primitive and civilized, contemporary and archaic. The entire spectacle is before us. We have only to read it, study its constant patterns, analyze its variations, and therewith come to an understanding of the deep forces that have shaped man's destiny and must continue to determine both our private and our public lives.[8]

The similarities to the rhetoric of *A Skeleton Key* are patent. Note, for example, how the psychologist, like Joyce the author, functions as proxy for Campbell the culture-hero. And yet in a sense the mythological approach to a literary work (*Finnegans Wake*) reverses itself to become a literary approach to mythology. Like *Finnegans Wake*, mythology becomes text, an assemblage of cultural-racial characters to "translate," "read," or "misread" in the effort to come to a fuller understanding of the ways of the human spirit.

Campbell's "reading" of mythology as text of course hardly aligns with post-structural notions of "world as text," as a realm of constantly shifting signifiers having no provable reference to a ground of signified meaning (transcendental or otherwise). On the contrary, Campbell's trope of "text," in line with the semiotics at work in *A Skeleton Key*, functions as a shell that covers the true interior of myth. "Reading" the text involves simply making transparent the signifier of the outer body in order to get to the signified, the mythic message or content represented by the body's interior. The title *The Hero with a Thousand Faces* perfectly illustrates Campbell's notion of the semiotic. Like the later *Masks of God*, Campbell's figure for mythic essence presupposes the essential substitution of myriad names (of peoples, cultures, religions) for the transcendental signified, the heroic or divine spirit or vitality that animates the earthly and divine realms.

Campbell's drive to strip away the linguistic peel to get at the metaphysical fruit, witnessed in both *A Skeleton Key* and *The Hero with a Thousand Faces,* overtly typifies the logocentric search for origins that post-structural efforts condemn. Indeed, Michel Foucault's description of how the search for absolutes "necessitates the removal of every mask to ultimately disclose an original identity" not only aptly assesses Campbell's efforts but echoes his metaphor for the procedure. Campbell's fluoroscope functions like the X-ray machine in *A Skeleton Key*: both are required to close the gap between word and spirit, between signifier and signified, and hence reach what Derrida calls the "lost presence." The last words of the recent Public Broadcasting interviews with Bill Moyers make only too clear the metaphysics of presence at work:

> MOYERS: The meaning is essentially wordless.
> CAMPBELL: Yes. Words are always qualifications and limitations.
> MOYERS: And yet, Joe, all we puny human beings are left with is this miserable language, beautiful though it is, that falls short of trying to describe—
> CAMPBELL: That's right, and that's why it is a peak experience to break past all that, every now and then, and to realize, "Oh . . . ah."[9]

Eric Gould in *Mythical Intentions in Modern Literature* emphatically asserts that "there can be no myth without *an ontological gap between event and meaning*," and that "a myth intends to be an adequate symbolic representation by closing that gap, by aiming to be a tautology" (6). In Campbell's semiotics of myth, event and meaning become the various manifestations of mythic signifier and signified, respectively—mythic narrative and message, profane and sacred, symbol and meaning, text and experience. Through the fluoroscopic capacities of the mythographer-psychologist, the gap between signifier and signified is closed and the lost presence recalled.

Gould solidly anchors his discussion of the mythicity of Modernist writing in the semiotic, but his structural orientation prevents him from substantially considering the issues of authorial power involved. Rather, for him when the truly "mythic" operates in the Modernist text (say, of Eliot or Joyce), then "the presence of an author is incidental" (*Mythical Intentions* 135), as authorial intention disappears into the larger structural intention of mythicity. He does not sufficiently consider (and the absence of Foucault as a source underlines the absence) that the author who shuttles between the mythic signified and signifier in the effort to recover the "power of myth" is necessarily involved in a complex play of dominations, often propelled by the drive toward authorial command and usually expressed through the shaping of mythic message into cultural-ideological allegory.

To understand Campbell's semiotics of myth, we must consider the role of Jungian psychology, which played a major role in Campbell's notion of the transcendental signifier, and the part played by Adolph Bastian, whose notion of Elementary Ideas to which all the world's spiritual manifestations can be reduced was central to Campbell. But for the rhetoric that inscribes those semiotics and, importantly, garners its authority from them, we must look elsewhere, to Frazer of course, but also to the literary Modernists. Campbell himself attests that Modernist writings were central to his development. As he states in *The Power of Myth,* James Joyce and Thomas Mann were his real "teachers" in his early years ("I read everything they wrote") because "both were writing in terms of what might be called the mythological traditions" (4). More specifically, these two Modernists exemplify the artist, who, in our century, "is the best prototype of the Modern Hero."[10] The artist in the modern world has stepped into the role of hero because, in the absence of belief in traditional myths, he has "created a new mythology."

Campbell refers to this new heroism as Creative Mythology, a restructuring of myth that first emerged in the Middle Ages, characterized by "expressions of individual experience" as opposed to a statement of "dogma."[11] The author's supplanting of the traditional hero, who "ventures forth from the world of common day into a region of supernatural wonder" (HTF 30), says much for the power of the Modern text. The traditional hero returns from his quest "with the power to bestow boons on his fellow man" (30); Campbell views the heroes of the narratives of Joyce and Mann as "persons daring enough not only to venture forth to a strange new world but also to return" (Segal, *Joseph Campbell* 138), and the applicability of this description of the hero to narrative has had a tremendous impact upon literary studies in the past forty years. But more germane to the issue of authorial control: what is the nature of the power wielded by the author who returns with a "new" mythology in hand?

The apparent answer lies in the *comprehensiveness* of the author-hero's interpretive strategies, his ability to "read" experience (again, the literary figure) from an angle that will not occlude any portion of the world's lively text. In *Creative Mythology,* the fourth volume of *The Masks of God,* Campbell champions Joyce over the orthodox Catholic Church because of his "ways of interpreting Christian symbols": for Campbell, "the artist reads" these symbols nonconstrictively, "as referring to an experience of the mystery beyond theology that is immanent in all things, including gods, demons, and flies," while "the priests, on the other hand, are insisting on the absolute finality of their Old Testament concept of a personal creator God 'out there.' "[12]

In *A Skeleton Key,* Campbell's assessment of Joyce's accomplishments underlines the power of the all-incorporative text. The *Wake* succeeds, according to Campbell, because it is "the first literary instance of myth utilization on a universal scale. Other writers . . . employed mythological symbolism, but their images were drawn from the reservoirs of the West.

Finnegans Wake has tapped the universal sea" (361). Similarly, the imagery of the *Wake* owes its complexity to Joyce's "titanic fusion of all mythologies." Clearly Joyce's authority as hero for a new age, as creative mythologist, is not due so much to his having "created a new mythology" as it is to his comprehensively mapping out, and then reading, the world's artifacts. Much like the rhetorical authority of Frazer, the power of the creative mythologist derives from the wholesale reorganizing, recycling, and rephrasing of traditional mythic materials.

In the preface to *The Hero with a Thousand Faces,* Campbell articulates the methodology of his own mythographic effort in language that echoes his description of Joyce's powers: he plans "to bring together a host of myths and folk tales from every corner of the world, and to let the symbols speak for themselves. The parallels will be immediately apparent; and these will develop a vast and amazingly constant statement of the basic truths by which man has lived throughout the millenniums of his residence on the planet" (viii).

Campbell's self-proclaimed charge is nothing less than the rearticulation of the voice of the cosmos. But the tremendous authority granted to the mythographer, the power of comparativism, is given the illusion of rhetorical humility: like Frazer and like Joyce the creative mythologist, Campbell merely lets the "symbols speak for themselves." That semiotic transparency is made possible in part through Campbell's all-inclusive organization of mythic materials; but, as he states at another point in the preface, the fluoroscopic powers of depth psychology are also essential to the process of allowing the mythic signifier to give voice to its primal message: "The old teachers knew what they were saying. Once we have learned to read again their symbolic language, it requires no more than the talent of an anthropologist to let their teaching be heard. But first we must learn the grammar of the symbols, and as a key to this mastery I know of no better tool than psychoanalysis" (HTF vii).

The mythographic text functions as a repository of voices, a version of the cosmic polyphonic whose voices are vented when the mythographer closes the gap between symbol and meaning. The humility of the mythographer's rhetorical stance (the mere "talents of an anthologist" coupled with the teaching of a simple grammar) thinly veils the mythographic authority at work, the will-to-power to become the agent of meaning for all that is primal, unconscious, "primitive." Indeed, the humble task of translation carries with it the authority to shape the semiotics of myth to the advantage of the mythographer. For Campbell, translating as he does supplants religion's deleterious function of making myth literally factual or true. In *Myths to Live By* Campbell insists that myths should not be seen as "historic facts" as religion insists that we do; rather, "such universally cherished figures of the mythic imagination must represent facts of the mind."[13] Mythic occurrences, then, are detached from historical process and become elementary semiotic entities, symbols to be read: "Whereas it must, of course, be the task of the historian, archaeologist, and prehistorian to show that the myths are as facts untrue . . . it will be more and more, and with increasing urgency, the task of the psychologist and comparative mythologist . . . to identify, analyze, and interpret the symbolized 'facts of the mind'" (12).

Relevant here is Campbell's claim, in *Hero,* that "the stressing of the historical element will lead to confusion; it will simply obfuscate the picture message" (17). The trope makes too clear that history acts as an unfortunate obstacle within Campbell's schema, much as it did for Frye. History is constituted, in Campbell's view, of pesky clumps of signifiers that dirty the lens through which we view the transcendental mythic signified. In *Hero* Campbell similarly claims that "we are concerned at present with problems of symbolism, not of historicity. We do not particularly care whether Rip Van Winkle, Kamar al-Zaman or Jesus Christ ever actually lived. Their *stories* are what concern us."[14] Campbell's denial of the role of history in myth, like Frye's, recalls Rahv's claim that myth critics fear history and change and thus "induce in themselves through aesthetic and ideological means a sensation of mythic time—the eternal past of ritual" ("Myth and Powerhouse" 114).

To Campbell mythic "events" cannot be read as facts (they are "false and to be rejected as accounts of physical history," Campbell says in *Myths to Live By,* 12) because, in the words of Gould, that would preclude the "ontological gap between meaning and event" (*Mythical Intentions* 6) that makes mythicity possible. Campbell requires the fundamental semiotic division between fact or reality versus symbol, of signified versus signifier, for without that division there would be no need for the mythographer to assume the role of the authority who closes that gap by providing what Gould calls the "adequate symbolic representation" (6) of mythic essence.

Paradoxically, although reading myths "literally" (as "facts" of "history") is "false," such interpretations have functioned effectively for traditional societies over the centuries: "For not only has it been the way of multitudes to interpret their own symbols literally, but such literally read symbolic forms have always been the supports of their civilizations. . . . With the loss of them there follows uncertainty, and with uncertainty, disequilibrium. . . . Today the same thing is happening to us" (MTLB 8–9).

Campbell's recollection of prelapsarian literalism serves the rhetorical function of making necessary a hero who will return from his perilous venture into the semiotic with an invaluable boon: a translation of the mythic text that will bring forth a bliss approximate to that which literalism had showered upon the ignorant.

Robert Segal pegs Campbell as "unabashedly elitist" in his conviction that "only the few are sensitive to the breakdown of tradition" (*Joseph Campbell* 149). Campbell's attitude ensures the prominence of the mythographer in much the same way that Eliot sought the recognition of a primitive substratum to experience that could revitalize modern society, but only if that "primitiveness" was welded to a civilized, and civilizing, intelligence: the literary artist, of course, was best equipped to perform that function. Campbell's semiotics of myth works much like Eliot's rhetoric of the primitive, in which, for example, the artist "is more *primitive,* as well as more civilized, than his contemporaries" (Eliot, "Tarr" 106).

Campbell's self-serving and self-constructed dichotomies look backward to Frazer's bifurcations of theory versus fact, artist versus fact-collector, and science versus literature. Campbell's segregations, like Frazer's divisions, enable Campbell to play both sides of the line to his advantage. Campbell's wide reputation and extensive influence, for example, like Frazer's is more integrally tied to his empirical ability to amass large amounts of raw mythic materials, sources, and "facts" than it is to creating a new system of ideas about his subject. William Doty in this respect notes that "Campbell's writings are referred to frequently in mythological criticism, but the manner of reference suggests that his works have had importance more as resources for comprehending a wide range of mythological perspectives than as contributions to a methodological posture."[15] The trope of multivocality that Campbell figures into the text, like Frazer's, promotes the notion that his work functions as a storehouse of mythological sources and facts that transparently announce themselves: see, for example, when Campbell in *Hero* describes "the host of myths and folk tales from every corner of the world" that are brought together and are permitted "to speak for themselves" (viii).

And yet, while his reputation benefits greatly from his role as collector, Campbell simultaneously crosses the self-created line of demarcation between disciplines when he asserts his status as translator and analyzer, much as Frazer cleaved to his role as armchair theorist while drawing upon his reputation as fact-collector. Campbell's insistence upon myths as literally untrue, for example, necessitates a mythologist with the capability to analyze "the facts of the mind." To the historian and archaeologist are left the supportive, more onerous, but insignificant task of demonstrating that myths are factually untrue (MTLB 12).

Thus, like Frye, Campbell bolsters his authority through an accumulative method that appeals to the empirical while simultaneously finding it necessary to elevate his own activities above those of other "fact"-oriented professions. "Whenever the poetry of myth is interpreted as biography, history, or science," Campbell states in Hero, "it is killed. The living images become only remote facts of a distant time or sky" (249). Mythology read by science, according to Campbell, is absurd—"the life goes out of it, temples become museums. . . . Such a blight has certainly descended on the Bible and on a greater part of the Christian cult" (249). Like Frazer, Campbell denigrates mere fact, in the process marking himself off from custodians of fact like historians; but at the same time he derives authority from the facts accumulated within his own text. Also like Frazer and Frye, Campbell warns of the damage done to the Bible when it is taken literally as "history" and not taken literarily as "poetry": for both Frazer and Campbell the aestheticization of the religious document denies a place to historical process.[16]

Again, Campbell's analytical adeptness and authority is masked by a humility claiming that only "the talent of an anthologist" is needed to let the "meaning" of myth "become apparent of itself" (HTF vii). But, as happens with Frye, the medium with which Campbell works is obscured, mystified. For Campbell's method, as exemplified in Hero, hardly involves the simple translation and evocation of the multiple mythic voices of the hero; rather, to achieve thematic simplicity and coherence the author sculpts, or more accurately chops from context, the representations of mythic voices. Doty accurately describes the method at work in Hero: "Campbell . . . presents a simple, easily graphed cycle, with great analytical power—as he exemplifies with many accounts of heroic figures from a wide range of cultures" (Mythography 176). This power has made Campbell's work more usable as an "analytical tool for literally hundreds of secondary studies," and hence more influential than "Raglan's or Rank's statistical accountings of the [hero] motif" (176).

Others have harshly isolated Campbell's neglect of culture-specific myths in his figuring of the hero, in critiques that recall Benedict's criticism of Frazer's Frankensteinlike method of comparison. Alan Dundes, for one, holds that Campbell's attempt to fuse all heroes into a "monomyth" damages the integrity of the particular heroes as they function in their own distinctive narratives. According to Dundes, "Campbell's pattern is a synthetic, artificial composite which he fails to apply in toto to any one single hero. Campbell's hero pattern, unlike the ones formulated by von Hahn, Rank, and Raglan, is not empirically verifiable, e.g., by means of inductively extrapolated incidents from any one given hero's biography."[17] Segal also states that although Campbell is praised as a storyteller, "in his writings he tells surprisingly few myths, at least whole ones" (*Joseph Campbell* 264), and Raphael Patai claims of Campbell's text that "no actual mythology contains such a pattern of composite myth" (*Myth and the Modern Man* 59).

Campbell's "synthetic" master-myth ignores cultural holism in the colossal authorial effort of fitting together a piecework universalism. In this respect it resoundingly recalls the monomyth that he projected onto Joyce's text, which in turn recalls Eliot's *Waste Land* and *The Golden Bough*. The notion of the text as brilliantly configured composite, as aggregation of "fragments" of culture, is crucial to understanding Campbell's authorial tactics. For Campbell's harmonic heroic cycle is, like Frazer's text, not the "real thing" but a simulacrum, constructed out of the severed parts of multiple heroes that are pulled from the great body of myths and sources.

Like Eliot, Campbell figures as archaeologist who pieces together a cultural mosaic out of the shards of myths, or, in another Campbellian trope, as geologist who reconstructs the whole of ancient myth from the survivals that trace the pattern of its glacial disappearance. Note in this regard how the metaphor of "terminal moraine" used to describe *Finnegans Wake* in 1943 is reintroduced almost forty years later, in the opening to the first volume of *The Atlas of World Mythology,* to describe what remains of mythic culture: "We live, today, in a terminal moraine of myths and mythic symbols, fragments large and small of traditions that formerly inspired and gave rise to civilizations."[18]

This rhetorical strategy, like that of *The Waste Land,* is predicated upon the assumption that culture lies in ruins at our feet and that the author must refit the pieces or fill out the whole from the partial pattern. Read in the light of a rhetoric of inclusive domination, the "fragments" of cultural artifacts that Campbell, like Eliot's persona, has "shored against [his] ruins" signify cultural authority regained, as the Promethean capacities of the creative mythologist forge out of the shards of ancient culture a new mythical coherence.

Like the reception of *The Golden Bough,* *Hero*'s appeal to a literary readership continues long after, and indeed usually in ignorance of, strong contemporary critiques that emerged from within the fields of folklore and mythology. In both cases, more circumspect experts in the "field" (anthropology, myth and folklore) posed the work as a repudiation of reigning functionalism in its disregard of important cultural differences. William Kerrigan, for example, claims that Campbell "has no respect for locality." Responding to a typical Campbellian assertion that various Oriental and Occidental holy men and artists are saying the same thing, Kerrigan states: "These figures did not have 'the same thought,' their voices are not interchangeable; the passage [quoted from *The Mythic Image*] comes to little more than the free associations of an educated mind. . . . At such times, as if a spell had been lifted, this lovely book metamorphoses into a crude collage done with scissors and paste" ("Raw, Cooked" 655).

Campbell himself, moreover, does not deny either his scorn for those who insist upon narrowing their focus to a single culture or his filiations with an earlier brand of comparativism. He claims that it is the functionalists who ignore holism in their insistence upon discrete cultures and their neglect of the more comprehensive perspective upon human culture in total. In "Bios and Mythos," published in 1951, Campbell holds that the functionalist insistence upon "stressing the differences between the dialects of the common human language" (again, note the trope of polyvocality at work) wrongly rejects the comparativist belief in "the uniformity of mankind's 'Elementary Ideas.'"[19]

In "Bios and Mythos," Campbell pays tribute to Adolph Bastian for his work in bringing to light "the local manifestations of universal forms," and goes on to claim that "Tylor, Frazer, and the other comparative anthropologists, likewise recognized the obvious constancy in mankind's Elementary Ideas." To Campbell, "the result" of the rejection of the comparativist notion of uniformity "has been a complete dismemberment of what [before the 1920s] promised to become a science" (16). According to Campbell, "no learned amount of hair-splitting . . . can obscure the fact that the primary problem here is not historical or ethnological but psychological—even biological . . . and no amount of scholarly jargon or apparatus can make it seem that the mere historian or anthropologist is dealing with the problem" (17).

Again, Campbell creates or emphasizes institutional dichotomies (in this case, history and anthropology versus mythology) that compel a comprehensive view only possessed by the comparative mythologist. The distinction between the mere fact-grubbing and "hair-splitting" historian or ethnographer and the more comprehensive mythologist (whose activities are rooted in the, oddly enough, more trustworthy fields of psychology and biology) is further enhanced by the rhetorical tactic of opposing the activities of objective science and art. In the following quotation Campbell's forced opposition of science and art, like Frazer's, looks forward to the

comparativist whose artistically intuitive faculties afford a more comprehensive vista:

> Since in poetry and art, beyond the learning of rhetorical and manual
> techniques, the whole craft is that of seizing the idea and facilitating
> its epiphany, the creative mind, adequately trained, is less apt than the
> analytic to mistake a mere trope or concept for a living, life-awakening
> image. Poetry and art, whether "academic" or "modern," are simply
> dead unless informed by Elementary Ideas: ideas not as clear abstrac-
> tions held in the mind, but . . . vital factors of the subject's own being.
> . . . Their force lies not in what meets the eyes but in what dilates the
> heart, and this force, precisely, is their essential trait. Since mythology
> is the compendium of such ideas effective at any moment, the historian
> or anthropologist proud of his objective eye has been gelded of the
> organ that would have made it possible for him to distinguish his ma-
> terials. He may note and classify circumstances, but can no more speak
> authoritatively of mythology than a man without taste buds of taste.
> On the other hand, however, though the poet or the artist, with im-
> mediate recognition, experiences the idea and grows to meet it . . .
> he is finally an amateur in the fields of history and ethnology. ("Bios
> and Mythos" 18)

Of course, Campbell's segregation of art and science leads to the inexorable conclusion that only the comparative mythologist can fuse the clas-
sificatory function of science to the intuitive faculty necessary to apprehend
myth. Indeed, this rhetorical move is consistent with Campbell's larger
assumption that science itself is becoming more mythic, is, as he reports
in *The Power of Myth,* "breaking through now into the mystery dimensions" (132). In "Bios and Mythos" the shortcomings of each field (science,
art) are obviated as the mythologist joins what a postlapsarian world has
torn asunder. At the heart of Campbell's conception of the commonality
of poetry and myth and the incongruity of myth and social science is his
version of transcendent semiotics: the poetic mind, in tune with myth, in-
tuitively recognizes "mere trope" and casts it aside in the search for "life-
awakening image," just as history must be shunted aside in order to clear
the view for the "picture-message" of pure myth. The scientist, caught in
the confines of objective literalism, effeminately confuses metaphor for the
real thing. Poetry, like myth, is not in essence figural but transcendent;
thus the poet does not negotiate meaning through the medium of language
(or history, for that matter) but, rather, follows a beeline to an ultimate

meaning that is eminently nonlogical and subjective (associated, after all, with the "heart" over the "eyes" and, one can surmise, the head).

Campbell holds that Bastian's hierarchy of Elementary Ideas is essential, but believes that depth psychology, as initiated by Freud and Jung, "now makes it possible to go beyond Bastian's mere listing and description of the Elementary Ideas to a study of their biological roots" ("Bios and Mythos" 18). Like Frazer, Campbell here is mapping out an institutional space which he himself is eminently qualified to fill: a mythologist with a stress on essentialist ideas and a background in biologically based depth psychology. His anticipation of the criticism to be leveled at his method once again fortifies the lines drawn between scientist and artist, as well as objective and subjective, in the interest of staking out a distinctly comprehensive position from which the comparative mythologist can hold sway.

The appeal to the experiential suffuses Campbell's texts and plays a large part in their popularity. Indeed, a key to Campbell's rhetorical authority, similar and yet distinct from Clifford's notion of ethnographic authority, lies in the appeal of the authentic, the "lived through" or "lived in," and especially the "felt." In the opening chapter of Creative Mythology, entitled "Experience and Authority," for example, Campbell distinguishes creative from traditional mythology by associating the "experience" of the individual with the creative and the "authority" of "socially maintained rites" with the traditional (4). Necessary to this experiential appeal is the supposition that the text is a medium in which the signified, in this respect experience, shines transparently through. This version of semiotics is supported in Creative Mythology when Campbell claims that the individual's "communication of 'experience' "—"if his realization has been of a certain depth and import"—"will have the value and force of living myth" (4).

The direct transmission of the real most characteristically takes the form of the panoply of human voices, those "dialects of the common human language" ("Bios and Mythos" 18) that culminate in a wide polycultural chorus absent from the work of the hair-splitting specialist. But for Campbell, as for Frazer, beneath the aural variation there runs the dominating bass of authorial resolution (the "common" in those "dialects" of the language). For both, the chorus reduces to an overdetermined generalizing chord—for Frazer, evolutionary in nature, for Campbell, both evolutionary and universalist—in which the mythic signifiers are firmly blended into a signified system of belief. In the conclusion to Hero, Campbell trots out the trope of polyvocality in his expression of the authorial narrowing of many into one: " 'Truth is one,' we read in the Vegas; 'the sages call it by many names.' A single song is being inflected through the colorations of

the human choir. General propaganda for one or another of the local so-
lutions is superfluous—or much rather, a menace. The way to become
human is to recognize the lineaments of God in all of the wonderful
modulations of the face of man" (389–90).

Campbell deploys a strategy of containment aimed toward reducing
multiplicity and chaos to uniformity, harmony, and order. Meisel's description of *The Waste Land*'s strategy of aiming to "resolve its apparent fragments into an isomorphic symbolism that yokes all myths, all religions, all
literature in a serene and pacifying conclusion" (*Myth of the Modern* 87) well
approximates the tactic behind Campbell's comparativism. As with Eliot,
Frye, and Frazer, the signifiers of the cultural-mythic universe are many,
but the signified message is one.

RITUALIST UNDERPINNINGS

Though Campbell's strategies promote his rendition of myth as an ultimate
opening up to a signified message, a comprehensive widening that defies
exclusion of any mythic signifier, in fact Campbell's primary representations of myth are quite determined historically, largely fixed within the
fragile confines of evolutionary ritualism. His most pronounced inheritance
from that line of thinking concerns the fate of spiritual and mythic forces
within a culture in the process of becoming civilized. As they progress
most cultures, according to Campbell, progressively suck the might and
magic out of myths by reducing mythic figures to their contemporary cor-
relatives, logical and anthropomorphized versions of the mighty signified:

> In the later stages of many mythologies, the key images hide like nee-
> dles in great haystacks of secondary anecdote and rationalization; for
> when a civilization has passed from a mythological to a secular point
> of view, the older images are no longer felt or quite approved. In Hel-
> lenistic Greece and in Imperial Rome, the ancient gods were reduced
> to mere civic patrons, household pets, and literary favorites. Uncom-
> prehended inherited themes, such as that of the Minotaur—the dark
> and terrible night aspect of an old Egypto-Cretan representation of
> the incarnate sun god and divine king—were rationalized and rein-
> terpreted to suit contemporary ends. (HTF 248)

Like Frye and other mythic critics, Campbell clears the ground of the
messy tangle of historical and social particularities in order to get at the
root of the myth, the ur-myth itself, the transcendental signified of mythic
power. Campbell's anathema, the merely "local," rears its ugly head as

specific cultures express themselves in variation from the ur-signified, "to suit" their own petty "contemporary ends." But in fact Campbell's figuration of local culture's warping of myth overtly replicates the Frazerian and Cambridge-Hellenist representation of late Greek culture's shaping of earlier mythic content: from the more primal and "natural" representations of mythic content (those elemental vessels of mana), on to plant and animal representations, and finally to the more intellectualized and anthropomorphized versions (the Olympian "gods" themselves).

In the conclusion to *Hero*, "The Hero Today," Campbell asserts that the true task of the modern hero is to "discover the real cause for the disintegration of all of our inherited religious formulae." The cause of the collapse, Campbell then informs us, is that "the center of gravity . . . has definitely shifted." Where there was originally in "primitive hunting peoples" no "psychological" link to nature around them, "an unconscious identification took place, and this was finally rendered conscious in the half-human, half-animal, figures of the mythological totem-ancestors." From there "the tribes supporting themselves on plant-food became cathected to the plant." But eventually "both the plant and the animal worlds" were "brought under social control," and at that point "the great field of instructive wonder shifted—to the skies—and mankind enacted the great pantomime of the sacred moon-king, the sacred sun-king, and the symbolic festivals of the world-regulating spheres" (390).

Anyone who has read *The Golden Bough*, or Harrison's *Themis* for that matter, will immediately recognize the pattern. Campbell's rhetoric promotes the notion that the unfortunate transmission from the primal to the local-specific is, once recognized (thanks to Campbell), obvious to the eye and indisputable. What is of course not acknowledged is the extent to which Campbell's reading of mythic transmission is dependent upon long-discredited ritualist notions. Like Frye, Campbell does not realize that the political and social uses of myth that he so scornfully points to (local cultures selfishly and narrowmindedly reading myth "to suit contemporary ends") apply as fittingly to those who influenced him and, by extension, to himself.

Although Campbell does not hold the classical ritualist position that all myths can be traced to rituals (for that matter, neither does Frazer), nonetheless the attractions for Campbell of an evolutionary ritualist view that highlights the vital and sensual in a culture are clear. Figured in Cambridge-Hellenist writings and most mid-century myth criticism is a call for the revitalization of culture, achievable by tapping into the sources of prime spiritual energy, or mana. Like Eliot, though far more blatantly, Campbell puts forth his own call to revivify the original energies that have since been drained. "To bring the images back to life," Campbell pronounces, "one has to seek, not interesting applications to modern affairs, but illuminating hints from the inspired past. When these are found, vast areas of half-dead iconography disclose again their permanent meaning" (HTF 249).

Campbell's urging for a renewal of ancient mythic images recalls the search in *The Waste Land* for the originary spiritual source, the mana that reanimates culture. Indeed, Campbell's description of those images as corpses that are "half-dead" and need to be brought "back to life" is redolent of a controlling figure of "The Burial of the Dead," the corpse planted in the garden, whose "bloom" is crucial to rebirth. In both instances the rebirth works, in part, as a reversal of the flow from live spiritual energy to dead gods. In Eliot's case the transition between half-death ("feeding / A little life with dried tubers," ll. 6–7) and rebirth ("Has it begun to sprout," l. 72) is wound within a complex semiotics: in fact, reams of Eliot criticism have been devoted to the debate over whether the poem presents a rebirth at all. But for Campbell the journey becomes simply and plainly a matter of spontaneous translation, as "iconography"—what Campbell terms in this same context "picture language" (256)—dissolves, with fluoroscopic ease, into the ultimate signified of "permanently human meaning."[20]

The logocentric oneness at the heart of this ritualist conception of primitive spirituality becomes replicated in Campbell's text, as in Eliot's poetry, in the form of figures that precede the unfortunate fall into duality. To borrow from the language of "Mr. Eliot's Sunday Morning Service," Campbell laments the loss of the originary "Word" that "produced enervate Origen" and thus has passed from the one to the many and lost the capacity to contain contraries. In Campbell's work that nostalgic cause for lament is strikingly figured, as in Eliot's early poetry, in the image of the androgyne. Once the "feminine" was abstracted from the notion of the "androgynous," according to Campbell, we see "the beginning of the fall from perfection into duality . . . the devolvement of eternity into time, the breaking of the one into two and then the many" (HTF 153).

Not coincidentally, Campbell follows his statement on androgyny with a note that cites the example of Tiresias, the "blinded seer" who is "both male and female" (HTF 153). Striking here is the parallel to Eliot's treatment of Tiresias, whose status as androgyne, in whom "the two sexes meet," makes him "the most important personage in the poem, uniting all the rest" (*Collected Poems* 72). For Campbell, the androgyne, like the primal antithetical "Word" of both Freud and Eliot, precedes the division into dualities, in this case of male and female, and so functions as a valuable figure in his own effort to bring together the fragments that the dissociation has torn asunder. Campbell's discussion of "Primal Bisexual Divinity" and androgyny in *The Way of the Animal Powers* (173–75) and his treatment of the "primal androgyne" in *Oriental Mythology* bear out this interest.[21]

In *Hero* the two myths Campbell initially provides as examples of the fall into the later "rationalized" attitude toward mythology concern fire-sticks, recalling again Rendel-Harris's treatment as chronicled by Eliot. The first, in which a hero escapes from the belly of a whale by making a fire, is interpreted by Campbell as follows: "Fire-making in this manner is symbolic of the sex act. The two sticks—socket stick and spindle—are known respectively as the female and the male; the flame is the newly generated life. The hero making fire in the whale is a variant of the sacred marriage" (248).

But the second tale, an Eskimo story in which Raven escapes from the whale, Campbell interprets as a "modification" of the "fire-making image" that helps to prepare for his point on the unfortunate transition from the "mythological to a secular point of view" (248). In that tale, according to Campbell, "the original fire sticks having become superfluous, a clever and amusing epilogue was invented to give them a function in the plot."

The primary function of both Eliot's and Campbell's use of fire-sticks/snakes is to chart the coordinates of the sexual-spiritual evolution, or devolution in this case, that progressively drains the vitality out of the mythic representation. The sexual fusion that creates the mythic fire, however, functions as a representation of the even more primal fusion of sexes figured in androgyny, the double- (or neither-) sexed version of ultimate spirit that Campbell refers to as "the first wonder of the Bodhisattva: the androgynous character of the presence" (HTF 162). In that ultimate state of androgyny, Campbell claims, two critical mythic functions, "the Meeting with the Goddess and the Atonement with the Father," come together (162), just as in *The Waste Land* the meeting with the Hyacinth Girl and the Test of the Thunders are the determining factors for the quester's salvation. Indeed, this fundamental meeting of male and female Campbell saw as integral to *Finnegans Wake* as well. In *A Skeleton Key*, Campbell claims that "HCE and ALP represent a primordial male-female polarity, which is basic to all life" (11). Referring to the anniversary at the end of Joyce's book, Campbell holds that "*despite* the complexity of HCE and ALP" (italics my own), "together they constitute the primordial, androgynous angel, which is Man, the incarnate God" (13).

Like Eliot, Campbell sees the return to the ultimate androgynous spirit-state as possible through an opening up to "Oriental" religion. Note, again, that Campbell's version of androgynous presence is the Bodhisattva. And in *Hero* Campbell holds that "the modern thinker wishing to know the meaning of a world religion (i.e., of a doctrine of universal love) must turn his mind to the other great (and much older) universal communion: that of the Buddha, where the primary word still is peace—peace to all beings" (159).

While Oriental religion in *Hero* is represented as a window to the comprehensive universal (as discussed below, this view will change in later works), Occidental religion is figured as insufficient precisely because it is narrow-mindedly "local," unable to liberate itself from social context. Campbell holds that the religions of the West fail because they are dominated by what Campbell calls in *Creative Mythology* "the priestly orthodox mind," which is "always and everywhere focused upon the local, culturally conditioned rendition" (8). The answer, Campbell baldly states in *Hero*, lies in opening oneself to the archetypal, in this case to the power of love:

> Once we have broken free of the prejudices of our own provincially limited ecclesiastical, tribal, or national rendition of the world archetypes, it becomes possible to understand that the supreme initiation is not that of the local motherly fathers, who then project aggression onto the neighbors for their own defense. The good news, which the World Redeemer brings . . . is that God is love, that He can be, and is to be, loved, and that all without exception are his children. . . . The World Savior's cross, in spite of the behavior of its professed priests, is a vastly more democratic symbol than the local flag. (158–59)

That Christianity at its best (which is, at its most universal) is figured as "democratic symbol" indicates just how ideologically fixed and locally determined Campbell's "universalism" really is. Campbell himself becomes, as translator into a mythic Esperanto, a spiritual version in human form of the United Nations. The mythographer, by standing on the heads of the priests, has become the empowered channel through which we pass on to the great universal.

Campbell's self-defined role as conduit to the Great Spirit hearkens back to Bedient's version of Eliot as architect of a poem whose signifiers all point to the otherworldly, the "unsignifiable." Again useful is Eagleton's point that the signifiers of Eliot's poem fail to link precisely in order that the poem's highly ideological "meaning" remains surreptitiously preserved. Just as Eliot's message of unutterable peace ("Shantih   shantih   shantih") is bracketed within an ideology of containment and conservatism, so Campbell's vision of mythic universalism functions as an ethnocentric valorization of Western power mechanisms: the privileged ability, arising from Western cultural expansion, to exercise a comparative method; "democracy" itself as ultimate religious standard; "Love" as translated, controlled, distributed by the comparative mythographer; gender pared down to the "androgynous angel, which is Man" (sk 13).

Campbell's rhetoric, like Frazer's, promotes a feint of openness and plurality that, in this case, graciously admits the Other—the woman, the Oriental—in order to appropriate it. Although, according to Lefkowitz, Campbell's portrait of mythic woman emphasizes her supportive role (earth mother, child bearer: "Myth of Campbell" 422–23), sexual difference is eliminated, quashed, in the journey toward the unsignifiably androgynous. Similarly, in the journey toward spirit, the "Oriental" is taken out of the Oriental, as all religions meld into a lump of prime spiritual energy. All the mythic signifiers, according to Campbell, have no value per se but, rather, illustrate "with clarity the anthropomorphic powers in the realm of myth. They are not ends in themselves, but guardians, embodiments, or bestowers, of the liquor, the milk, the food, the fire, the grace, of indestructible life" (HTF 173). We do not see the unsignifiable milk, food, fire, however. What we are left with is the trace of the journey toward that ineffable mana, a path that bears the signature of the pathfinder. The drive toward the absence of nation, gender, and religion effectively functions as a logocentric tactic of assimilation. For it is only the author who, by a self-created contagion, wields the mana that proceeds from the sacred source.

The Politics of Myth

Campbell's ideological aspiration as set before us in the preface to *Hero* is integrally tied to his method: "my hope is that a comparative elucidation may contribute to the perhaps not-quite-desperate cause of those forces that are working in the present world for unification, not in the name of ecclesiastical or political empire, but in the sense of mutual human understanding" (viii). Comparative arrangement, the compiling of the multiple voices and sources of various cultures, reveals the truth about human fellowship. The task as set before us is great indeed: "a transmutation of the whole social order is necessary," Campbell states near the end of *Hero* (389). And Campbell's rhetoric makes clear that only through a comparative lens is such a vision of unified humanity possible.

For Campbell, the unification of the world's peoples has self-evident, ultimate value; it is ideologically timeless (unrelated to current, local, or national trends) and pure (note, for example, how his motives are presented as untainted by colonialism, as having no link to the Western expansion and dominance that makes his comparative culture-reading possible). In fact, as Florence Sandler and Darrell Reeck point out, Campbell's *Hero* was popular with its audience in part because "appearing as it did in the aftermath of the Second World War, the book reads as a sincere attempt to demonstrate the similarities of the mythical traditions and thus enhance 'mutual human understanding.'"[22] What Sandler and Reeck do not explicitly suggest is that the postwar climate that gave birth to the United Nations was actually formative in shaping Campbell's "universalist" perspective.

One striking example of the period-bound nature of Campbell's universalism is found in the 1950s and 1960s, when his ideology of unification takes a different turn. The opening to "The Separation of East and West" (composed in 1961, appearing in *Oriental Mythology* and later in *Myths to Live By*) lays the groundwork for a new dichotomization of East and West:

> It is not easy for Westerners to realize that the ideas recently developed in the West of the individual, his selfhood, his rights, and his freedom, have no meaning whatsoever in the Orient. They had no meaning for primitive man. They would have meant nothing to the peoples of the early Mesopotamian, Egyptian, Chinese, or Indian civilizations. . . . And yet . . . they are the truly great "new thing" that we do indeed represent to the world and that constitutes our Occidental revelation of a properly human spiritual ideal, true to the highest potentiality of our species. (MTLB 61)

The easy conflation of "primitive" to "Oriental," and the equation of Western individualism to the higher reaches of the species, reveal some evolutionist assumptions inherited from turn-of-the-century social theory and anthropology (Tylor, Frazer, the Cambridge Hellenists, Leo Frobenius, Spengler).[23] The call for liberty of spirit, it is true, correlates to Campbell's earlier condemnation of the priestly class (then figured as Occidental) that has denied individuals of their potentials, but now Campbell's ire is directed toward the Oriental, rather than the Western, Other.

Campbell gives to his vilification of Oriental Other a pseudo-social-scientific (historical, anthropological) foundation that is, again, anchored in an earlier brand of social evolutionism. Essentially, the Oriental is tied to the ideology of a prehistorical period and thus, quite simply, has not sufficiently evolved: "the great point I most want to bring out is that this early Bronze Age concept of a socially manifest cosmic order, to which every individual must uncritically submit if he is to be anything at all, is fundamental in the Orient—one way or the other—to this day" (MTLB 65).

In *Oriental Mythology,* the second volume of *The Masks of God,* Campbell's opinion of the Oriental is based upon an oddly skewed reading of world history that prefers prehistoric hunting cultures over agricultural ones: Orientals, we are to believe, derive primarily from the agricultural cultures. The cultivators, according to Campbell, embody the passive and sacrificial aspects of culture that gave rise to the Bronze Age and produced the priestly class, which in turn bound religion to the morality of fully anthropomorphized, removed gods. Campbell prefers the hunting class because, in brief, it preserves the vitality of "primitive" worship that was lost with the postlapsarian predominance of "moral authorities." As Sandler and Reeck point out, for Campbell the liberating mentality of the hunter is figured in "the bands of lusty barbarians, usually Aryans (Greeks, Vedic Indians, Celts, and Germans), who erupt into civilization from time to time, usually on horseback, usually as smashers and destroyers, but all the same self-sufficient and freedom-loving. Their religion does not bind them to the collective super-ego, and therefore does not fill them with guilt and moral intolerance" ("Masks of Campbell" 12).

Campbell's cultural, ethnic, and religious divisions fan out from this highly dubious evolutionist reading of world culture. Orientals differ from Westerners in their steadfast cleaving to the "collective superego"; at the same time, the Germanic tribal mentality of individualism is distinguished from both the Oriental and Levantine mentality of sacrifice that encourages the formation of priest classes and states. As Sandler and Reeck indicate, the ideological filiations of Campbell's rhetoric are frightening: "to differentiate the freedom-loving non-state-forming Germano-Celtic type from the state-and-priest-ridden Levantine is so transparent a revival of the old prejudice of Aryan culture against Jewish that one blushes for an author so disingenuous, especially when that author knows and deplores Nazi politics" ("Masks of Campbell" 15).

The recent controversy over Campbell's alleged anti-Semitism, surfacing in editorials in *The New York Review of Books* and *The New Yorker,* is then nothing new to one who has read with care Campbell's corpus.[24] And yet the point really is not that Campbell, in what he thought were small and safe private audiences, seems to have passed on anti-Jewish anecdotes; more pressing and fundamental is the kind of dichotomizing that constitutes and remains inscribed in his extremely popular writings. Intention is not the issue (certainly Campbell was not purposefully establishing a parallel between his set of contrasts and those of Hitler). More to the point is that his entire rhetoric matches quite neatly the structure of Said's Orientalism, described by Clifford as the "tendency to *dichotomize* the human continuum into we-they contrasts and to *essentialize* the resultant 'other'—to speak of the Oriental mind, for example" (PC 258). Said's attacks on "essences and oppositional distinctions" (PC 274) apply only too fittingly to Campbell's self-constructed dichotomies, "primitive" versus "civilized," Oriental versus Occidental, Aryan versus Oriental and Levantine.

Campbell's Orientalist rhetoric surfaces most blatantly in the conclusion to *Oriental Mythology*, and indeed it is here where we find the underpinnings of the anti-Orientalist rhetoric of the 1950s and 1960s. Campbell's fiercely antagonist responses to Communist China and, more important, the generalizations on the Orient that proceed from his contemplation of China's reception of communism, tell much about this turn against the Oriental mind:[25]

> The first point of interest here for the student of mythology is that there has taken place a juncture between the old Chinese yin-yang dichotomy and the dialectical materialism of Marx. And, as many manifestations in the modern Orient suggest, there is in the Oriental mind a deep sense of affinity with the Marxist view. . . . The notion of a cosmic law is disregarded as irrelevant, but that of law in human affairs is retained: a law to be known to be followed, without the necessity or even possibility of individual choice and freedom of decision. So that, whereas formerly it was the priest, the reader of the stars, who knew and taught the Law, now it is the student of society. (507)

Campbell's interpretation of the Oriental reception to communism points up, again, the evolutionary immaturity of the Oriental mind: it has not had "to face the crucial Occidental problem of what Dr. C. G. Jung has termed individuation" (*Oriental Mythology* 507). But when the Marxist is equated to the law-enforcing priest, the Oriental shifts from being harmlessly backward to dangerous, even horrifying. Chinese communists are to be dreaded because they are forcing themselves "into the modern world on wholly modern terms" (507). In one important sense, they will no longer remain comfortably marked off as "primitive," "exotic," "fading" from view, so become instead the threatening Other.

Sandler and Reeck refer to Campbell's treatment of the Oriental in *Oriental Mythology* as "Cold War Rhetoric" ("Masks of Campbell" 13). Like the ideology of unification surfacing just after the Second World War, Campbell's packaging of the deadly threat of Chinese communism follows a decade of rightist dichotomizing ideology in the United States. Once again, Campbell presents local, nation-bound ideology as a universalist statement that transcends the petty ideologies of the local, the nation-bound. Specifically, Campbell's strong ideological response has been triggered, we find out at the conclusion of *Oriental Mythology,* by horror stories from the Orient, accounts of atrocities by the communist Chinese.

This final chapter, entitled sardonically "Tibet: The Buddha and the New Happiness," serves as an interesting example of Campbell's variety of comparativist rhetoric. Here Campbell, like Frazer, quotes from and paraphrases a plethora of sources that build to seemingly irrefutable, and oftentimes implicit, generalizations on the nature of the "Oriental" mind. Multiple voices of the sufferers are vented, evoking tales of murder, torture, rape, and horrifying scientific experimentation; those voices are carefully placed against each other and against Campbell's own editorializing comment. After quoting from an account of people burned alive and crucified, Campbell mentions Mao's "All Power . . . to the Peasant's Association" (*Oriental Mythology* 510). Quoting from an eyewitness account of a public execution by shooting, Campbell places the powerful line "as their brains spattered the Chinese called them the flowers in bloom" against " 'Let a thousand flowers bloom,' wrote Mao Tse-Tung, 'and let a hundred schools of thought contend' " (513). The careful selection of quotation and retort is belied by the powerful impression, calculated on Campbell's part, of multiple sources giving way to universal truths. As example is heaped upon example, quotation layered upon quotation, Campbell's rhetoric, like Frazer's, is calculated upon the belief that the more "facts" that are produced, the truer the generalizations drawn from those examples become. Kerrigan is speaking of such a rhetorical tactic when stating that Campbell "collects coincidences with great rapidity until, incapable of explaining away every one of them, opponents forfeit their skepticism" ("Raw, Cooked" 651).

The last of Campbell's examples (and he reminds us there are many more: "the reports go on and on") recounts Tibetan monks "taken to the fields, yoked together in pairs, pulling a plow, under the supervision of a Chinese who carried a whip" (*Oriental Mythology* 515). In the paragraph that follows, Campbell explains how, in the Tibetan Book of the Dead, a lama counsels the soul "to recognize all the forms beheld as projections of its own consciousness." The lama says of the time when the soul encounters visions from hell, " 'Fear not, fear not, O nobly born! The Furies of the Lord of Death will place around your neck a rope and drag you along; cut off your head, extract your heart, pull out your intestines, lick up your brains, drink your blood, eat your flesh, and gnaw your bones; but in reality, your body is of the nature of voidness; you need not be afraid' " (515).

Campbell makes no explicit comment on the purport of his selection from the Book of the Dead, or of its connection to the account of the tortured monks, but the message comes clear: the monks typify that mentality of sacrifice that sadly deemphasizes individual initiative and thus encourages state formation.[26]

While the monks are represented as members of the wretched and foolish cult of sacrifice, not unlike Western Christian ascetic groups, Campbell figures the Chinese communists as Furies of the Lord of Death. With broad strokes, Campbell paints a grandly staged mythic allegory of the good (the Westerner who *has* achieved individuation), the bad (the modern Oriental communist), and the indifferent (the silent, suffering Tibetan monks). But, like Frazer's allegorizing, Campbell's figuration is posed as the truth come plain and simple. In the paragraph following the quotation from the Tibetan Book of the Dead, Campbell presents his highly skewed reading of Oriental culture as the virtual manifestation of myth, the fluoroscopic visualization of the grand mythic structure: "And with this sobering, terrifying vision of the whole thing come true, the materialization of mythology in life, I shall close—in silence; for no Western mind can comment on these two aspects of the one great Orient in terms appropriate to the Orient itself, which, as far as any words from its leading contemporary minds would seem to show, is rather proud and hopeful of both" (*Oriental Mythology* 516).

Campbell's concluding "in silence" represents an ultimate Frazerian ploy: his own figuration is figured as pure representation, so that the author himself is posed as a speechless conduit to mythic truth (after we have seen the pictures, what is there to say?). And the author promotes his own humility by flourishing a bow to the voices of an Orient that he himself has created (we mere Westerners are not capable of talking about Orientals, but this is what they say about themselves).

In the book's concluding paragraph, Campbell extends his gesture of humility to Oriental mythology, "the one timeless doctrine of eternal life" (*Oriental Mythology* 516). And yet, in speaking of that doctrine as "the nectar of the fruit of the tree that Western man . . . failed to eat" (516), Campbell closes his volume with firm separate-but-equal rhetoric that announces implicitly, "and thank God we didn't take that bite." Instead, Campbell's next two volumes of *The Masks of God* (*Occidental Mythology* and *Creative Mythology*) tend to applaud the Western mythic mind. As Sandler and Reeck testify, Campbell at this stage of his career shifts his interest from East to West "to celebrate the Western worldview and a hero like Parzival whose style is not dissolution [like the suffering monks] but individuation, and who will be nobody's victim" ("Masks of Campbell" 14). Though Parzival the knight is but one of a number of figures who exemplify for Campbell Western individualism, as quester he is highly appropriate for Campbell's ideological purposes. For Parzival becomes a powerful signifier of Campbell's creative mythologist, who, like the knight, must go on a dangerous quest through the wasted modern world in search of the Grail of mythic meaning. That Campbell in *Creative Mythology* would allude to Eliot in his articulation of this allegory is only appropriate: "In Christian Europe, already in the twelfth century, beliefs no longer universally held were universally enforced. The result was a dissociation of professed from actual existence and that consequent spiritual disaster which, in the imagery of the Grail legend, is symbolized in the Waste Land theme" (5).

Campbell borrows from Eliot the notion of *dissociation* to indicate, as did Eliot, a spiritual-material split in civilized consciousness: little matter that one sites that split in the twelfth century and the other in the seventeenth. In both cases the dichotomization is figured in the loss of the Grail itself; and in both cases the knight must restore a spiritual-mythic wholeness to existence. The dissociative quality in *The Waste Land* is discussed by Campbell throughout his career. When Bill Moyers, in *The Power of Myth,* talks about "the curse of modern society, the impotence, the ennui that people feel," Campbell responds with, "this is exactly T. S. Eliot's *The Waste Land* that you are describing, a sociological stagnation of inauthentic lives and living that has settled upon us, and that evokes nothing of our spiritual life" (131).

In *Creative Mythology* the quester as knight is made to signify the creative mythologist, the author who initiates a new mythology to give the modern world meaning, or, to put it in Eliot's words, "makes the modern world possible for art." Indeed, in *Creative Mythology* the modern questers are figured as the literary Modernists (Joyce, Mann, Eliot), who like "young people today" are "facing in their minds, seriously, the same adventure as thirteenth century Gottfried [another knight-quester]: challenging hell" (38). Campbell parallels the careers of Mann and Joyce according to their proximity to mythic patterns of heroic quest. Early works by both, for example, figure as "accounts of the separation of a youth from the social nexus of his birth to strive to realize a personal destiny" (38–39). Campbell then creates a narrative of the life experience of the hero-Modernist that shaped his later literary masterpieces: "He will have arrived in this world in one place or another, at one time or another, to unfold, in the conditions of his time and place, the autonomy of his nature. And in youth, though imprinted with one authorized brand or another of the Western religious heritage, in one or another of its historic states of disintegration, he will have conceived the idea of thinking for himself, peering through his own eyes, heeding the compass of his own heart" (40). Significantly, Campbell's own history quite neatly fits the pattern that he has constructed: Campbell rejected the Catholicism of his youth and constructed his own mythic symbology. The ideal of individualism becomes a vessel for the ultimate aggrandizement of the self.

Campbell's essentializing portrait of Western individualism functions, then, as allegorically as his conception of Oriental submissiveness. It is not only a matter of Campbell's creating his own Orientalism as a useful tool for the promulgation of Western ideology, rather, both East and West ultimately serve the purposes of a strategy conceived by the omnipotent culture-reader. And the portrait of the West that Campbell paints sells not because it is true but because it flatters the Westerner. This is especially true of Campbell's depiction of America as mythic site and source. It can come as no surprise that Campbell's promotion of the individual and condemnation of the submissive and sacrificial should be intimately related to a celebration of mythic America. As Sandler and Reeck relate, "Wolfram's Parzival may be the paradigm for modern man in general, but as the *parvenu*, pursuing his chivalric quest according to his own sense of direction to become the deliverer of Anfortas and be recognized as the new Grail king, he is the paradigm for American man in particular" ("Masks of Campbell" 16).

Campbell does view the ascendancy of America as the introduction of a special mythic force, and yet he also states that the American myth functions as a paradigm for myths to come. In *The Power of Myth* Campbell, holding to the need for "myths that will identify the individual not with his local group but with the planet," goes on to claim that "a model for that is the United States. Here were thirteen different little colony nations that decided to act in the mutual interest, without disregarding the individual interests of any of them" (24). Campbell illustrates the mythic significance of the American experience with a score of high-flying numerological parallels that enter into the whacky and occultish. For example, waxing on the significance of the Great Seal of the United States as it is displayed on the dollar bill, Campbell claims,

> When you count the number of ranges on this pyramid, you find there are thirteen. And when you come to the bottom, there is an inscription in Roman numerals. It is, of course, 1776. Then, when you add one and seven and seven and six, you get twenty-one, which is the age of

reason, is it not? It was in 1776 that the thirteen states declared independence. The number thirteen is the number of transformation and rebirth. At the Last Supper there were twelve apostles and one Christ, who was going to die and be reborn. Thirteen is the number of getting out of the field of the bounds of twelve into the transcendent. You have the twelve signs of the zodiac and the sun. (25)

In Campbell's mythical-magical universe, America has stood to signify the "eye of the pyramid" on the Seal that can see all impartially (PM 25–28). Contrary to Sandler and Reeck's claim, Campbell's promulgation of a superior mythic America does *not* simply translate into a paean to America's status as newfound world power. Indeed, in *The Power of Myth* Campbell holds that with America's entry into the First World War, "we canceled the Declaration of Independence and rejoined the conquest of the planet. And so we are on one side of the pyramid. We've moved from one to two. . . . We do not represent the principle of the eye up there" (28).

In a sense the loss of a mythic America is necessary to the authorial program of the comparative mythographer who, like Joyce or Eliot as creative mythologist, requires a wasted civilization that can then be reconstructed. The nostalgic appeal to the lost wholeness of American life parallels Campbell's logocentric impulse to reclaim the indivisible unity of the androgynous spiritual source. It is significant in this sense that we have moved from "one to two" in our fall from mythic grace. And of course Campbell's program strongly suggests the rhetorical dynamics of *The Waste Land.* Tiresias is the equivalent of that mythic eye, the "spectator" (see Eliot's Notes) seeing all, in whom "the two sexes meet," in whom the two have rolled back to the one. But Tiresias is old and impotent; like America he has lost the full power of myth: so enter the author, whose genius at arrangement can evoke the forces to recall us.

In Campbell's vision of fallen America, the rhetoric of the comparative mythologist as pedagogue, as great mythic teacher, is most explicitly at work. According to Campbell in *Myths to Live By,* with the loss of belief in the old myths, enforced by traditional society, "there is nothing secure to hold on to, no moral law, nothing firm" (10). Citing the collapse of "primitive communities unsettled by the white man's civilization" (again, trotting out the allegory of extinction), Campbell proclaims, "Today the same thing is happening to us. With our old mythologically founded taboos unsettled by our own modern sciences, there is everywhere in the civilized world a rapidly rising incidence of vice and crime, mental disorders, suicides and dope addictions, shattered homes, impudent children, violence, murder, and despair" (11). The evolutionary nature of his use of "primitive communities" becomes clear: we, after all, are just like primitives in our general behavioral patterns, only more evolved: and it is important that we keep evolving to keep the distance between us. In this respect, Campbell sounds much like Frazer when he tells Moyers that "by overcoming the dark passions, the hero symbolizes our ability to control the irrational savage within us" (PM xiv).[27]

Ironically, what's right about America, the nonbinding individualism, the breaking free from enforced group belief, is also what's wrong. In "Bios and Mythos" Campbell laments both the loss of traditional social cohesion that comes with the fall of the old mythologies and the maladjustment that follows: "Hence we find today, after some five hundred years of the systematic dismemberment and rejection of the mythological organ of our species, all the sad young men, for whom life is a problem" (22). What aimless "young men" need, Campbell claims in a conversation with Moyers, is the swift kick in the rear that a traditional (read here, primitive) society, through its rituals, provides:

> MOYERS: What happens when a society no longer embraces a powerful mythology?
> CAMPBELL: What we've got on our hands. If you want to find out what it means to have a society without any rituals, read the *New York Times*.
> MOYERS: And you'd find?
> CAMPBELL: The news of the day, including destructive and violent acts by young people who don't know how to behave in a civilized society.
> MOYERS: Society has provided them no rituals by which they become members of the tribe, the community . . .
> CAMPBELL: That's exactly it. That's the significance of the puberty rites. In primal societies, there are teeth knocked out, there are scarifications, there are circumcisions, there are all kinds of things done. So you don't have your little baby body anymore, you're something else entirely. (PM 8)

Andrew Klavan, after quoting from the above conversation, retorts: "Those young people! Bring back Torquemada with his powerful mythology, his rituals, his civilized society—and, oh yeah, those hot pincers too."[28] Now Campbell, given his hatred of organized religion, ought not to be described as an apologist for the Inquisition. And yet he certainly does hold up ritualized violence as a model and articulates it as such, and he appears to relish its effects upon the unruly young.

Campbell's tips on returning to primal disciplinary tactics most blatantly reveal the particular ideological underpinnings of his mythography; but to assert, as does Klavan, that by the time of *The Power of Myth* Campbell had "followed the path of his study into dogma" severely oversimplifies the issue and bypasses the purport of the anthropological authority that runs throughout his works. Klavan, in claiming that in Campbell's case "a scholar of mythology becomes a guru and forgets that he is just another teller of the tale" ("Myth Master" 62), is mistakenly assuming that Campbell before the late stages of his career was simply telling stories, giving vent to the multiple voices of myth. Rather, the multiplicity of voice in *A Skeleton Key* and *Hero* operated through a comparativism that strained the multiple chords to an even frequency of ideology.

The only feature that stays substantially the same in Campbell's corpus is the authorial rhetoric that dissolves the disparate mythic sources and voices into sameness. As with Frye, the social criticism that operates out of the later work is deeply embedded in the early literary criticism; the semantics of that criticism may shift, but the rhetorical structure stays the same. The self-serving dichotomies persist but with different tags attached: "fact" versus "symbol," historian versus mythologist, Aryan versus Semite, Oriental versus Westerner. In each case whole entities are divided so that the comparativist may step in and become the agent who fluroscopically mediates them. Like Frazer, Eliot, and Frye, Campbell as comparative culture-reader divides only to bind the world.

Afterword

In this book I delineate how the participants in the rhetoric of authority (to borrow from Fredric Jameson) "construct the objects of their study and the 'strategies of containment' whereby they are able to project the illusion that their readings are somehow complete and self-sufficient."[1] In the case of Frazerian comparativism, each writer, whether anthropologist, literary artist, critic, or mythologist, projects the illusion of comprehensiveness and autonomy through the welding of several rhetorical tactics: profusion of voice and source funneling to the single authorial chord; transparency and transcendency masking incessant figuring; hard "facts" and overarching theories shielding time-bound notions and delimiting ideologies.

And yet any study of the operations of such an authority must contend with the question of whether reading the texts of these authors in terms of rhetorical authority is not itself a strategy of containment, whereby I achieve completeness and self-sufficiency by drawing a linguistic or semiotic circle around the texts and the cultural phenomena that fall within their purview. I do not wish to avoid the contentiousness of the issue, but I have to admit that on a certain level any act or inscription of cultural criticism is a delimiting process. I also must conclude, however, along the lines of Jameson, that even if I were to agree that texts do not have ultimate primacy (there *is* a world out there), they nonetheless are the most telling manifestations of the ideologies that shape culture. In the simplest of terms, only through texts and the rhetoric that shapes them can we begin to grasp the cultural forces that animate them—Jameson terms this process "the unmasking of cultural artifacts as socially symbolic acts" (*Political Unconscious* 20)—and thus perceive continuities between them.

Some might maintain that by persistently reading cultural representations in terms of their authorial dominance and seeking out their "socially symbolic" functions we lose the appreciation of an ennobling and pleasurable aesthetic (perhaps even metaphysical) experience. Such analyses of power, some might say, truly drain the "mythic" power of texts like *The Golden Bough* and *Four Quartets*. In this respect I am in agreement with

Gould, whose assertions on the genuine fascination readers (including myself) have with texts that enter into the mythic is firmly grounded in the assumption that "we have no meaning without interpretive processes" (*Mythical Intentions* 7). Knowing that the mystery of mythic moments in text are grounded in a semiology does not nullify the awe we feel when, as Gould notes, we encounter the "tautology" of myth that attempts to close the "ontological gap between event and meaning" (6).

Still, this volume, in its insistence upon authorial rhetoric, attempts to illumine the modes by which these four authors appropriate such mythic moments in narrative. Fundamental to my approach is the notion that such transcendent textual moments are constructed and therefore (apart from any narrow sense of intentionality) are usable and used by the authors who do the constructing. But this is not to say that the authors involved in building mythic moments are incapable of generating responses that can undercut their own authorial powers or motives, or that they are prevented from creating "gaps" that leave themselves, and their subsequent readers, wondering for some time to come what has happened. Of course some authors are better than others at leaving these gaps or fissures of potent undecidability open—Eliot in this respect, along with Joyce, goes much further than Campbell or Frye. And in any case such openings, into which the author and reader may momentarily vanish, are fleeting: "We know that such disappearances in reading and writing are never final," Gould reminds us (*Mythical Intentions* 133). What endures, after such vanishings, is the signature of the acclaimed author.

In another important sense I have also run the risk of repeating the strategy I disclose: the persistent reading of difference as similarity. This is why I do not claim that Campbell and Eliot have the same thoughts, are inscribing the same things, or should be held in the same regard for that matter (like Frye, I thinly veil my valuations, so it is not hard to discern my respect for Eliot's complex hermeneutic sense and my impatience with Campbell's fairly simplistic semiotics). I have earnestly tried not to dodge some clear and fundamental dissimilarities. For example, on a certain basic level Frazer was an evolutionist in ways that Campbell, Frye, and certainly Eliot were not. Frazer was an ardent secularist, whereas Eliot and Frye were committed church members, and Campbell propounded a broader belief that scorned cleavage to particular faiths. But, as I hope this book has made clear, differences exist alongside similarities, and in some cases mask even more essential similarities, such as the powerful rhetoric of evolutionism, the pattern of the anthropomorphization of totems, and the semiotics of transcendence that run through the texts of all four authors.

Disclosing the rhetoric of authorial dominance has been a primary concern here, and in this respect I have participated in a "post"-critique of so called postmodern anthropological aspirations, especially in my insistence that profusion of voice can serve the interests of authorial dominance. Clifford's promotion of polyvocality in anthropology, for example, does not sufficiently account for the power relations at work in the joining of voices. In this respect Paul Rabinow's characterization of the new anthropology's "specific historical constraints" indicates the narrative of progress at work: "Experimentalists (almost all male) are nurturing and optimistic, if just a touch sentimental. Clifford claims to be working from a combination of sixties idealism and eighties irony. Textual radicals seek to work toward establishing relationships, to demonstrate the importance of connection and openness, while being fuzzy about power and the realities of socioeconomic constraints."[2]

And yet even if one were to grant the justness of such critiques, an equally just reply might be made to a study such as mine: once I have exposed the will to power at work in the inscription of anthropological encounter, how do I justify further cultural representation? Is there, quite simply, no way ethically and accurately to compare and assess cultures? Does the very representation of cultural subjects, in this case in a comparative framework, translate inevitably into forced figurations of them? And what does that say about writings (such as mine) that put into question others' discursive efforts to represent?

These important (though perhaps in some cases simplistic) questions cannot all be answered here, but they are addressed in current anthropological theory. Stephen Tyler's conception of an ethnography of evocation, whereby the anthropologist does not hope to "represent" but rather "evokes," represents an interesting, and conspicuously postmodern, response to the dilemma. For Tyler, stressing "dialogue" over "monologue," collaboration over control, notes that "evocation is neither presentation or representation. It presents no objects and represents none. . . . It is thus beyond truth and the judgment of performance." But critiques of Tyler's alternative have stressed other problems. Marilyn Strathern discerns in Tyler's reconception of anthropology a "hidden aesthetic form," in which the anthropologist, despite the removal of "representation," is still the "tourist" of other cultures and thus at center stage. "The journey takes place for one person," Strathern remarks, "It is the traveler in whom the experiences of these locations are juxtaposed who becomes renewed."[3]

There is no ready answer to the conclusion I find implied in Strathern's response: that any and all cultural readings inevitably foreground the author, that a true dialogic encounter with otherness is unattainable. And yet

I think a modulation of my own tone of urgency is necessary here. Cultural observation is always a hermeneutic process always already enmeshed in discourse, but that certainly does not mean that crosscultural encounter cannot be useful, enriching, exciting, entertaining. When we begin calling it "science," however, we need to pose different kinds of questions, having to do with, among other things, the applicability of scientific paradigms to the social realm, the limits or shifting bases of empirical validation as applied to the study of human population, and the possible motives for transplanting the status of scientific activity (scientism) to the social sciences. These issues have been with anthropology since its inception, and further responses to them demand a complexity and length that I cannot take on here. More to the point is that my own persistent analysis of the rhetorical power at work in cultural representation does not mean to suggest that all forms of comparative culture reading are to be shunned. But I do hold that this particular strain of comparativism, given its roots in evolutionary theory and colonial encounter, its persistent focus upon maintaining an elitist power structure, and its power to appeal to fairly large masses of the population, has quite hazardous effects and deserves serious attention.

But, again, it needs to be asserted that all types of comparativism neither work in these rhetorical patterns nor produce these effects. Indeed, the focus of this book is not comparativism as a whole, or even more specifically, comparative anthropology. While I discount the impact upon the humanities of comparative studies in anthropology after Malinowski, and I make clear that such studies represent a deviation in the norm of anthropology from 1922 to the present, comparative studies do exist in substantial form: in the whole-culture comparisons of Mead and Benedict; in the "controlled comparisons" method, in which a study is made of a few neighboring or related communities; in larger regional studies, initiated by Boas, in which cultural ties are brought to light through statistical distribution analysis; and in the form that inherits most from the classical comparativism of Tylor and Frazer, the crosscultural survey method, in which worldwide comparisons of cultures are made (the Human Research Area Files located at Yale University serve as a prominent example).[4] Nor does this book encompass the entire rhetoric of the comparative method as originating in evolutionary anthropology. If it were the latter, certainly other figures could have been included in more extensive discussion: William Robertson Smith, Emile Durkheim and Lucien Lévy-Bruhl, the Cambridge Hellenists (most notably Jane Harrison), Francis Fergusson, Heinrich Zimmer, S. E. Hyman and other prominent myth critics of the 1950s and 1960s, and others.

Perhaps the authors selected were chosen because it is hard to imagine four Anglo-American comparativists who are more notable in their fields. For all of them that prominence has much to do with how a conscious literariness is merged to a systematizing capability, so that each creates what seems to be an autonomous, self-sustaining "imaginative" structure. In this light it is significant that all of them, in eminently comparativist fashion, denied their fields, balking at over-specialization and traversing disciplinary boundaries. For each, comparativism meant more than selecting cultural material from a wide array of peoples past and present; it also involved each man's carving out a new pan-institutional space, which was achieved precisely by identifying a profusion of professional activities (anthropologist, classicist, poet, critic, mythologist, folklorist, social critic) and figuring himself as the powerful agent capable of welding them.

Notes

Introduction

1 John Vickery, Introduction to *Myth and Literature,* ed. John Vickery (Lincoln: University of Nebraska Press, 1966), ix.

2 For general assessments of the contribution of these movements to theories of discursivity in anthropology, see James Clifford's introduction to *Writing Culture: The Poetics and Politics of Ethnography* (Berkeley: University of California Press, 1986), 1–26, and my introduction to *Modernist Anthropology: From Fieldwork to Text,* ed. Marc Manganaro (Princeton: Princeton University Press, 1990), 3–47.

3 James Boon, "Functionalists Write, Too: Frazer/Malinowski and the Semiotics of the Monograph," *Semiotica* 46 (1983), 131; James Clifford, introduction to *Writing Culture,* 2.

4 Friedrich Nietzsche, *Early Greek Philosophy,* trans. Maximilian Mügge. Part II of *The Complete Works of Friedrich Nietzsche* (New York: Russell & Russell, 1964 [1909–11]), 180.

5 Johannes Fabian, *Time and the Other: How Anthropology Makes Its Object* (New York: Columbia University Press, 1983); George Marcus and Michael Fischer, *Anthropology as Cultural Critique: An Experimental Moment in the Human Sciences* (Chicago: University of Chicago Press, 1986).

6 Clifford Geertz, *Works and Lives: The Anthropologist as Author* (Stanford: Stanford University Press, 1988), 4. See James Clifford's seminal essay, "On Ethnographic Authority" [1983], in his *Predicament of Culture: Twentieth-Century Ethnography, Literature, and Art* (Cambridge: Harvard University Press, 1988), 21–54.

7 I am referring here to Clifford's treatment of pre-Malinowskian fieldwork in "On Ethnographic Authority," 26–29.

8 James Clifford, *Predicament of Culture,* 34. Referred to hereafter as PC within the text. See also George Stocking, "The Ethnographer's Magic: Fieldwork in British Anthropology from Tylor to Malinowski," in *Observers Observed: Essays on Ethnographic Fieldwork,* ed. George Stocking (Madison: University of Wisconsin Press), 70–120.

9 James Clifford, "On Ethnographic Allegory," in *Writing Culture,* 117. Referred to hereafter as WC within the text.

10 For other challenges to what have been perceived as utopian narratives of prog-

ress at work in Clifford's critique of ethnography, see Joseph Tobin, "The HRAF as Radical Text?" *Cultural Anthropology* 5 (1990), 482–84, and Paul Roth, "Ethnography without Tears," *Current Anthropology* 30 (1989), 555–61; see also Clifford's response to Roth's essay in the same issue (561–62).

11 Alan Dundes, "The Anthropologist and the Comparative Method in Folklore," *Journal of Folklore Research* 23 (1986), 125, 130–31. It needs to be emphasized that there is no *one* comparative method. Marilyn Strathern points out, for example, the gap between the comparative method as practiced by Frazer and other evolutionary comparativists and the method practiced by "modern anthropologists" after Frazer, involving not the collecting together of diverse customs but "the comparison of distinct systems." See "Out of Context: The Persuasive Fictions of Anthropology," in *Modernist Anthropology,* 87.

12 Andre Köbben, "Comparativists and Non-Comparativists in Anthropology," in *A Handbook of Method in Cultural Anthropology,* ed. Raoul Naroll and Ronald Cohen (New York: Columbia University Press, 1970), 583.

13 James Boon, *Other Tribes, Other Scribes: Symbolic Anthropology in the Comparative Study of Cultures, Histories, Religions, and Texts* (Cambridge: Cambridge University Press), 27, ix.

14 I am reminded here of Marianna Torgovnick's recent *Gone Primitive: Savage Intellects, Modern Lives* (Chicago: University of Chicago Press, 1990), 40–41, where she cautions that James Clifford's notion of the carnivalesque possibilities of the mixing of West and third world cultures ought not to obscure the harm the West has done to those other cultures.

15 Jacob Gruber, "Forerunners," in *Main Currents in Cultural Anthropology,* ed. Raoul Naroll and Frada Naroll (Englewood Cliffs, N.J.: Prentice-Hall, 1973), 39; See Torgovnick, *Gone Primitive,* for a recent general treatment of modern appropriations of the "primitive" in both the arts proper and popular culture.

16 J. F. Lafitau, *Customs of the American Indians Compared with the Customs of Primitive Tribes,* ed. and trans. William Fenton and Elizabeth Moore (Toronto: Champlain Society, 1974), 27.

17 Robert Ackerman, *James George Frazer: His Life and Work* (Cambridge: Cambridge University Press, 1987), 73. Referred to hereafter as JGF within the text; Andrew Tuck, *Comparative Philosophy and the Philosophy of Scholarship: On the Western Interpretation of Nagarjuna* (New York: Oxford University Press, 1990), 5; An especially important comparative mythologist-philologist was Max Müller, who in the latter half of the century attempted to trace the "disease of language" back to its pristine origins. On the conflict between Müller's school (called the solarists) and later evolutionists such as Andrew Lang and Edward Tylor, see Ackerman, JGF, 32, and Robert Fraser, *The Making of* The Golden Bough (New York: St. Martin's Press, 1990), 13–14.

18 Edwin Ackerknecht, "On the Comparative Method in Anthropology," in *Method and Perspective in Anthropology: Papers in Honor of Wilson D. Wallis,* ed. Robert F. Spencer (Gloucester, Mass.: Peter Smith, 1969), 119.

19 George Stocking, *Victorian Anthropology* (New York: Free Press, 1987), 178. Cited as va within the text; Gruber states that Spencer "stripped [evolution] of its metaphysical elements," rigorously defined it, "demonstrated its universal application, and left it the guiding principle of all the historical sciences" ("Forerunners" 59).

20 Quoted in E. A. Hammel, "The Comparative Method in Anthropological Perspective," *Comparative Studies of Society and History* 22 (1980), 146. Also, on the rise of anthropology in relation to other disciplines, see Gillian Beer, "Speaking for the Others: Relativism and Authority in Victorian Anthropological Literature," in *Sir James Frazer and the Literary Imagination,* ed. Robert Fraser (New York: St. Martin's Press, 1990), 42–43.

21 Edward Tylor, *Primitive Culture,* 2 vols. (New York: Harper & Row, 1958 [1871]), I: 2.

22 In *Victorian Anthropology* (162) Stocking presents this quotation with the prefatory comment that there was no "hint of irony at its easy ethnocentrism." See Gillian Beer, "Speaking for Others," 42–43, on "the confidence displayed in evolutionary patterns."

23 On Galton's problem, see also Hammel, "Comparative Method in Anthropological Perspective," 147; Raoul Naroll, "Galton's Problem," in *Handbook of Method in Cultural Anthropology,* 974–89; Stocking, va, 318; and Dundes, "Anthropologist and the Comparative Method," 129, 142; Reprinted in Franz Boas, *Race, Language, and Culture* (New York: Macmillan, 1940), 276.

24 Ruth Benedict, *Patterns of Culture* (Boston: Houghton Mifflin, 1934), 49.

25 Robert Thornton, "'Imagine Yourself Set Down . . .': Mach, Frazer, Conrad, Malinowski and the Role of Imagination in Ethnography," *Anthropology Today* 1 (1985), 10.

26 The background to comparativism in anthropology I am providing here does not mean to suggest that one can look only to anthropology to explain Frazer's rhetoric and method. The chapters on Frazer within will broaden the scope of Frazer's cross-disciplinary interests.

27 On the relation of Malinowskian ethnography to earlier accounts of travel (travel books, memoirs, missionary accounts, etc.), see Mary Louise Pratt's excellent essay "Fieldwork in Common Places," in wc, 27–50. Pratt examines how "some tropes of ethnographic writing" originate in these early forms of writing and how indeed ethnographers have tended to mystify the connections between them.

28 This increasingly cited remark was made by Malinowski to B. Z. Seligman, quoted in *Man and Culture: An Evaluation of the Works of Bronislaw Malinowski,* ed. Raymond Firth (London: Routledge & Kegan Paul, 1957), 6, and discussed in Clifford, pc, 96.

Chapter 1. James Frazer

References to Frazer's first edition of *The Golden Bough,* originally published in two volumes in 1890, are to *The Golden Bough: The Roots of Religion and Folklore* (New

York: Avenel Books, 1981). This edition was published under the title *The Golden Bough: A Study in Comparative Religion*. Citations from the twelve volumes of the third edition refer to *The Golden Bough: A Study in Magic and Religion* (London: Macmillan, 1907–1915). The title of the volume cited will be provided within the text.

1 Edmund Leach, "On the 'Founding Fathers,'" *Current Anthropology* 7 (1966), 561. Leach in fact was replying to I. C. Jarvie's Freudian reading, in the same volume, that Frazer has been much maligned since "Malinowski ousted Frazer from the leadership of the anthropological world in a father-killing revolution" ("In Defence of Frazer" 568). See also Jarvie's *Revolution in Anthropology* (London: Routledge & Kegan Paul, 1964).

2 Strathern herself admits that Frazer is "a person whom postmodernism allows us to countenance. It is salutary to think of Frazer because it is salutary to think about what the modernists [of anthropology: Malinowski and others] found so distasteful in him—taking things out of context" ("Out of Context" 111).

3 Charlotte Burne, in "Reviews" of the second edition of *The Golden Bough, Folk-Lore* 12 (1901), 243; Stanley Edgar Hyman, *The Tangled Bank: Darwin, Marx, Frazer, and Freud as Imaginative Writers* (New York: Atheneum, 1962), 267. Referred to hereafter as TTB within the text; Steven Connor, "The Birth of Humility: Frazer and Victorian Mythography," in *Sir James Frazer and the Literary Imagination*, 77.

4 *Edinburgh Review* 172 (1890), 544.

5 R. R. Marett, "De Mortuis," Review of Frazer's *Fear of the Dead, Quarterly Review* 267 (1936), 41. John Vickery recently has endorsed this assessment when commenting that Frazer's "ceaseless tattoo of documentation . . . compels assent if only through thwarting refutation by the sheer weight and diversity of authority." See "Frazer and the Elegiac: The Modernist Connection" (*Modernist Anthropology* 51–68), 64.

6 James Frazer, *Totemism and Exogamy*, 4 vols. (London: Dawsons of Pall Mall, 1968 [1910]), I: x. Referred to hereafter as TE within the text.

7 See also Frazer's preface to the late *Garnered Sheaves* (London: Dawsons of Pall Mall, 1968 [1931]), where Frazer represents his collection of previously published essays as "sheaves . . . reaped in harvest long years ago" that, significantly, require no "pruning": "On the whole I have not seen reason to change my views on any essential point" (v).

8 Robert Alun Jones, "Robertson Smith and James Frazer on Religion: Two Traditions in British Social Anthropology," in *Functionalism Historicized: Essays on British Social Anthropology*, ed. George Stocking (Madison: University of Wisconsin Press, 1984), 38.

9 John Vickery, *The Literary Impact of* The Golden Bough (Princeton: Princeton University Press, 1973), 23.

10 James Frazer, *Man, God, and Immortality: Thoughts on Human Progress* (New York: Macmillan, 1927), 30.

11 Robert Ackerman, "Frazer on Myth and Ritual," *Journal of the History of Ideas* 36
     (1975), 122; Note Jarvie's argument (pejoratively cast against Malinowski) that,
     while Frazer "was not given to going on about 'science' . . . Malinowski's rev-
     olution took terribly seriously the claim to scientific status and made it the basis
     for his revolution" (*Revolution in Anthropology* 174).

12 R. R. Marett, *Psychology and Folk-Lore* (Oosterhout, The Netherlands: Anthro-
     pological Publications, 1971 [1920]), 195. Geertz in *Works and Lives* might be
     said to qualify the rhetorical authority of Frazer's fact-collecting when he states
     that if it were true that "ethnographic texts convince . . . through the sheer
     power of their factual substantiality," then "J. G. Frazer would indeed be king"
     (3). I would note that, first, Frazer *was* considered king, once; second, Frazer is
     not an ethnographer of course but a comparativist; and third, "facts" do not
     constitute the only source of Frazer's authority.

13 Edmund Leach, "Golden Bough or Gilded Twig?" *Daedalus* 90 (1961), 381.

14 Indeed, Leach holds that Frazer's reputation had "passed its peak by 1900," and
     that in that year "the anthropologists were notably cool" to the publication of
     the second edition of *The Golden Bough*: "Andrew Lang was positively insulting;
     Hartland and Haddon praised Frazer's zeal but were caustic about his theories"
     ("'Founding Fathers'" 562).

15 On the fallacious nature of Frazer's King of the Wood and the "error" it per-
     petuated in ritualist circles (especially among the Cambridge Hellenists), see
     Joseph Fontenrose, *The Ritual Theory of Myth*, Folklore Studies no. 18 (Berkeley:
     University of California Press, 1966), 1; and Richard Hardin's "'Ritual' in Re-
     cent Criticism: The Elusive Sense of Community," PMLA 98 (1983), 849.

16 James Frazer, "Baldwin Spencer as Anthropologist," in *Spencer's Last Journey*,
     ed. R. R. Marett and T. K. Penniman (Oxford: Clarendon Press, 1931), 9.

17 James Frazer, *The Gorgon's Head and Other Literary Pieces* (Freeport, New York:
     Books for Libraries Press, 1967 [1927]), 299–300.

18 In the original version of this manuscript I discussed at this point the ways in
     which the mechanics of Frazer's source borrowing lend a greater authority to
     Frazer as author: through both the omission of quotation marks around quoted
     material and the use of a single set of quotation marks around a large section of
     directly quoted material, Frazer blurs the distinction between his own words
     and those of his sources.

19 Frazer's negligent handling of the "facts" culled from his sources has been noted
     and criticized with some consistency since the first edition of *The Golden Bough*.
     See, for example, the *Edinburgh Review* (1890), 554, and Marilyn Strathern,
     "Out of Context," 261; Alexander Goldenweiser, quoted in Abram Kardiner
     and Edward Preble, *They Studied Man* (Cleveland: World Publishing Company,
     1961), 107.

20 Strathern reacts against the application to Frazer of "postmodern" features, par-
     ticularly what she calls the "metaphor of play" ("Out of Context" 267), and
     states quite resoundingly that "to construct past works as quasi-intentional lit-

erary games is the new ethnocentrism" (269). I readily admit her point that textualization if carelessly employed can lead to the violation of the text's very real historical and social contexts. And it is true that postmodernism usually involves a particular response to a particular time frame and cultural context (first half of the twentieth century, Modernism). But Strathern herself finds useful the originally literary or at least artistic categories of Modernism by applying them to the historical framework of anthropology. More to the point, my own application of "play" to Frazer is not done in a postmodernist haze. In fact, Hyman, who we can safely assume never heard of postmodernism as we conceive it, states that "Frazer keeps referring to his theories as *playful fancies* rather than scientific conjectures" (TTB 244). My point is not that Frazer is a postmodernist but that he does strike a pose of "playing" precisely because he is deadly serious about his ultimate rhetorical end. In that respect I am in agreement with Strathern—"playing" is not a game for Frazer.

21 Marty Roth, "Sir James Frazer's *The Golden Bough*: A Reading Lesson," in *Modernist Anthropology,* 75–76; Mary Douglas, "Judgements on James Frazer," *Daedalus* 107 (1978), 151.

22 Vickery's choice of romance as the genre of *The Golden Bough* is supported by others, but for quite different reasons. George Marcus and Michael Fischer, for example, adopting Hayden White's conception of romance as "the empathetic self-identification by the writer with quests that transcend specific periods of world history," categorize *The Golden Bough* "as a quest of reason battling through centuries of superstition" (*Anthropology as Cultural Critique* 13).

23 Northrop Frye, *Anatomy of Criticism: Four Essays* (Princeton: Princeton University Press, 1957), 109.

24 *Norton Anthology of English Literature,* fifth edition (New York: Norton, 1986), I: 2182. See also where Robert Fraser writes of Frazer's "Augustan" tendencies, citing Pope in the process (*Making of Golden Bough* 133).

25 Joseph Addison, *The Spectator,* number 62 (11 May 1711), ed. Donald F. Bond (Oxford: Clarendon Press, 1965), I: 268. Further page references to this number will be made within the text.

26 In this respect Frazer's brand of comparativism is considerably more extreme than that of either of his chief mentors, Tylor and Robertson Smith. On the relatively tame use of the comparative method in Tylor, see Stocking's discussion of Tylor's "methodological sobriety" (VA 300). On Smith's tamer version of the comparative method, see Robert Alun Jones in "Robertson Smith and James Frazer."

27 John Vickery, "Frazer and the Elegiac: The Modernist Connection," in *Modernist Anthropology,* 51–68.

28 James Frazer, *Anthologia Anthropologica,* viii, cited in Leach, " 'Founding Fathers,' " 561.

29 Stocking parallels "savage" magic to what he terms the "ethnographer's magic" at work in Malinowski's text: the latter is intimately tied to the ethnographer's literary authority ("Ethnographer's Magic" 106).

30 James Frazer, *Passages of the Bible Chosen for Their Literary Beauty and Interest,* 2nd ed. (London: Adam and Charles Black, 1909), viii.

31 Relevant here is Ruth Benedict's analogy, in *Patterns of Culture,* of Frazer's use of the comparative method to the construction of Frankenstein's monster.

32 Though Hyman valorizes Frazer's dramatistic tendencies, he does occasionally poke fun at Frazer's penchant for the dramatic. At one point, exclaiming that Frazer "dramatizes everything," he tells how in *Adonis, Attis, Osiris* "a reconstruction of the conservative magical mind becomes an elaborate Colonel Blimp music-hall turn" (TTB 256).

33 Philip Rahv attacks the myth critic's "fear of history" in his 1953 essay, "The Myth and the Powerhouse," that startingly anticipates current moods in criticism: "One way certain intellectuals have found of coping with their fear [of history] is to deny historical time and induce in themselves through aesthetic and ideological means a sensation of mythic time—the eternal past of ritual." In Vickery, *Myth and Literature,* 114.

34 On Hyman's importance to Frazer studies, see Ackerman, who claims that "it was not until 1962 [with the publication of *The Tangled Bank*] that Frazer's ideas received serious study" (JGF 2). Attesting to the centrality of Hyman as a myth critic, Hardin in his "'Ritual' in Recent Criticism" calls Hyman's 1958 "Ritual View of Myth and the Mythic" in *Myth and Literature,* ed. John Vickery, "the most confident assertion of [myth and ritual criticism's] beliefs" (846).

35 My conflation of New Criticism and myth criticism is quite deliberate. Though obviously the myth criticism of, say, Northrop Frye is consciously opposed to many aesthetic notions of New Criticism, nonetheless for both types of criticism literature remains curiously autonomous from historical process. And both schools use figures, such as that of the web and the thread, that privilege complex patterning and ambiguity. See, for example, Frank Lentricchia, *After the New Criticism* (Chicago: University of Chicago Press, 1980), which quotes Frye's phrase "the shifting ambiguities and complexities of unidealized existence" as an example of the latter's "New-Critical" terminology (22).

36 Robert Fraser, having quoted Frazer's web-thread passage in *The Making of* The Golden Bough, also replicates Frazer's strategy. At the conclusion to his book, Fraser states that "We are further along the web than he, and the way ahead is no clearer" (212). Frazer's figure for reading culture as the penetration of a darkened dense fabric or thick web is not unique in the development of modern anthropology; indeed, in some respects Frazer's use of the figure anticipated later anthropological figuration of cultural interpretation. Renato Rosaldo, in *Culture and Truth: The Remaking of Social Analysis* (Boston: Beacon Press, 1989), notes that "anthropology's classic norms prefer to explicate culture through the gradual thickening of symbolic webs of meaning" (2). In a sense what Frazer called the "web" or "fabric" of culture would later be figured as cultural texture.

37 Roger Poole, Introduction to Claude Lévi-Strauss, *Totemism,* trans. Rodney Needham (London: Penguin Books, 1969), 28. Indicative of totemism's meta-

phorical nature is Lévi-Strauss's opening line: "Totemism is like hysteria" (1). For Lévi-Strauss on the history of the reception and rejection of Frazer's paradigm of totemism, see *Totemism,* 4–5.

38 Though Frazer himself would barely acknowledge the filiation, his attention to the mystical and social sides of totemism is closely approximated in the approach of the French sociologists, Emile Durkheim and Lucien Lévy-Bruhl. Indeed, in *Elementary Forms of the Religious Life* (1912) Durkheim would later double, with modifications, Frazer's stress upon the social solidarity of totemism. And Frazer's notion that, to quote Kardiner and Preble, "the essence of totemism" was "the individual's complete identification with the totem" (*They Studied Man* 100) anticipates Lévy-Bruhl's "law of participation" that mystically makes the native and the totem one. Lévy-Bruhl's *Les Fonctions mentales dans les sociétés inférieures* (first published in 1910 and translated into English as *How Natives Think*) contains the fullest expression of his law of participation.

39 This quotation is taken from the second edition of *The Golden Bough* (London: Macmillan, 1900), I: xxi.

40 Jane Harrison, *Themis* (London: Cambridge University Press, 1927 [1912]), 476.

41 Robert Ackerman, "Frazer on Myth," 115–116; 131. See also Richard Hardin's "'Ritual' in Recent Criticism," 846–62.

42 Also, Vickery notes that reviewers of the first edition "continually reiterated" and were impressed by Frazer's notion of ritual preceding myth (*Literary Impact* 80).

43 See where Vickery identifies Frazer as "one of the four major figures in what came to be called the Cambridge School of Anthropology. Only one of these, Frazer himself, could really be termed an anthropologist" (*Literary Impact* 89); Jones notes that Frazer in his thinking on ritual and myth "changed his mind frequently, but in doing so deleted neither the 'theories' he no longer believed nor the 'facts' he had gathered to support them" ("Robertson Smith and James Frazer" 38), and Ackerman holds that though Frazer gave contradictory positions on ritualism, one could "extract a ritualist Frazer that will not do excessive violence to the truth. This is not as opportunistic as it sounds if only because Frazer himself, in his devaluation of theory, seems to have invited it" ("Frazer and Myth" 132).

44 After completing this chapter, I came across Steven Connor's "Birth of Humility." Connor makes a point similar to mine using essentially the same figure, when he states that "*The Golden Bough* fluctuates between the centripetal desire to consolidate, organize, and simplify, and the centrifugal force of the data, which keeps threatening to spin out of conceptual control" (78).

45 What I see as Frazer's essentially logocentric semiotic leads me to agree with Robert Thornton, "If Libraries Could Read Themselves: The New Biography of Frazer," *Anthropology Today* 4 (1988), 21–22, and Robert Fraser, in *Making of Golden Bough,* 209, on the point that Frazer was *not* simply antireligious and wholly rationalistic.

Chapter 2. T. S. Eliot

1 T. S. Eliot, "A Prediction in Regard to Three English Authors," *Vanity Fair* 21 (1924), 98.

2 T. S. Eliot, Review of *The Growth of Civilization* and *The Origin of Magic and Religion,* by W. J. Perry, *Criterion* 2 (July 1924), 489–90.

3 This account of the paper is taken from *Josiah Royce's Seminar, 1913–14: As Recorded in the Notebooks of Harry T. Costello,* ed. Grover Smith (New Brunswick: Rutgers University Press, 1963), 72–77. William Skaff in *The Philosophy of T. S. Eliot: From Skepticism to a Surrealist Poetic, 1909–1927* (Philadelphia: University of Pennsylvania Press, 1986), 69–72, provides a good summary of Eliot's shift toward Frazer and away from the other anthropologists, particularly Lévy-Bruhl.

4 T. S. Eliot, *Selected Essays* (New York: Harcourt, 1950), 19. Referred to hereafter as SE within the text; Jacob Korg, "Ritual and Experiment in Modern Poetry," *Journal of Modern Literature* 7 (1979), 135.

5 Michael Levenson, *A Genealogy of Modernism: A Study of English Literary Doctrine, 1908–1922* (Cambridge: Cambridge University Press, 1984), 119.

6 Richard Shusterman, *T. S. Eliot and the Philosophy of Criticism* (New York: Columbia University Press, 1988), 41.

7 Louis Menand's *Discovering Modernism: T. S. Eliot and His Context* (Oxford: Oxford University Press, 1987) contributes significantly to our understanding of Eliot's mastery of cultural politics.

8 T. S. Eliot, "Experiment in Criticism," *The Bookman* 70 (1929), 228.

9 Piers Gray, *T. S. Eliot's Poetic and Intellectual Development, 1909–1922* (Sussex: Harvester Press, 1982), 128; See *Josiah Royce's Seminar,* 76. My own reading of the paper, housed in the library of King's College, Cambridge, confirms this treatment of Harrison.

10 T. S. Eliot, Introduction to *Savonarola: A Dramatic Poem,* by Charlotte Eliot (London: Cobden-Sandersen, 1926), viii.

11 On the relation of "interpretation," as contemplated in Eliot's paper "The Interpretation of Primitive Ritual," to his later literary criticism, see Grover Smith, *Josiah Royce's Seminar,* 73, and Piers Gray, *Eliot's Development*; T. S. Eliot, "Ulysses, Order, and Myth," *Dial* 75 (1923), 483.

12 Sanford Schwartz, *The Matrix of Modernism: Pound, Eliot, and Early Twentieth-Century Thought* (Princeton: Princeton University Press, 1985), 7, 164. Schwartz quotes Eliot's essay on Swinburne.

13 T. S. Eliot, Review of *Elementary Forms of the Religious Life,* by Emile Durkheim, *Monist* 28 (1918), 158; Louis Menand and Sanford Schwartz, "T. S. Eliot on Durkheim: A New Attribution," *Modern Philology* (February 1982), 314. Single quotation marks denote Eliot's direct quotation from Durkheim. Eliot discusses Durkheim's book in 1913, in his paper on primitive ritual, one year after the book's publication. Throughout his career Eliot cites Durkheim, often in conjunction with Lévy-Bruhl. For another related example of Eliot's discussion of

theories of totem, see where he notes "the union of the worshiper with his god, the identity of the individual and his totem," in his review of Clement C. J. Webb's *Group Theories of Religion* in *New Statesman* 7 (29 July 1916), 405.

14 T. S. Eliot, *The Waste Land,* l. 431. Unless otherwise noted, all references to Eliot's poetry are to *Collected Poems, 1909–1962* (New York: Harcourt, 1970). Copyright 1970 by Esme Valerie Eliot.

15 Richard Poirier, "The Literature of Waste," in *The Performing Self* (London: Chatto & Windus, 1971), 58; Perry Meisel, *The Myth of the Modern* (New Haven: Yale University Press, 1987), 87. James Longenbach, in "Matthew Arnold and the Modern Apocalypse," PMLA 104 (1989), 844–55, argues against Meisel's claim that Eliot constructs *The Waste Land* as a kind of ultimate apocalyptic expression. Rather, Longenbach maintains, Eliot's apocalyptic rendering is part of a tradition of apocalypse "that fully contains its own critique" (851) and thus recognizes the "figural status" of its own apocalyptic expression (846). I agree that Eliot probably had a deep understanding of the figures of apocalypse that preceded his own, and that in at least one instance he "divest[ed] himself of responsibility for the wasteland myth" by pointing to the poem's "figural status" (846). Nonetheless, I hardly think that Eliot's disclaimer, or his awareness of previous figures, prevents him from exercising the authorial power of apocalypse. To the contrary, the knowledge of the tradition's workings encourages that use, and the recognition of past apocalypse in itself further empowers Eliot the critic. Longenbach engages in a kind of dubious intentionalism when he accepts some of Eliot's own comments at their face value and makes claims such as the following: "Eliot knew that his wasteland was not the embodiment of a generation's predicament but a young man's interpretation of a narrow range of experience" (847).

16 See Grover Smith's brief discussion, in *Josiah Royce's Seminar* (73), of the relation between "interpretation" as conceived in the primitive ritual paper and Eliot's conception of "the modifying effect, upon the past, of successive interpretations," particularly as that latter idea works into "Tradition and the Individual Talent." On the relation of these interpretive concepts to Eliot's poetry, see also James Longenbach, "Guarding the Hornéd Gates: History and Interpretation in the Early Poetry of T. S. Eliot," ELH 52 (1985), 503–27.

17 Richard Poirier notes that "Eliot is anxious to dislodge works or writers from the place previously assigned to them. He deprives them of those contexts" ("Literature of Waste" 54).

18 Calvin Bedient, *He Do the Police in Different Voices: The Waste Land and Its Protagonist* (Chicago: University of Chicago Press, 1986), 216; Terry Eagleton, *Criticism and Ideology* (London: New Left Books, 1976), 148–49.

19 Lucien Lévy-Bruhl, *How Natives Think,* trans. Lilian A. Clare (New York: Washington Square Press, 1926 [1910]), 50–52 (referred to hereafter as HNT within the text); Emile Durkheim, *Elementary Forms of the Religious Life,* trans. Joseph Ward Swain (London: George Allen and Unwin, 1915 [1912]), 305; Sigmund Freud, *Totem and Taboo,* trans. James Strachey (New York: Norton, 1950

[1913], 54–57. On Eliot's reading and appropriation of Lévy-Bruhl, see William Harmon, "T. S. Eliot, Anthropologist and Primitive," *American Anthropologist* 78 (1976), 797–811, and my "The Primitive Mind in the Early Poetry of T. S. Eliot," *Journal of Modern Literature* 13 (March 1986), 96–110.

20 T. S. Eliot, *Old Possum's Book of Practical Cats,* ll. 25–31, in *The Complete Poems and Plays, 1909–1950* (New York: Harcourt, 1950), 149. Copyright 1971 by Esme Valerie Eliot.

21 William Harmon, "T. S. Eliot's Raids on the Inarticulate," PMLA 91 (1976), 454.

22 Freud's idea corresponds to Frazer's notion that the original seamless totemic energy breaks into increasingly more identifiable anthropomorphic gods.

23 Claude Lévi-Strauss, quoted and discussed in Jacques Derrida, "Structure, Sign, and Play in the Discourse of the Human Sciences," in *The Structuralist Controversy,* ed. Richard Macksey and Eugene Donato (Baltimore: Johns Hopkins University Press, 1970), 261–62.

24 Eric Gould, *Mythical Intentions in Modern Literature* (Princeton: Princeton University Press, 1981), 7.

25 J. Hillis Miller, *Fiction and Repetition: Seven English Novels* (Cambridge: Harvard University Press, 1982), 68, 61.

26 T. S. Eliot, Review of *The Ascent of Olympus,* by James Rendel-Harris, *Monist* 28 (1918), 640.

27 The notion of the fire of thunder striking the oak and making it sacred is one of Frazer's central explanations for the sacredness of the golden bough itself, which he identifies with the mistletoe. See, for example, the penultimate chapter of the 1922 edition, 701–11.

28 Jacques Derrida, *Of Grammatology,* trans. Gayatri Spivak (Baltimore: Johns Hopkins University Press, 1976), 140.

29 What Poirier calls "the extraordinary fusion of diffidence and dogmatism" at work in Eliot's text closely parallels Frazerian rhetorical qualities. Poirier could well be commenting on Frazer when he notes that Eliot's "reluctance of self-assertion, by acknowledging all the possibilities open to it, emerges as a kind of frighteningly controlled strength" ("Literature of Waste" 58).

30 Gregory Jay, *T. S. Eliot and the Poetics of Literary History* (Baton Rouge: Louisiana State University Press, 1983), 150; Sandra Gilbert, "Costumes of the Mind: Transvestism as Metaphor in Modern Literature," *Critical Inquiry* 7 (1980), 397–98.

31 For an especially interesting anthropological treatment of thunder, familiar to Eliot, see Jane Harrison's discussion of the early Greek Rite of the Thunders in *Themis* (52–69), and my treatment of the relevance of Harrison's discussion to *The Waste Land* in "T. S. Eliot and the Primitive Mind," Ph.D. diss., University of North Carolina, 1985, 108–13.

32 T. S. Eliot, "War-Paint and Feathers," review of *The Path on the Rainbow,* ed. George W. Cronyn, *The Athenaeum* 4668 (1919), 1036.

33 T. S. Eliot, "Tarr," *Egoist* 5 (1918), 106.

34 We know Eliot read Lévy-Bruhl's *Les Fonctions mentales dans les sociétés inférieures*

by 1913, for he discusses it in the primitive ritual paper presented in Royce's seminar.

35 T. S. Eliot, *The Use of Poetry and the Use of Criticism* (Cambridge: Harvard University Press, 1933), 141. Referred to hereafter as UPUC within the text.

36 The concept of "collective representations" is central to the philosophy of both Durkheim and Lévy-Bruhl. See HNT, 13.

37 T. S. Eliot, Preface to *For Lancelot Andrews* (London: Faber, 1970 [1928]), vi.

38 William Skaff in *The Philosophy of T. S. Eliot* considers the relevance of Eliot's comments on rhythm to his readings on then-current anthropology (82–87). Skaff is incisive when he ties "primitive" rhythm to Eliot's sense of the "physiological unconscious" and rightly cites Harrison's *Themis* as one possible source for Eliot's notion of rhythm. I differ with Skaff, however, on his identification of "mystical participation" with Eliot's version of "immediate experience" and also believe that Skaff's conclusion, that the anthropological impact upon Eliot led ultimately to a "surrealist poetic," is dubious.

39 T. S. Eliot to Ezra Pound, quoted in Grover Smith, *T. S. Eliot's Poetry and Plays: A Study in Sources and Meanings,* 2nd ed. (Chicago: University of Chicago Press, 1956), 220.

40 T. S. Eliot, *On Poetry and Poets* (London: Faber & Faber, 1957), 15–16. Referred to hereafter as PP within the text.

41 For an excellent treatment of the ritualist workings in Eliot's plays, especially as relating to the Cambridge-Hellenist F. M. Cornford, see Carol Smith, *T. S. Eliot's Dramatic Theory and Practice* (Princeton: Princeton University Press, 1963).

42 T. S. Eliot, *After Strange Gods: A Primer of Modern Heresy* (London: Faber & Faber, 1934), 18. Referred to hereafter as ASG within the text.

43 T. S. Eliot, *The Idea of a Christian Society* (New York: Harcourt, 1940), 34. Referred to hereafter in the text as ICS.

44 For a perspective on Eliot that stresses the relation between Eliot's fascination with the primitive to urban space, see Robert Crawford, *The Savage and the City in the Work of T. S. Eliot* (New York: Oxford University Press, 1987).

45 T. S. Eliot, *Notes toward the Definition of Culture* (London: Faber & Faber, 1948), 104. Referred to hereafter as NDC within the text.

46 Relevant here is David Bleich's claim, in *Subjective Criticism* (Baltimore: Johns Hopkins University Press, 1978), that, in line with our culture's longstanding "association of religious interests and the objective paradigm," in Eliot's criticism "two aspects of the objective paradigm are combined—the religious assumption that ministers have special access to the absolute truth and the scientistic assumption that an object of art is independent of human perception" (33–34). Bleich does not mention here Eliot's social criticism, but we can easily replace the "scientistic assumption" toward "an object of art" with that of the "scientistic assumption" toward "an object of culture." On Bleich's claims, see also Shusterman, *Philosophy of Criticism,* 10.

47 T. S. Eliot, "The Beating of a Drum," *Nation and Athenaeum* 34 (6 October 1923), 12.

Chapter 3. Northrop Frye

1 Northrop Frye, *Fearful Symmetry: A Study of William Blake* (Princeton: Princeton University Press, 1947), 424. Referred to hereafter as FS within the text.

2 Northrop Frye, "World Enough without Time," in *Northrop Frye on Culture and Literature,* ed. Robert Denham (Chicago: University of Chicago Press, 1978), 100. This volume contains previously uncollected early reviews and essays by Frye. Referred to hereafter as NFCL within the text; Northrop Frye, "Forming Fours," in NFCL, 123.

3 Robert Denham, *Northrop Frye and Critical Method* (University Park: Pennsylvania State University Press, 1978), 223. Referred to hereafter as NFCM within the text.

4 Frank Mc'Connell, "Northrop Frye and *Anatomy of Criticism,*" *Sewanee Review* 92 (1984), 624.

5 Northrop Frye, *Anatomy of Criticism,* 341. Referred to hereafter as AC within the text.

6 Northrop Frye, "The Instruments of Mental Production," in *The Stubborn Structure: Essays on Criticism and Society* (Ithaca: Cornell University Press, 1970), 4–5. Referred to hereafter as SS within the text.

7 Northrop Frye, *T. S. Eliot: An Introduction* (Chicago: University of Chicago Press, 1963), 29. Significantly, Frye follows this statement with one of Eliot's central quotations on how great poetry bridges the gap between primitive and civilized states: "such poetry," Frye documents, "'fuses the old and obliterated and the trite, the current, and the new and surprising, the most ancient and the most civilised mentality'" (29).

8 M. H. Abrams, review of *Anatomy of Criticism, Toronto University Quarterly* 28 (1958–59), 196.

9 Terry Eagleton, *Literary Theory: An Introduction* (Minneapolis: University of Minnesota Press, 1983), 91. On Frye's scientism, its relation to other "scientific" criticism of the century, and the general tendency of scientific criticism to lose objectivity and become "interpretive," see also Roger Seamon, "Poetics against Itself: On the Self-Destruction of Modern Scientific Criticism," PMLA 104 (1989), 294–305.

10 Northrop Frye, *Spiritus Mundi: Essays on Literature, Myth, and Society* (Bloomington: Indiana University Press, 1976), 95. Referred to hereafter as SM within the text.

11 In "Conflict and Consensus in the History of Recent Criticism," NLH 12 (1981), 356, Evan Watkins comments that in 1957 "value-free" seemed "the only basis possible from which to maintain the authority of criticism."

12 This act of mystification or naïveté on Frye's part has been noted by a number of critics, particularly in regard to Frye's own implicit evaluations. See M. H.

Abrams in his review of *Anatomy,* 192; P. J. M. Robertson, "Northrop Frye and Evaluation," *Queen's Quarterly* 90/1 (1983), 153; and Gene H. Bell-Villada, "Northrop Frye, Modern Fantasy, Centrist Liberalism, Antimarxism . . . ," in *Reinventing the Americas,* ed. Bell Gale Chevigny and Gari Laguardia (Cambridge: Cambridge University Press, 1986), 282.

13 Harold Bloom, *A Map of Misreading* (Oxford: Oxford University Press, 1975), 30; Critics as various as Hartman, Lentricchia, Said, and Todorov also stress how Frye's ornate schema, mapping out literary tradition with its charts and diagrams, deprives literary texts of their unique temporal contexts.

14 Northrop Frye, *The Critical Path: An Essay on the Social Context of Literary Criticism* (Bloomington: Indiana University Press, 1971), 18. Referred to hereafter as CP within the text.

15 See where Hayden White in *Tropics of Discourse* (Baltimore: Johns Hopkins University Press, 1978), 83, holds that Frye locates the *fictive* in the space between the polarities of the *mythic* and the *historic.*

16 Northrop Frye, *The Educated Imagination* (Bloomington: Indiana University Press, 1969), 63–64. Referred to hereafter as EI within the text; Fredric Jameson, *The Political Unconscious* (Ithaca: Cornell University Press, 1981), 130.

17 Northrop Frye, *The Great Code: The Bible and Literature* (San Diego: Harvest, 1982), 46. Referred to hereafter as TGC within the text.

18 See also where Denham notes the confluence between Frye's interpretations of Toynbee and Frazer in NFCM, 45. Finally, see where Frye notes that Spengler has produced "a vision of history which is very close to being a work of literature" (SM 187).

19 See Sanford Schwartz, "Reconsidering Frye," *Modern Philology* (1981), 289.

20 George Woodcock, "Diana's Priest in the Bush Garden: Frye and His Master," from *The World of Canadian Writing* (Vancouver: Douglas & McIntyre, 1980), 226, 229; Graham Hough, *An Essay on Criticism* (London: Gerald Duckworth & Company, 1966), 154.

21 Northrop Frye, *The Secular Scripture: A Study of the Structure of Romance* (Cambridge: Harvard University Press, 1976), 9, and SM, 136.

22 Several years later this passage would appear almost verbatim in *Anatomy of Criticism.*

23 Frye is engaging in that "backward tracing of the evolutionary pattern" that Wallace Douglas sees as characteristic of myth critical works ("The Meaning of 'Myth' in Modern Criticism," in *Myth and Literature,* 126). On the ritualist basis of some of Frye's literary concepts, see also A. C. Hamilton, *Northrop Frye: Anatomy of His Criticism* (Toronto: University of Toronto Press, 1990), 100.

24 Frank Kermode, review of *Anatomy of Criticism, Review of English Studies* 10 (1959), 323.

25 W. K. Wimsatt, "Northrop Frye: Criticism and Myth," in *Northrop Frye in Modern Criticism,* Selected Papers from the English Institute, ed. Murray Krieger (New York: Columbia University Press, 1966), 98.

26 Both Eliot and Frye here owe much to the Tylorian concept of the survival, the relic of an earlier culture whose original purpose in its own cultural context has been lost and replaced by other, usually less socially central and empowering, functions.

27 T. S. Eliot, review of *Group Theories of Religion and the Religion of the Individual,* by Clement C. J. Webb, *International Journal of Ethics,* 27 (1916), 116.

28 Note Frye's emphasis in *Anatomy* upon "making total human form out of nature" (105). In his first book, Frye defines Blake's cosmology as essentially "a revolutionary vision of the universe transformed by the creative human imagination into a human shape" (FS ii).

29 See also Frye's *Study of English Romanticism* (New York: Random House, 1968), 4–5, on myth as the "direct ancestor of literature." A. C. Hamilton links Frye's notion of the progression from nonhuman to human concerns with the development of literary forms from myth to romance and beyond. See *Frye: Anatomy of His Criticism,* 162–63.

30 Frye's use of the metaphor-metonymy dichotomization recalls Frazer's opposition of magic and science. Indeed, in *The Great Code* Frye speaks of "verbal magic in the metaphoric phase, arising from a sense of an energy common to words and things," and holds that "in the metonymic phase this sense of verbal magic is sublimated into a quasi-magic inherent in sequence or linear ordering" (11). Missing from Frye's version of course is the sense of positive progress that Frazer attributes to science, as magic improved upon, but the notion of science as a complication or realignment of magical processes in Frye's version does hearken back to Frazer.

31 My point is not to deny the "ambiguities" in Blake's corpus but to show that Frye found Blake's structurations amenable to his own need to bracket and systematize.

32 Northrop Frye, *The Well-Tempered Critic* (Bloomington: Indiana University Press, 1963), 103. Referred to hereafter as WTC within the text.

33 Geoffrey Hartman, *Beyond Formalism: Literary Essays 1958–1970* (New Haven: Yale University Press, 1970), 11.

34 See *The Fantastic* (Cleveland: Press of Case Western Reserve University, 1973), 5–23, where Tzvetan Todorov criticizes Frye for his failure to recognize the fantastic as a genre.

35 George Woodcock, "Frye's Bible," *University of Toronto Quarterly* 52 (1982–83), 149–50.

36 Northrop Frye, *Fables of Identity: Studies in Poetic Mythology* (New York: Harcourt, Brace, 1963), 149.

Chapter 4. Joseph Campbell

1 Mary Lefkowitz, "The Myth of Joseph Campbell," *The American Scholar* 59 (1990), 429.

2 Robert Segal, "Frazer and Campbell on Myth: Nineteenth- and Twentieth-

Century Approaches," *The Southern Review* 26 (1990), 471–72. Segal notes that whereas Frazer's view of myth is essentially rationalistic, Campbell's is romantic. See as well his essay "Following Your Bliss: The Romantic Appeal of Joseph Campbell and Modern Myths," *Cultural Vistas: Louisiana Endowment for the Humanities* (Summer 1991), 19–20. In "Frazer and Campbell on Myth" Segal also points out that both authors garnered wide popular readerships but have "mixed professional receptions" (470).

3 Joseph Campbell and Henry Morton Robinson, *A Skeleton Key to* Finnegans Wake (New York: Harcourt, Brace, & World, 1944). Referred to hereafter as SK within text. Throughout this chapter I refer to Campbell as author of *A Skeleton Key* not because I want to deny that Robinson had a part in writing the book, but because, as I hope my treatment of the book demonstrates, *A Skeleton Key* functions so clearly as a blueprint for Campbell's later works. Campbell is listed as primary author of the book for reasons other than alphabetical.

4 Shari Benstock, "The Letter of the Law," *Philological Quarterly* 63 (1984), 163, 206–07.

5 Margot C. Norris, "The Consequence of Deconstruction: A Technical Perspective of Joyce's *Finnegans Wake*," in *Critical Essays on James Joyce,* ed. Bernard Benstock (Boston: G. K. Hall, 1985), 206.

6 In *Beyond Modernism: A New Myth Criticism* (Lanham, Maryland: University Press of America, 1988), Ted Spivey wrongly sees the promotion of difference in deconstruction as closely approaching the "collision of forces" and "tension of opposites" found in the writings of Jung, Eliade, and Campbell (9).

7 Raphael Patai, in *Myth and Modern Man* (Englewood Cliffs, N.J.: Prentice-Hall, 1972), writes of Campbell as the example of "the transformation of a historian of religion into mytho-poet" (58).

8 Joseph Campbell, *The Hero with a Thousand Faces* (Princeton: Princeton University Press, 1949), 256. Referred to hereafter as HTF.

9 Michel Foucault, "Nietzsche, Genealogy, and History," in *Language, Counter-Memory, Practice,* ed. Donald F. Bouchard (Ithaca: Cornell University Press, 1977), 142; Joseph Campbell, with Bill Moyers, *The Power of Myth,* ed. Betty Sue Flowers (New York: Doubleday, 1988), 231. Referred to hereafter as PM within the text.

10 See Robert Segal's discussion of Campbell's notion of the modern artist as hero in *Joseph Campbell: An Introduction* (New York: Mentor, 1990 [1987]), 124–40.

11 See Segal's treatment (*Joseph Campbell* 123–26) of Campbell's conception of creative mythology; also, see Lefkowitz ("Myth of Campbell" 432) on the importance of individualism to Campbell.

12 Joseph Campbell, *Creative Mythology,* volume 4 of *The Masks of God* (New York: Viking, 1968), 260–61.

13 Joseph Campbell, *Myths to Live By* (New York, 1973), 12. Referred to hereafter as MTLB within the text.

14 Joseph Campbell, quoted in H. A. Reinhold, "A Thousand Faces—But Who

Cares?" *Commonweal* (8 July 1949), 322. See also William Kerrigan, "The Raw, The Cooked, and the Half-Baked," *VQR* 51 (1975), 651.

15 William Doty, *Mythography: The Study of Myths and Rituals* (University, Alabama: University of Alabama Press, 1986), 176.

16 Segal makes the point that both Frazer and Campbell condemn taking myth *literally*—that is, as true—but that Frazer has no use for myth symbolically either, as Campbell does. See "Frazer and Campbell on Myth," 472, 474.

17 Alan Dundes, *Interpreting Folklore* (Bloomington: Indiana University Press, 1980), 232; See also Stanley Hyman, "Myth, Ritual, and Nonsense," *Kenyon Review* 11 (1949), 455–56.

18 Joseph Campbell, *The Way of the Animal Powers,* volume 1 of *The Historical Atlas of World Mythology* (San Francisco: Harper and Row, 1983), 8.

19 Joseph Campbell, "Bios and Mythos: Prolegomena to a Science of Mythology," in *Myth and Literature,* ed. John Vickery, 16.

20 Campbell's notion of "picture-language" is integrally related to the use of illustrations in his books. In volumes such as *The Mythic Image, The Power of Myth,* and especially *The Historical Atlas of World Mythology,* the pictures function as irrefutable testimony to his assertions. On the authority of such illustrations, see also Kerrigan's review of *The Mythic Image,* "The Raw, The Cooked, and the Half-Baked," 455–56.

21 Joseph Campbell, *Oriental Mythology,* volume 2 of *The Masks of God* (New York: Viking Press, 1976 [1962]), 9–13. See, for example, *The Way of the Animal Powers,* where Campbell states that "a commonly recognized corollary of the male-female polarity theme is represented in the image of a single, androgynous, higher source of power out of which opposites have sprung" (173).

22 Florence Sandler and Darrell Reeck, "The Masks of Joseph Campbell," *Religion* 11 (1981), 9.

23 Segal comments that with *Myths to Live By* and *Creative Mythology,* the West becomes Campbell's "ideal, and the East becomes his nemesis" (*Joseph Campbell* 140).

24 The piece that began this debate in the press is Brendan Gill's "Faces of Joseph Campbell," *New York Review of Books,* 36 (28 September 1989), 16–19; following that were "Joseph Campbell: An Exchange," *New York Review of Books,* 36 (9 November 1989), 57–61, and editorials by Robert Segal and Arnold Krupat in the *New York Times* (2 December 1989), 26. Segal maintains that Campbell condemns Judaism as he does all organized religion, only with an added intensity. Like other religions, Judaism for Campbell is narrowly local (versus universalist) and reads myth literally rather than symbolically. Added to Judaism's shortcomings, according to Campbell, are its patriarchal, nationalistic, and anti-mystical tendencies. See Segal, "Campbell on Jews and Judaism," *Religion* 22 (1992), in press.

25 I should like to avoid giving the impression that there is one definitive shift in Campbell's writing from a pro- to an anti-Orientalist position. Campbell is

pro-Eastern (and anti-Western) at many points in his later writings. I focus on the anti-Orientalist rhetoric of the 1950s and 1960s primarily because it most blatantly illustrates his brand of essentializing. Segal discusses the inconsistencies and multiple shiftings of Campbell's anti-Orientalist rhetoric in *Joseph Campbell*, 142–43.

26 See Sandler and Reeck, "Masks of Campbell," 14.

27 Campbell's attitude toward so-called savages—usually Africans, in fact—can be traced back to *Hero*, which begins with the words, "Whether we listen with aloof amusement to the dreamlike mumbo jumbo of some red-eyed witch doctor of the Congo, or read with cultivated rapture thin translations from the sonnets of the mystic Lao-tse . . . it will always be the one, shape-shifting yet marvelously constant story that we find" (3). These words, in fact, are reverentially quoted by Bill Moyers in his introduction to *The Power of Myth*.

28 Andrew Klavan, "Joseph Campbell, Myth Master," *Village Voice* (24 May 1988), 60.

Afterword

1 Fredric Jameson, *The Political Unconscious: Narrative as a Socially Symbolic Act* (Ithaca: Cornell University Press, 1981), 10.

2 Paul Rabinow, "Representations Are Social Facts: Modernity and Post-Modernity in Anthropology," in WC, 255. For other criticisms of so-called postmodern anthropology, see P. Steven Sangren's "Rhetoric and the Authority of Ethnography," *Current Anthropology* 29 (1988), 405–35, and note 10 of the introduction (above).

3 Steven Tyler, "Post-Modern Ethnography: From Document of the Occult to Occult Document," in WC, 123; Marilyn Strathern, "Partial Connections," Distinguished Lecture, 1988 Meeting of the Association for Social Anthropology in Oceania.

4 For a good summary of post-evolutionary comparative anthropology, see Ronald Cohen and Raoul Naroll, "Method in Cultural Anthropology," in *A Handbook of Method in Cultural Anthropology*, ed. Raoul Naroll and Ronald Cohen, 13–14. For another useful account of modern comparative work in anthropology, with a focus on the Human Relations Area File in particular, see Joseph Tobin, "HRAF as Radical Text?" 473–87.

Index

Abrams, M. H., 116–17
Ackerknecht, Edwin, 11–14 *passim*
Ackerman, Robert, 11, 12, 20, 30, 31, 32–33, 35, 37, 38, 44, 46, 62–63
Addison, Joseph, 44–45, 46, 65, 116–17
allegory of salvage, 26, 33, 78–79, 101, 157–58, 166, 183
Anatomy of Criticism, 113–29, 131–37, 139; as comprehensive, 113–14, 128–29; as literary, 128–29; genre of, 114–15. *See also* Frye, Northrop
androgyny, 85–89, 172–75, 183, 207n21
anthropology: branches of, 3–4, 7, 11; discursive nature of, 1–2, 15–16, 49, 188–89, 191n2; ties to colonialism of, 9; institutionalization of, 11–12, 25, 26–27; textual approach to, 1–2, 102–03, 188–89; justifications for, 188–89. *See also* comparative method; ethnography; evolutionary comparativism; Frazer, James
anthropomorphism: in Frazer, 59, 61–63; in Eliot, 84, 87, 89; in Frye, 135–38, 140; in Campbell, 170–71, 175, 177. *See also* evolutionary totemism
anti-Semitism, 99, 177, 207n24

Bastian, Adolph, 160, 167, 169
Bedient, Calvin, 80, 83, 87, 89, 174
Beer, Gillian, 193nn20,21
Bell-Villada, Gene H., 149
Benedict, Ruth, 14–15, 72, 91, 165–66, 189, 197n31

Benstock, Shari, 153, 156–57
Bible, 48–49, 126–27, 140, 142, 161, 165
Bloom, Harold, 124–25, 145
Boas, Franz, 14, 15, 19, 189
Boon, James, 2, 8, 9, 10, 16, 66

Cambridge Hellenism, 189; in Frazer, 61–63, 65, 198n43; in Eliot, 85, 87, 101, 108; in Frye, 131, 135–38; in Campbell, 171, 176. *See also* Harrison, Jane; ritual, theories of
Campbell, Joseph: and cultural holism, 165–67, 170–71; as fact-collector, 164, 179; reduction of cultural difference to sameness by, 153–59, 167, 169–70, 185; on gender, 175; on language, 153–56, 159–60; as social critic, 158, 175–85; on religion, 161–63, 174, 181–82, 184; on myth, 151, 159–62, 163–65, 168–70, 172; on the rhetorical authority of the mythologist, 161, 163–64, 167–68, 174, 181, 185; as anti-historical, 163, 165, 170; evolutionary tendencies of, 176–77, 183; popular appeal of, 151–52, 155, 169; on Modernism, 152, 154, 155–56; on the artist as hero, 161–62; relation to Frazer of, 151–52, 154–55, 164, 166, 167, 169, 171, 176, 184; anti-Semitism of, 177, 207n24; orientalism of, 174–80, 182, 207–08n25; on democracy, 174–75, 182; on America, 182–83; on communism, 178–80. Works: *The Atlas of World Mythology,* 166, 207n20; "Bios and Mythos," 167–